Constructing
Bangladesh

Islamic

Civilization

& Muslim

Networks

Carl W. Ernst and

Bruce B. Lawrence,

editors

Sufia M. Uddin

Constructing Bangladesh

Religion,

Ethnicity,

and

Language

in an

Islamic

Nation

THE UNIVERSITY OF
NORTH CAROLINA PRESS
CHAPEL HILL

Designed by Heidi Perov
Set in Garamond
Manufactured in the United States of America

The paper in this book meets the guidelines
for permanence and durability of the Committee
on Production Guidelines for Book Longevity of the
Council on Library Resources.

Library of Congress Cataloging-in-Publication Data
Uddin, Sufia.
Constructing Bangladesh : religion, ethnicity,
and language in an Islamic nation / Sufia Uddin.
p. cm.—(Islamic civilization and Muslim networks)
Includes bibliographical references and index.
ISBN-13: 978-0-8078-3021-5 (cloth: alk. paper)
ISBN-10: 0-8078-3021-6 (cloth: alk. paper)
1. Bangladesh—History. 2. Islam and state—Bangladesh—
History. 3. Bangladesh—Civilization. 4. Group identity—
Bangladesh—History. 5. Bengali language—Social aspects.
6. Nationalism—Bangladesh—History. I. Title.
II. Islamic civilization & Muslim networks.

DS394.5.U33 2006

954.92—dc22   2006004325

10 09 08 07 06   5 4 3 2 1

To *Mahir Thadani*
Born 5 December 2004, 6:29 P.M.
and *Sunil Thadani*

Contents

Illustrations, Maps, & Table

Foreword

Constructing Bangladesh: Religion, Ethnicity, and Language in an Islamic Nation is the fifth volume to be published in our series, Islamic Civilization and Muslim Networks.

Why make Islamic civilization and Muslim networks the theme of a new series? The study of Islam and Muslim societies is often marred by an overly fractured approach that frames Islam as the polar opposite of what "Westerners" are supposed to represent and advocate. Islam has been objectified as the obverse of the Euro-American societies that self-identify as "the West." Political and economic trends have reinforced a habit of localizing Islam in the "volatile" Middle Eastern region. Marked as dangerous foreigners, Muslims are also demonized as regressive outsiders who reject modernity. The negative accent in media headlines about Islam creates a common tendency to refer to Islam and Muslims as being somewhere "over there," in another space and another mind-set from the so-called rational, progressive, democratic West.

Ground-level facts tell another story. The social reality of Muslim cultures extends beyond the Middle East. It includes South and Southeast Asia, Africa, and China. It also includes the millennial presence of Islam in Europe and the increasingly significant American Muslim community. In different places and eras, it is Islam that has been the pioneer of reason, Muslims who have been the standard-bearers of progress. Muslims remain integral to "our" world; they are inseparable from the issues and conflicts of transregional, panoptic world history.

By itself, the concept of Islamic civilization serves as a useful counterweight to that of Western civilization, undermining the triumphalist framing of history that was reinforced first by colonial empires and then by the Cold War. Yet when the study of Islamic civilization is combined with that of Muslim networks, their very conjunction breaks the mold of both classical Orientalism and Cold War studies. The combined rubric allows no discipline to stand by itself; all disciplines converge to make possible a refashioning of the Muslim past and a reimagining of the Muslim future. Islam escapes the timeless warp of textual norms; the additional perspectives of social sciences and modern technology forge a new hermeneutical strategy that marks ruptures as well as continuities, local influences as well as cosmopolitan accents. The twin goals of the publication series in which this volume appears are (1) to locate Islam in multiple pasts across several geo-linguistic, sociocultural frontiers, and (2) to open up a new kind of interaction between humanists and social scientists who engage contemporary Muslim societies. Networking between disciplines and breaking down discredited stereotypes will foster fresh interpretations of Islam that make possible research into uncharted subjects, including discrete regions, issues, and collectivities.

Because Muslim networks have been understudied, they have also been undervalued. Our accent is on the value to the study of Islamic civilization of understanding Muslim networks. Muslim networks inform the span of Islamic civilization, while Islamic civilization provides the frame that makes Muslim networks more than mere ethnic and linguistic subgroups of competing political and commercial empires. Through this broad-gauged book series, we propose to explore the dynamic past, but also to imagine an elusive future, both of them marked by Muslim networks. Muslim networks are like other networks: they count across time and place because they sustain all the mechanisms—economic and social, religious and political—that characterize civilization. Yet insofar as they are Muslim networks, they project and illumine the distinctive nature of Islamic civilization.

We want to make Muslim networks as visible as they are influential for the shaping and reshaping of Islamic civilization.

Carl W. Ernst
Bruce B. Lawrence
Series editors

Acknowledgments

I am deeply grateful to the many people and institutions who have aided me on this project. My work on Bengali translations of the Qur'an was conducted with funding from the Council of American Overseas Research Centers and the American Institute of Bangladesh Studies (AIBS). The Bangladesh liaison office for the AIBS, the Centre for Development Research Bangladesh (CDRB), provided me with a tremendous amount of logistical support, even when I was no longer an AIBS fellow, and put me in contact with many other people who also helped me. Ahmed Sarwerruddawla at CDRB was always available for consultation whenever I came to the office. The numerous wonderful lunches with the staff sustained me on those hot and sticky Dhaka days. Dr. Mizanur Rahman Shelley, chair of CDRB, introduced me to the relatives of Mohammad Naīmuddīn. Without that introduction, I would never have found copies of some of his most important works. I thank Naīmuddīn's family members for trusting me with their only copies of his work. At Dhaka University, I am most grateful and indebted to Professor Anisuzzaman, who has been a great teacher to me over the past ten years. I have learned much from him about Bengali literature written by Muslims and about Muslim issues of identity. Our rich discussions at Dhaka University, the Dhaka Club, and his home have strongly influenced my thinking about questions of community identity, and his support and encouragement have been crucial. Anisuzzaman also introduced me to many others who have helped me along the way. At the Bangla Academy I received a great deal of assistance from librarian Amirul Momenin, who knows his collection well and provided me with many cups of tea. Razia Sultana introduced me to Razib Ahmed, who has assisted me with great enthusiasm and energy. Ahmed, an aspiring journalist and graduate of Dhaka University, agreed to work with me because he believed in the project. He spent long days helping me interview and do library research and served as a sounding board on many aspects of this project during our walks, during rides in rickshaws, and at our lunches at Dhaka's great Bengali restaurants. I have great respect for his opinions and appreciate his careful consideration of the questions I raised. I cannot forget my dear friend, Eleanor Leyden, who provided great dinners in the evening, wonderful coffee in the morning, and great conversation on the weekends.

At the University of Vermont, I am indebted to Peter Seybolt, chair of the Asian Studies program, and to the program for providing financial support for three research trips to Bangladesh. The University of Vermont's Committee on Research and Scholarship also provided funding for a three-month visit to Bangladesh. I thank the late Dean Joan Smith for her support of my leave to conduct research. Pat Hutton and Bob Taylor of the university and Carol Salomon, Frank Korom, and Jason Fuller took the time to discuss elements of some of the later chapters, for which I am most grateful.

Grants from the Wabash Center for Teaching and Learning in Theology and Religion and the National Endowment for the Humanities enabled me to complete this manuscript. At Duke University in April 2003, I participated in the South Asia Triangle workshop, From Competition to Conflict: South Asian Muslim Communities between Local, Day-to-Day Practice and National/Trans-National

Religious Ideology, where I fleshed out some of the main ideas about Bengali Muslim identity. My visit included fruitful discussions with the many symposium participants and organizers—David Gilmartin, Bruce Lawrence, and Tony K. Stewart. Stewart read drafts of chapters and spent many hours providing feedback on several chapters. He also helped me work through several issues in this manuscript, especially my use of the term "identity," and suggested the more useful and more accurate term "visions of community," which made possible a more textured engagement with the issue.

My dear friends and colleagues, Kevin Trainor and Anne Clark, supported me with encouragement, advice, and critiques. Finally, I thank Elaine Maisner, Bruce Lawrence, Carl Ernst, and the reviewers for seeing what this small book has to offer on our current understanding of Islam and Muslim community in the contemporary world.

The book's remaining faults are mine and cannot be attributed to the many wonderful people and the institutions that have provided support for this study on one of the largest Muslim nations today.

Note on Transliteration

For Bengali terms, I used the conventional transliteration method. However, the final *a* is left off of all words where this vowel is not sounded in Bengali. Bengali Muslim names are transliterated in the same way except for those names that are commonly spelled in another form. In this case, I use those more common spellings. I have omitted diacritical marks from Arabic terms in the text.

Constructing
Bangladesh

Introduction

In March 1948, only six months after Pakistan gained independence, Muhammad Ali Jinnah, the country's first governor-general, visited the province of East Bengal, where he addressed students and faculty at Dhaka University's convocation. Well respected for his role in leading Muslims to nationhood status in 1947, Jinnah was known as *qa'id-e-azam,* or the "Great Leader." His speech addressed the question of national language, which was already on many citizens' minds as Pakistan began to formulate policies on governance. Said Jinnah, "Let me restate my views on the question of a state language for Pakistan. For official use in [East Bengal], the people of the province can choose any language they wish. The question will be decided solely in accordance with the wishes of the people of this province alone, as freely expressed through their accredited representatives at the appropriate time and after full and dispassionate consideration.

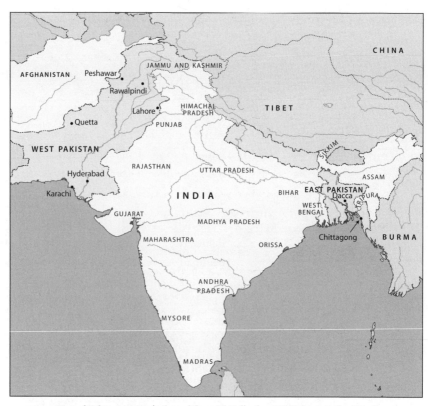

MAP 1. United Pakistan, 1947. (Adapted from H. Fullard and F. Treharne, eds., *Muir's Historical Atlas: Ancient, Medieval, and Modern*, 9th ed. [London: Philips and Son, 1962].)

There can, however, be only one lingua franca—that is, the language for intercommunication between the various provinces of the state— and that language should be Urdu and cannot be any other."[1] Even in 1948, Bengali speakers outnumbered speakers of any other language in Pakistan. An obvious choice for state language is the language spoken by the majority of the nation's inhabitants. Yet the nation's leader demanded that Urdu be accepted as the national language. What was at stake? What made Urdu, in Jinnah's eyes, more appropriate than Bengali when the majority of the nation's inhabitants spoke Bengali? Jinnah responded to these concerns by saying that Urdu "has been nurtured by a hundred million of this subcontinent, [it is] a language understood throughout the length and breadth of Pakistan and above all a language which, more than any other provincial language, embodies

MAP 2. Independent Bangladesh. (Adapted from Ali Riaz, *God Willing: The Politics of Islamism in Bangladesh* [Lanham, Md.: Rowman and Littlefield, 2004].)

the best that is in Islamic culture and Muslim tradition and is nearest to the languages used in other Islamic countries."[2]

Jinnah believed that promoting and nurturing the adoption of a single national language of communication was crucial. More importantly, however, that language should represent the people as an Islamic nation. Though Bengali was the language most spoken, Jinnah and many other Muslims of West Pakistan saw that language as totally foreign to Muslim culture: for this reason alone, it was not an acceptable national language. Conversely, throughout the nineteenth century, Urdu had gained status and wide recognition among the educated elite as the preeminent South Asian Muslim language because of its script, though it was linguistically connected with Hindi. As the educated Muslims of the subcontinent increasingly employed the Perso-Arabic-scripted Urdu, northern Indian Hindus increasingly employed the Devanagari-scripted Hindi. Both Muslims and non-Muslims in the subcontinent associated Urdu with the language of the Qur'an. This rhetoric of association was extremely powerful, as Jinnah's speech suggested. Muslim identity, as we shall see, was directly linked not only to religious tradition but also to select languages and northwestern regional customs of the Muslims. As a result, language and even Bengali regional customs came to lie at the center of the public debate over national language and culture during the united Pakistani era. This debate eventually led to the partition of this Muslim nation less than three decades later. The common bond of Islam ultimately was not enough to hold this nation together. This book explores the questions that remain on the minds of Muslims throughout the world—what does it mean to be a part of a Muslim *umma* (community) in the contemporary world? How best can the needs of the *umma* be met? Is religious nationalism the answer?

Among today's Muslims, diverse views about actualizing Islam hinge not only on historical memory but also on historical amnesia. History comprises not just a compilation of events that are remembered but also what we selectively omit from our collective memories. Let us take, for example, one Islamist view and how it relates to an idealized Islamic past. The Salafiyya of Saudi Arabia employ a rhetoric of returning to the pure faith of Islam and to the ways of the first Muslims. In their view, Muslims have deviated from the "true path" of Islam. The Taliban too, argue that they want to bring Islam to its true practice, the way of Muhammad. However, close historical analysis suggests many striking differences between their ideas and historical evidence from Muhammad's time. In premodern Muslim societies, administrative law, tribal law, and custom also constituted influential sources of law and thus way of life. Shari'a was never fully realized as the source of all legislation. Islam was perhaps never so narrowly conceived as it is today by Islamists and extremists who are themselves a product of modern social problems and conflicts. They too, are selective in what they recall as the great Islamic past.

As Partha Chatterjee, Peter van der Veer, and others have found, something unique to the colonial experience heralded modern ways of thinking and has led to today's particular public struggles and declarations about religion, community, and nation.[3] These concerns most often are addressed in terms of religion and of the struggle to claim one's own interpretation of religious tradition as legitimate and authoritative. India provides a case in point: the nation is being increasingly defined by many groups such as the Bharata Janata Party, which employs only those symbols that define and reinforce India's Indic roots, selectively excluding Islamicate contributions. In Afghanistan, the Taliban's destruction of the Bamiyan Buddhist statues can also be read as an effort to erase from national memory the cultural artifacts that tie the nation's roots to cultures other than Islam. Such examples illustrate efforts to create a historical memory that reinforces one way in which a religious community is envisioned. In the name of rebuilding infrastructure and reviving a proper Islamic way of life, organizations from the Gulf states have bulldozed major Muslim monuments in Bosnia and Kosovo to reconstruct them according to puritanical ideals. In some cases, local Muslim monuments that had survived Serb and Croat militia attacks were destroyed soon thereafter by the donors of this aid under the guise of "reconstruction." To receive this so-called reconstruction aid to rebuild towns and villages demolished by Serb and Croat militia attacks, Bosnians and Kosovars had to agree to the destruction of tombs, mosque complexes, and libraries, erasing evidence of a Bosnian-informed Muslim culture.[4] Muslims from the Gulf states export their versions of orthodoxy to rid regionally informed Muslim cultures of their regional character, replacing it with what Gulf Muslims argue is orthodox Islamic culture, which most closely resembles their own regionally informed Islam.

Western media have a tendency to reinforce a portrayal of Islam and the Muslim world that is more in line with only two insider Muslim perspectives, one Islamist, the other extremist. We hear little about Islamic diversity. Further distorting our understanding of the Muslim world, the media, politicians, and some scholars erroneously conflate these two insider perspectives. The extremists' violent tactics are assumed to be the strategies of all Islamists, and this stereotyping of Islamists is wrongly applied to the majority of Muslims. Thus, many in the West see the entire Muslim world as not only monolithic but also inherently violent. This distorted image ignores the cultural diversity that is widely evident throughout Islamic history.

Since the days of early European contact with the Islamic world, Islamic civilization has been characterized as violent, ideologically driven, and hostile toward the West. The history of Bangladesh, the country with the world's third-largest Muslim population, is one of many examples suggesting otherwise. Furthermore, even if we rely on the term "Islamic civilization," plurality and diversity of representative Islamic cultures exists. These cultures demonstrate the limited utility of "Islamic civilization" to define the entire Muslim world exclusively as one culture or one people with a singular ideology. What does it mean to talk about one people? In a sense, we may certainly refer to Muslims as one people, but the term is no more precise than the word "Christian." As is the case with all other religious people, Muslims' values, ethics, and general worldview are always conditioned by particular regional experiences, the historical moment, and other social, political, and pragmatic factors. The complexity of this experience leads to great diversity in "Islamic civilization" itself.

What makes Islamic civilization Islamic are not any essential, unchanging factors. Rather, Islam is a dynamic tradition that relies on debate and discourse to elicit notions of orthodoxy in different times and places and among different ethnolinguistic groups. The Qur'an and Sunna of the Prophet Muhammad provide the timeless foundation for this discourse all over the Islamic world. To understand Islam and the Islamic world, Talal Asad has argued, one must recognize and give due attention to Muslim peoples' continual and historically situated interaction with their foundational texts. The Qur'an and the hadith are the common bond from which any and all discussions take place that result in the assertion of orthodoxy in a given period. Interpretations of orthodoxy change in different periods and among different groups. Moreover, in addition to the consideration of historically situated intersections to which Asad has rightly pointed, one must also consider regional context because orthodoxy is also determined by regional culture. In fact, multiple and sometimes conflicting notions of orthodoxy exist even within a particular region. This point is crystallized in the discussion of Bengali Muslim literary discourse on Islam precisely because the discourse focuses on what it means to be a Muslim in the modern world. The way Islam in Bengal articulates itself—or its many selves—at pivotal moments in the nineteenth and twentieth centuries captures the tensions existing between the universal or transnational and the local that foster a culture that is both unique to the region and common to Muslims everywhere. Moving closer to the present, the example of Bangladesh also proves instructive because we find here the tensions surrounding the meaning of membership in a global community that is experimenting with modern concepts of nationhood. Examining the point where tensions between universal and local exist reveals the diversity and the unity that are Islamic civilization.

Linguists generally argue that Bengali is the oldest modern Indo-European language and therefore is most closely related to Sanskrit. Not coincidentally, as Islam began to appear in Bengal, literature about Islam also began to appear in Bengali. Islam and literature about Islam took on a unique flavor, appearing not just as the religion practiced by conquerors but as a tradition becoming influential among the people from the general region of Bengal who moved farther into areas that had formerly been dense forest. Although most people who populated this region were not literate in Bengali, the content of the literature was indeed transmitted. Bengali culture has been and to a great extent remains an oral culture that relies on oral forms of transmission to spread knowledge. In the premodern period, like Bauls (Sufi religious communities of Bengal known for their devotional songs and rejection of normative religious practice), performers of all types and social gatherings were the means for communicating what is preserved in *puthi* (a genre of Bengali literature written by Muslims and with a preponderance of Arabic, Urdu, Persian, and Hindi). The same logic can be applied to the way knowledge of the great Indian epics is communicated. Most individuals cannot say they have read the *Mahabharata*, *Ramayana*, or *Bhagavad Gita*; nevertheless, their meanings and stories are known to a wider public. In the nineteenth and twentieth centuries, printed material was disseminated in many of the same ways. Even today in Bangladesh, daily newspapers are displayed on walls of buildings, and groups gather to read and discuss the content of the day's news.

The premodern foreign Muslim encounter with the rich Bengali language and culture led to a further enrichment of Bengali culture to the point that it gave rise to a Bengali-Muslim culture. After hundreds of years of interaction between Bengalis and non-Bengali Muslim transplants, a transformation and enrichment of the local culture was bound to occur. Islam in Bengal inevitably would become Bengali Islam. Therefore, we are obliged to take seriously the transformative experience of the introduction of Islam into the Bengali cultural milieu. Islam was not simply imported by the ruling elite. Instead, a more complex picture suggests the ways in which global traditions spread around the world. What happens here happens elsewhere in the Muslim world and is therefore instructive. This book will demonstrate the complex and dynamic relation between a rich local linguistic heritage and the greater Islamic global community.

Scholars who cite Muhammad Ali Jinnah's many statements promoting Muslim nationhood as an illustration of identity politics claim that it has become the source of religious conflict. It is therefore worth exploring briefly this question of identity politics. The characterization of current moves for independence as growing from identity politics is flawed. In most cases, people's desire to belong to a community has long existed, of course, as has their desire to publicly assert their membership in that community. But how community is defined is a dynamic variable. The term "identity politics" is too narrow to describe the problematic discussed here. Identity can refer to individual questions of self. One might infer only the psychological aspects and thus neglect the most important element of the problematic—community. Here I will refer to the question as a question of how community is imagined. With the rise and fall of ideologies come new ways of imagining communities associated with the ideologies. Nationalism, for example, did not exist prior to the modern period but is a product of modernity that has greatly influenced much of the contemporary world. The way communities identify themselves today is often conveyed through the concept of "nation," a people with a shared history and culture. Common bonds of language, history, religion, and ethnicity increasingly determine the parameters of nationhood. Take, for example, the Pledge of Allegiance in the United States. During the Cold War, the United States increasingly defined itself as a religious nation in opposition to what were commonly regarded as the "godless" communists: in this environment, lawmakers added the phrase "under God" to the pledge in 1954. In 2003 a dispute occurred in Alabama over the existence of a granite monument of the Ten Commandments in the Rotunda of the state Supreme Court. The monument was eventually removed, but not without protests from Americans who view this religious symbol as a testament to their national heritage. Religion and religious language dominate the public stage in much of the contemporary world. Thus, the conditions under which communities' religious identities are articulated and how they are articulated are matters of great importance in understanding the meaning of nationhood, even in a "Christian" nation such as the United States. Today this is also true of Islamic nationhood and the conditions under which it thrives and asserts a religious character.

The term "Islamic nationhood" is intended here in a very broad sense. If Muslims living in a predominantly Muslim state are motivated to create an Islamic nation, a debate will necessarily ensue as to the nature of Islamic nationhood. Our task must be to understand the various aspects of the particular regional culture and the nature of power relations therein and to grasp how the larger products of modernity such as globalization influence that debate. Understanding the nature of who articulates orthodoxy and how it gets articulated are also paramount to this task. As Asad has stated, "Orthodoxy is not a mere body of opinion but a distinctive relationship—a relationship of power."[5] Orthodoxy concerns the ability of those who have the power to persuade the wider community that may have doubts about certain practices and beliefs. Orthodoxy is determined through participation in discourse and argument about the relevance of the Qur'an and Sunna for a society and how they might best be actualized. Local Muslim communities around the world recognize the participants in this debate as authoritative figures, be they Sufis in one region, Sunni or Shi'ite religious scholars in another, or charismatic leaders who portray themselves as having authority. Passing on a tradition and a notion of correct practice involves persuading a community of believers of the relevance of this practice to a correct understanding of the Qur'an and the customs of Muhammad. Figures from different times and regions have asserted notions of orthodoxy because of the power they wield to change laws and move society in a particular direction or because of their ability to resist the power—either raw power or the power of persuasion—wielded by others. What is considered orthodox today may not have been considered orthodox centuries ago. Furthermore, what is orthodox among one group may not be orthodox among another. Among the Taliban, women have no role in public life, whereas in Bangladesh, Pakistan, and elsewhere in the Muslim world, women serve as public officials and in some cases have held high political office. Asad's position accounts for the changes over Islam's fourteen centuries that are denied by current media portrayals of Islam. As explored here, the tensions between elite classes, scholars, Sufis, and nonelites in precolonial, colonial, and postcolonial Bengal will demonstrate this relation between power and articulations of orthodoxy. This analysis will reveal the nature of realized visions of community that are regionally bound yet religiously tied to other communities of Muslims and nations around the world.

A "vision of community" suggests the dynamic nature of group identification much more subtly than the overpsychologized (and grossly overworked and therefore often reified) concept of identity. This vision also suggests the plurality of group definition. One broad type of vision of community is "Islamic nation," by which I mean a nation that is defined in some way through governmental or popular recognition of Islam. In an Islamic nation, civic law is not necessarily totally replaced by some form of Islamic law. An Islamic nation recognizes or acknowledges the common bond of religion among many of its citizens and sets out in some way to actualize that bond in public national life. This book does two things. First, it examines a small number of defining moments and events in colonial and postcolonial Islamicate Bengali history that reveal the profound impact and legacy of colonialism on these competing visions of community. Second, it examines the formation and contestation of Muslim community in these periods, revealing the multivalent ways that Islam and nationhood are currently being negotiated and contested among one of the world's largest Muslim populations. The greatest attention will go to the roles of reform literature and colonial experience in the formation of a particularly Bengali Muslim vision of community and the current struggle within Bangladeshi society to determine the role of Islam in public life. In broader terms, this book addresses the basis of current misrepresentations of Islam and the roots and nature of today's debates among Muslims about how Islam is defined and articulated as the faith of a world community and a nation.

This book does not provide either a comprehensive historical narrative or a political history of Bengal; instead, it offers a glimpse of select critical moments that led to the contemporary nation-state of Bangladesh. I chose these moments because of their power to highlight critical factors in the shaping of current debates about the relationship of global Islam to nationhood. The stage is set with a sketch of the precolonial Bengali environment in which Islamic influence emerged. This picture allows us to examine the earliest attempts to develop an Islamic literature in Bengali, with direct reference to its creators and audience. The story then moves on to the important individuals and their associated nineteenth-century reform movements that spurred a new ethical literature in Bengali. The late-nineteenth-century Qur'anic translations and exegetical texts in Bengali represent the peak of this literature. From there we turn to the Pakistan era and the struggle over language that led to Bangladeshi independence, a struggle foreshadowed in the story that opens this book. Our study ends with an examination of contemporary contestations of nationhood and the place of Islam in public life among Bangladesh's secularists, religious nationalists, and Islamists.

This analysis of the Bengali Muslim example demonstrates how language and popular ritual life play a central role in the formation of hyphenated, mutually influencing ethnic and religious communal self-perceptions. We see here how Islam as the universal framework interacts with regional particularities, some of which seem unique to Bengal. The tension between the universal framework and these regional particularities shapes localized notions of community. Islam is inevitably regionally informed unless one regional and time-specific form that makes claims to universality is actualized through either the power of persuasion or force. As will become apparent, many of the issues explored in this book constitute part of larger debates about modernization theory, nationalism, community identity formation, and even civilizational clash. A significant piece of the puzzle in the debates mentioned earlier is the role of the widespread use of print technology during the colonial period and the way community consequently is constructed in the modern period. In this regard, Benedict Anderson's theory that highlights some examples from Western Europe does not address the transformative effect of colonialism on both colonizer and colonized, a point Veer highlights in *Imperial Encounters.*[6] As a result, Anderson's theory does not account for the rise of religious group identity in public life, which constitutes a significant element of the colonial experience.

In *Religious Nationalism*, Veer argues that religious nationalism is a product of discourse informed by precolonial and colonial experience. Precolonial conditions will inform the way colonialism is experienced in South Asia. Veer deconstructs the relationships among modernity, secularism, and nationalism, thus demonstrating that secularism does not constitute an essential element of modernization, as Anderson assumes. The secular does not merely represent an absence of the religious in the public sphere but rather constitutes a move to transcend the differences of religious group identity in the public sphere, which happens in a number of ways and to different degrees globally.[7] Therefore, simply applying modernization theory to the South Asian context will not produce a viable explanation of the rise of religious nationalisms taking shape there. We need to examine carefully the impact of colonial experience. This does not mean simply blaming the colonial rulers, Orientalist scholars, and missionaries but suggests a full assessment of the interactions and the products of these interactions, such as the new genres of religious writings that are central to group formation. In the assessment of these interactions and products of the colonial experience, we are obliged to consider the many articulations of how community should be defined, the process of contestation, and its result. Therefore, a limitation of Ernest Gellner's work on nationalism, as Veer points out, is that it gives too much weight to homogenization and devotes scant attention to those who contest the process. Veer aptly suggests that "the centralizing force of nation building itself sprouts centrifugal forces that crystallize around other dreams of nationhood: nationalism creates other nationalisms—religious, ethnic, linguistic, secular—but not a common culture. The modernization paradigm makes too much of homogenization, while it overlooks 'antagonization' and 'heterogenization.' The forging of identity always simultaneously creates diversity."[8] The contesting visions must be examined to understand current struggles over the way Muslim community and nationhood are defined. The first and second partitions of Bengal bear out this contention. Referring specifically to the 1905 partition of Bengal, Partha Chatterjee rightly states that as one project of imagining a nation developed, so did a rival imagining of a nation. Bangladesh today provides another case in point whose identity is further complicated by the 1947 and 1971 partitions.[9] Muslim leaders thought that the 1947 partition would solve the problem of protecting the rights of the subcontinent's Muslims. Shortly after this first partition, however, dissension, frustration, and disillusionment about the viability of one Muslim nation grew, ultimately leading to the 1971 partition. A decade after Bangladeshi independence, fundamentalist groups and others again were envisioning this new nation in terms of Islamic nationhood.

As this volume will show, the current debates regarding nationhood have roots in the colonial past and in the competing visions of community the experience offered up. When we look at specifically Muslim activity in South Asia—as illustrated in language, literature, and religious ritual—the missionary and colonial past emerges as a period in which discourse focused on the role of Islam in individual and national life. At this juncture, religion crystallized as a source of community identity. As Arjun Appadurai and the subalternists point out, missionaries and colonial administrators used this process to identify the colonized peoples, first through caste and later through religion. In unprecedented numbers, Muslim reformers and intellectuals began to write and hold debates in response to colonial and missionary critiques of Muslim values, religious beliefs, and Islam's role in public life. This discourse about religion inevitably took place in the public sphere, and these reformers did not transcend religious difference. Rather, their debates centered on the question of the community's correct practice and beliefs. At the same time, nineteenth-century colonial experiences provided the means by which the European ideas of a nation-state were introduced to South Asia. The interaction of these factors would play a crucial role in the way both colonized and colonizer as well as later generations increasingly envisioned community. These religious and ethnic identities become the cohesive force that allows for the maturation of nationalist identities, in contrast to some Western forms of nationalism.

The colonial experience and Orientalist enterprise, which go hand in hand, had impacts that modernization theory fails to measure. Modernization theory also does not consider the human agency of a colonized people and how it potentially affects the appropriation of concepts and ideologies. This crucial omission dangerously neglects the question of how religious identity will influence the way nationalism is adopted. Furthermore, this lacuna also neglects the question of who articulates orthodoxy and how groups and individuals gain the power to assert their visions. Nationalism as a modernizing project is not always secular, as is clearly demonstrated by the examples of postcolonial India, Bangladesh, Pakistan, and Sri Lanka, where religion plays a central role.

Among the nineteenth-century Muslim elite and reformers, the religious community comes to represent a political (national) community. But did the Muslim elite really have common social, economic, and political interests with the rural, Bengali-speaking Muslims? The elite's and the reformers' representation of religious interests as political interests superficially muted other real and significant political interests (gender, class, and race). These conflicting interests later rose to the surface and produced internal conflict, as we see with Bengal's several partitions and competing visions of community. The result is not just an opportunistic exploitation of religious commitments but rather particular public representations of religion that engage religious commitments, giving them priority over other factors. These new articulations then are themselves religious; they do not simply marshal religious rhetoric for political ends. Therefore, it is misleading to argue, as have some scholars, that religion is simply being exploited to serve common political, economic, and social purposes in the twentieth and twenty-first centuries. In *The Color of Violence*, Sudhir Kakar asserts that "there may not be any great ferment taking place in the world of religious ideas, beliefs, rituals, or any marked increase in the sum of human spirituality. Where the resurgence is most visible is in the organization of collective identities around religion, in the formation and strengthening of communities of believers. What we are witnessing today is less the resurgence of religion than (in the felicitous Indian usage) of communalism where a community of believers not only has religious affiliation but also social, economic, and political interests in common which may conflict with the corresponding interests of another community of believers sharing the same geographical space."[10]

The problem here lies in the assumption that common bonds of religion means shared political, social, and economic interests. For that matter, this view even wrongly assumes that the notion of common religious roots suggests common practices or shared notions of orthodoxy. We again are confronted by another dilemma—the possibility of identifying the exploitation of religious ties for political and economic purposes. As difficult as it is to conflate the religious with the social, political, and economic, it is also difficult to excise the religious from the political and economic issues. Motives are always multiple and fluctuating.[11] How are we to know what is purely a political, religious, or economic motive? The individual and group desire to obtain and maintain power certainly is a motivating factor, but there is no way to measure the extent of this motive. In chapter 2, I explain that in the late nineteenth century, the Muslim elite likely felt vulnerable, as did the village mullahs (who were finally co-opted into the effort for reform), but there is no way to completely disentangle the religious motive from the political. Participants in the movements have diverse reasons for their different levels of involvement.

The Bengali Muslim nineteenth-century reform experience undermined the religious nationalism on which Pakistan would eventually be based. When Muslims gained nationhood as Pakistan in 1947, an ethnic divide between Bengali and Urdu speakers emerged. Bengali Muslims coalesced as a group, primarily identifying with their ethnolinguistic identity, which had been thoroughly affirmed in the nineteenth century through prolific literary productivity that took place in their regional language. The utility of a common religious affiliation that had been an effective unifying force in the nineteenth and early twentieth centuries faded while "Bengaliness" gained prominence. The instability of ethnolinguistic and religious nationalisms results from the contestation of visions of community not only from within the nation-state but also, as the book's final chapter will demonstrate, from transnational influences such as global fundamentalism. We glimpsed some examples of Middle Eastern Islamist assertions of orthodoxy in

Bosnia and Kosovo. Bangladesh, as we shall see, has not been immune to these influences. Global representations of Islam interact in a number of ways with local practices and interpretations, yielding contesting visions of community and nationhood. My interest in the formation of Bangladesh has less to do with an interest in politics of independence or nation-building and more to do with a keen interest in the changing role of religion in the public sphere, how our modern ways of thinking shape the way we view the Muslim world, and how those views have influenced Muslims and their responses. As we shall see here, a much more complex picture of "Muslim identity" and Islamic civilization exists than is depicted by contemporary scholars such as Samuel Huntington, Benjamin Barber, and Sudhir Kakar.[12]

Islamic Themes in Premodern Bengali Literature and Life

THE FOUNDATION OF CREATION: THE METAPHYSICS OF LIGHT (*nur-tattva*)

In the beginningless space the prime mover and creator (*karatā*) alone existed. The Stainless One (*nirañjana*) was a creamy essence in the thick of the enveloping universe of bleak inertia (*tama guṇa*). When the one called Stainless (*nirañjana*) rent the interior of that orb, he transformed into the Lord Īśvara. Forms (*ākāra*) began to differentiate within that universe and the unitary formless (*nirākāra*) metamorphosed into seventy-one forms. When the formless (*nirākāra*) assumed form, the Stainless (*nirañjana*) took the name of Viṣṇu. The blazing effulgence (*ujjvala*) of the formless (*nirākāra*) quickened the form (*ākāra*); and the darkness enveloped the blazing light with its dazzling colors: white (*sattva*), black (*tamaḥ*) and reddish-orange (*rajaḥ*) were latent and undifferentiated. No one could distinguish among the three qualities (*guṇa*) what was pleasing.
—Excerpted from Āli Rajā's *Āgama*

This chapter explores two distinct literatures that arose among residents of Bengal. The first to be discussed is the Arabic and Persian literature that was introduced by the ruling class after its conquest of Bengal and that proliferated under subsequent Muslim rulers. For our purposes, I have classified the Arabic and Persian literature as one type, a heuristic categorization based on the literature's origins and target audience. Here, the Arabic and Persian literature is imported and patronized by the ruling class. The second literature addressed a Bengali-speaking audience and introduced Islam as well as provided general religious instruction. In contrast to literature written in Persian and Arabic, Bengali literature dealing with Islamic topics generally did not receive sultanate or Mughal patronage. Some of this latter literature also deals thematically with the Islamic mystical tradition, as in the passage by Āli Rajā that opens this chapter. Tony K. Stewart suggests that Āli Rajā's piece is not, as Abdul Karim and Enamul Haq had described, some hybrid of Islamic and yogic literature but an early premodern example of an author's attempt to introduce Sufi cosmology in a new linguistic environment. Richard M. Eaton has described the literature about Islam in Bengal as the literary product of a petty religious class. As we shall see, although there is no evidence of Bengali translations of the Qur'an or *tafsir* (exegesis) before the nineteenth century, works written in Bengali served the purpose of their authors: to introduce Islam and affirm an Islamic worldview. Stewart convincingly demonstrates this crucial point, arguing that Āli Rajā's distinct vocabulary has very Islamic objectives: "The result is a thoroughly Islamic view of the world in a text that uses an ostensibly Hindu terminology to express it."[1] With little appreciation for what these early Bengali Muslim authors were doing, nineteenth-century reformers and critics perceived this literature as having weak religious affiliation with Islam or as a distorted form of Islam when in fact Āli Rajā was known in his time as a well-respected Sufi *pir* (master or saint) of Chittagong (known also as Kanu Fakir). Before I discuss these works in greater detail, however, I will provide an overview of Muslim rule in Bengal to demonstrate the relation between patronage and the spread of Islam in Bengal.

Bengal under Muslim Rule

The effects of political upheaval and transition in the thirteenth-century Middle East and Central Asia were felt as far east as Bengal.

The decline of the Ghaznavid and Seljuk powers in Central Asia led to the eastward emigration of Turkish conquerors, and in 1204 the Turkish Muslim Muhammad Bakhtiyar conquered Bengal. After 1204, Muslims ruled much of Bengal, with capitals at Gaur, Pandua, Dhaka, and Lakhnauti, until the British colonial period, which began in the late eighteenth century and ended in 1947.[2]

The Turks governed Bengal until 1342. Although nominally under the rule of the Delhi sultanate, the region achieved significant political independence, possibly as a result of its geographic distance from the capital. Bengal's real independence arrived later with the rule of Shams al-Dīn Ilyas Shah (1342–57) and the weakening of the Tughluq Sultanate in Delhi.

Shams al-Dīn Ilyas Shah was the first Muslim ruler of Bengal to break away from the Delhi sultanate. Until approximately 1400, the Ilyas Shahis governed an independent Bengal. On several occasions, the Delhi sultan attempted to regain control of Bengal, but even under the rule of Sikandar Shah, son and successor to Ilyas Shah, such attempts failed. The Ilyas Shahi dynasty therefore maintained its sovereignty, and Bengal remained independent for two centuries.

At the turn of the fifteenth century, a Hindu landowner (*zamīndār*), Raja Ganesh, came into political prominence. Although he never became ruler, he nonetheless was a powerful figure in Bengal, disrupting the rule of the Ilyas Shahis and orchestrating his young son's ascension to the throne in 1415.[3] After the death of this son, Sultan Jalaluddin, in 1432, the Ilyas Shahis regained authority and ruled until 1486. The following seven years were a time of great political upheaval in Bengal, as the Abyssinian military slaves (*Habshi*) of the Ilyas Shahi rulers vied for power. But at the end of the period of turbulence, a Meccan Arab, 'Ala al-Dīn Husayn Shah (1493–1519), assumed control of the region.

Husayn Shah, in his official role as a minister of the last *Habshi* ruler, Muzaffar Shah, sought to undermine his master's political authority by reducing the pay of the *Habshi* soldiers and collecting revenues at an unbearably high rate. Momtazur Rahman Tarafdar has contended that Husayn Shah also spread rumors that Muzaffar Shah had instituted these policies.[4] Tarafdar has persuasively argued that Husayn Shah single-handedly sabotaged Muzaffar Shah's reign, making possible Husayn Shah's ascension to power. The nobles were divided in their support for Muzaffar Shah, allowing Husayn Shah to take advantage of Muzaffar Shah's weakened political position. Husayn Shah eventually gained the support of the nobles and became ruler in 1494.

During Husayn Shah's twenty-seven-year reign, he expanded the territories under his suzerainty in the northern frontier. Husayn Shah is also known for the extent to which he employed Hindus in his service and for the religious tolerance he extended to all people under his rule.[5] In 1519 he was succeeded by his son, Nusrat Shah. During the latter's reign, the Lodi Dynasty of Afghans in Delhi was defeated by Babur, the first of the Mughals and a descendant of both Timur and Chingiz Khan. As a result, the Afghans moved eastward, and Nusrat Shah welcomed those who chose to settle in Bengal. During this eastward migration, Sultan Nusrat Shah lost control of areas west of the Gandak to the Mughal ruler Babur after refusing to allow his army to pass through Bengali territories during his military campaign against the Afghans.[6] The demise of the Husayn Shahi dynasty was completed after the defeat of Sultan Mahmud, the last of the Husayn Shahis, in the battle against the de facto Afghan ruler of Bihar, Sher Khan. Unable to fight off Sher Khan alone, Mahmud sought the assistance of the Mughal ruler, Humayun, which gradually led to the Mughals' takeover of Bengal. By 1612 the Mughals were firmly established as the rulers of Bengal, which they continued to govern until the British colonial period.

Islam in Bengal and the Spread of Islamic Influence

Bengal's rulers thus included Turks, Abyssinians, Arabs, and Afghans. Indeed, except for the reign of Sultan Jalaluddin, Muslims of foreign descent reigned in Bengal for more than five centuries. As will be discussed later in the chapter, the political and economic policies of these various Muslim dynasties have profoundly shaped the culture and religious beliefs of the people of Bengal.

In *The Rise of Islam and the Bengal Frontier*, Eaton provides a plausible argument for the spread of Islam in Bengal, rejecting a number of previous theories such as the immigration theory and the "religion of the sword" theory. According to the immigration theory, for example, Muslims from points west, such as Central Asia and the Middle East, account for the large Muslim population in Bengal and South Asia. This theory certainly does apply to some extent to parts of South Asia, but it does not convincingly explain the growth of a rural Muslim population so far east in areas that were formerly dense forest. Another theory suggests that because Islam was a militant religion, conversion occurred primarily through military campaigns. This theory, a favorite among Orientalists and first suggested by British administrators such as Sir Henry Elliot, falls apart when we try to explain how forcible conversion takes place.[7] Furthermore, neither evidence of nor a plausible motive for coerced conversion exists. A third theory explains the growth of Islam as a function of the people's desire to win the economic and political favor of the ruling class. If this theory were valid, then we would find that as we move away from the Muslim centers of power, Muslim populations would decrease, but such was not the case. Instead, the majority of Muslim populations of Bengal were located in rural areas. Yet another theory postulates that because the Hindu tradition was a socially stagnant and discriminatory system, many Hindus chose to convert to Islam to obtain freedoms they would otherwise not have enjoyed. According to Carl Ernst, however, "whatever value this observation has may be limited to the extreme south of India, where Muslims have generally had a high social status and converts have not been subjected to the limitations of their former caste. This stands in contrast to northern India, where the majority of Muslims in modern times hold relatively low social status."[8] It is not surprising to find that the source of this theory is a sixteenth-century Muslim whose positionality informs this stereotype about Indic traditions of the time.

Eaton argues that none of these theories sufficiently explains the rise of Islam in this region: although Bengali Muslims comprise one of the largest Muslim populations in the world today, the ruling elite did not play a significant role in the people's religious transformation. Rather, a petty religious class of Sufis and men with varying degrees of and specialization in Islamic knowledge imparted their understanding of Islam to the people of Bengal. Indeed, throughout the history of Muslim rule in Bengal, Muslim rulers demonstrated little interest in converting the indigenous people to Islam.[9] Instead, the rulers were primarily concerned with their economic interests, which indirectly affected the expansion of Islam in Bengal. Over time, particularly in the Mughal period, Bengal became a thriving economic zone involved in the export of muslin, cotton textiles, and rice.

The Mughal period in particular witnessed a significant rise in the production of cash crops such as rice, cotton, and silk, which spearheaded a booming Bengali economy.[10] The proliferation of these cash crops played a major role in the political landscape. In fact, an important part of the sultans' economic policies and especially those of the Mughals was the transformation of dense forest into rice-cultivating lands. The concept of cultivating dense forest regions via the disbursement of land grants to those willing to till the land was not new to Bengal under the sultans and Mughals. Land grants previously had been donated to Buddhist monasteries and to Brahmans in the period under the Palas (750–1161) and Senas (1097–1223). However, land grants had occurred predominantly in northern and western Bengal, with less activity in the dense forest regions of the eastern delta.[11] In the sultanate and Mughal periods, the delta moved eastward. As the Ganges River changed course, populations and economies expanded eastward. Eaton explains that the "regions in the west, which received diminishing levels of fresh water and silt, gradually become moribund. Cities and habitations along the banks of abandoned channels declined as diseases associated with stagnant waters took hold of local communities. Thus the delta as a whole experienced a gradual eastward movement of civilization as pioneers in the more ecologically active regions cut virgin forests, thereby throwing open a widening zone for field agriculture."[12]

The Mughals' primary interest in high productivity yields in the eastern delta held paramount significance for the growth of Bengali Muslim literature. Eaton's summary of the process of subinfeudation demonstrates how land cultivation ultimately fell into the hands of a petty religious class, which was responsible for the growth of Bengali literature with Islamic topics. Eaton concisely describes this subinfeudation process: An "absentee Hindu acquired *zamīndārī* rights from the Mughal governor, permitting him to extract as much wealth as he could from a given *ta'alluq*[13] so long as he remitted a stipulated amount to the government as land revenue. The *zamīndār* then contracted with some enterprising middleman, typically a member of the Muslim petty religious establishment, to undertake the arduous tasks of organizing the clearing of the jungles and preparing the land for rice cultivation."[14] Indeed, the Mughals' success at bringing as much land as possible under cultivation through the dissemination of land grants led indirectly to the growth of this literature. More specifically, this land grant policy unintentionally created a religious class whose members constructed rural mosques and shrines and subsequently produced educational literature on Islam for the local Bengali population.

Because the ruling powers had limited interest in the people's religious orientation, these grants went to any potential cultivator, without regard for his religious affiliation. The grantee then set up religious institutions on the tax-free land given to him for personal use. Moreover, the grant allowed the recipient's heirs to use this tax-free land. This system stood in direct contrast to the system that affected the growth of Islamic religious institutions in the rest of the Islamic world, providing further evidence that the rulers were not particularly interested in spreading Islam. For example, Central Asian and the Middle Eastern Islamic religious and educational institutions such as the madrassa, *masjid*, library, and college flourished under the *waqf* system of grants. A *waqf* grant is generally given to an Islamic religious institution to fund the existence of the institution in perpetuity; unlike the aforementioned grant system, a *waqf* grant would not allow for personal use of the land. If the rulers had specifically intended to encourage the conversion of local people to Islam, they could have granted *waqf* lands in this eastern frontier zone, thereby more directly meeting such an objective. Instead, this subinfeudation process did not secure the spread of Islam, especially as it was practiced by the ruling class.

Bengal's *sanad* documents (the documents of agreement between the ruling authority and individuals to relinquish tax-free lands to those individuals who agree to bring additional lands under cultivation) demonstrate how this system worked. For example, a 1735–36 *sanad* document granted to Raja Ramkanta, a *zamīndār* of Rajshahi, states that he would "pay into the royal treasury the peishcush, etc., and the balances, according to kistbundy (contract stating portions of the annual assessment, dates when due and like terms of agreement); and discharge year by year at the stated times and periods, the due rents, after receiving credit for muzcoorat (items of deductions allowed to cover the *zamīndār's* expenses of managing and collecting the revenues, fees and personal allowance of the *zamīndār*, and some petty assignments for religious or charitable purposes), nankar, etc. agreeable to usages."[15] Thus the *zamīndārs* and the government concluded agreements for taxed and tax-free lands, with the *zamīndārs* then responsible for distributing tax-free land to the enterprising individuals willing to cultivate it.

In the Mughal *sanad* documents, the titles of the men who were granted these lands and who oversaw cultivation of land (including *shaikh, chaudhurī, khwāndkār, hājjī, taʿalluqdar, shāh, faqīr, saiyid, darvīsh,* and *khān*) suggest that most were Muslims.[16] Eaton convincingly argues that these middlemen were central to the creation of the Muslim identity of this rural population.

Land grants went mainly to *zamīndārs*, many of them Hindus, who did not directly oversee the cultivation of land. Rather, they turned over lands to those who then organized the people to transform dense forest areas into productive wet rice-cultivating regions. Those pioneering efforts to cultivate the land were led mostly by a Muslim petty religious class. Because Islam recognizes no priesthood, classes of scholars, religious teachers, and preachers developed, with varying degrees of Islamic knowledge. One can only surmise the education of these itinerant preachers based on the preserved writings attributed to them, although their level of knowledge and education in Islam had no bearing on their ability to erect mosques and shrines. The critical factor was economic. The tax incentive succeeded, facilitating the task of building a mosque or shrine, but the petty religious class lacked the financial means to build ornate mosques, so the landscape became dotted with simple, small mosques and shrines. Predictably, as the petty religious gentry became the leaders of these farming communities, their religious role simultaneously increased in importance.

As the next section will demonstrate, this religious class introduced Islam to the communities of Bengali speakers partly through written works composed in the Bengali language. However, before going on to a discussion of this group of pioneers and their literature, we must consider the possible reasons for the Brahmanical tradition's lesser influence in the eastern delta region. Stewart suggests that a Brahmanical hesitance about moving beyond the Ganges persisted, leaving the region and its new residents open to the development of Islam: "Those areas east of the Ganga tended to yield more readily to Muslim development because of certain explicit restrictions on brahmana settlement and the more general fact that much of that land was insufficiently domesticated for Hindu habitation of a kind favored elsewhere."[17] In addition, though Brahmans attempted to harmonize Vedic religion with the region's indigenous cults, the results were mixed at best. While the Shiva and Vaishnava cults enjoyed state patronage from Hindu kings such as the Senas prior to the arrival of Indo-Turkish conquerors, the conquerors did not provide such patronage. The Shiva cult suffered, yet a popular devotional Vaishnava movement inspired by Chaitanya (d. 1533) gained some momentum in Bengal. Eaton attributes the success of Vaishnavism to its non-Brahmanical inclusiveness—for example, devotionalism over ritual—and to the power placed in the hands of the devout, especially with the use of Bengali over Sanskrit.[18]

At the beginning of Muslim rule, the class distinctions (*ashraf*/non-*ashraf*) were clear, and the two broad categories of literature—Arabic and Persian on the one hand and Bengali with Islamic topics on the other—represented the literature of the *ashraf* and non-*ashraf* audiences, respectively. However, over time these distinctions became blurred, providing room for a group I designate "lesser *ashraf*." This lesser *ashraf* likely plays the important role of transmitter of Islamic knowledge in the Bengali medium.

Ashraf and Non-*Ashraf* and Their Literatures

The petty religious gentry, not the ruling class, played a direct and significant role in the spread of Islam in Bengal. To fully appreciate the purposes and diversity of Islamic literature during Muslim rule in Bengal, however, it is crucial to examine the class distinctions between *ashraf* and non-*ashraf* audiences and authors. We need to understand the distinctions in terms of the dichotomy between the ruling elite of foreign descent (*ashraf*) and the indigenous people (non-*ashraf*) and those who fell into a more ambiguous category, the lesser *ashraf*.

All the Arabic and Persian literature produced in Bengal resulted from direct royal patronage. The authors and the intended audience were the *ashraf*—that is, the Muslim elite class of foreign descent. This

Muslim elite included non-Bengali soldiers, administrators, and a highly educated class of urban Sufis and *'ulama'*. The fact that this literature, as discussed earlier, consisted predominantly of Persian poetry and literature of the religious sciences in Persian and Arabic provides further evidence of its intended audience. The members of the *ashraf* class desired the production of this literature as a way of maintaining their cultural identity in a foreign land. The literature was both of a religious and nonreligious nature. Had this literature been intended for consumption by the indigenous population, the ruling elite would have patronized Bengali translations, which was not generally the case. (Kings did, however, sponsor a few examples of Bengali works, which will be discussed in the next section.) We find no Bengali or bilingual texts of *tafsir, fiqh* (works of Islamic jurisprudence), or hadith (traditions of the Prophet) from this early period. This absence provides further evidence that the Muslim rulers had a policy of not imposing their religion on the people of Bengal. Such works would require royal patronage to support the existence of a body of scholarly readers and authors. In fact, in the introductions of some seventeenth-century Bengali works, authors often mention *ashraf* opposition to the rendering of any Islamic literary topics in Bengali.[19] The rulers—*ashraf* Muslims—clearly avoided feeling alienated from their culture, language, and way of life in Bengal by bringing with them their own literary culture, such as recitations of Persian poetry and the patronage of the Islamic sciences in Arabic and Persian.

Although the members of the *ashraf* regarded their culture and way of life as superior to the indigenous, distinctions regarding one's "*ashraf*-ness" or nobility did not always remain clear.[20] As the *ashraf* assimilated and their culture became intermingled with Bengali regional culture, descendants of *ashraf* Muslims gradually became regarded as less *ashraf*. Some *ashraf* became more integrated into Bengali culture by intermarriage and place of birth. According to Abdul Majed Khan, "Nobility was determined by immigration from the west in direct proportion to the nearness in point of time and distance in point of land of origin from Bengal to Arabia."[21] *Ashraf* status in Bengal was synonymous with foreign descent and high culture.

Though distinctions between *ashraf* and non-*ashraf* were important to the *ashraf*, after approximately 150 years of Muslim rule, a Muslim artisan class arose in urban areas. The artisans' origins are not certain, but they may be descendants of both *ashraf* and non-*ashraf* peoples. This uncertainty exemplifies the increased ambiguity attached to *ashraf*/non-*ashraf* class distinctions over time. Their social and occupational distinctions mimicked the Hindu castes or *jātis* in that they were endogamous social networks organized by occupation. For example, as early as the sultanate period every city had weavers (*jolā*), livestock herders (*mukeri*), cake sellers (*piṭhāri*), fishmongers (*kābāṛi*), loom makers (*sānākār*), circumcisers (*hājām*), bow makers (*tirakar*), papermakers (*kāgajī*), wandering holy men (*kalandar*), tailors (*darji*), weavers of thick cord (*benaṭā*), dyers (*rangrej*), users of hoes (*hālān*), and beef sellers (*kasāi*).[22] Mukundarām Cakravartī's *Caṇḍī-maṅgal* (1589) describes some of the Muslim residents of a typical town in Bengal.

> Some marry according to Islamic usage; others marry according to Hindu usage. The *Maulanā* performs Islamic marriage ceremonies and receives many rupees in exchange. He blesses [those married] and recites a *kalamā* prayer. He sacrifices cocks with a sharp knife and receives a gift of forty cowries in return. Whenever there is a sacrifice of a she-goat, they give the *Mollā* the head; in addition he receives a gift of twenty-four cowries. Many young Muslims erect a sitting platform; there the *Maulvī* teaches them to read.
>
> Those who did not fast or make *namāz* became inferior Muslims [*golā*]. Those among them who weave cloth are called *Jolā*. Those who carry loads on bullocks are called by the name *Mukeri*. Those who sell *piṭha* sweets are called *Piṭhāri*. Those who sell fish are *Kabāṛi*; they always tell lies and do not have beards. Hindus who have become Muslims are *garsāl* [converts]. Those who become blind only at night, beg during the night. Those who card thread have the name Sānākār. Those who perform circumcision are named Hājām. Some wear turbans and hawk their goods in the town. Those who make arrows are Tirakars. Those who make paper are named Kāgajī. Those who wander from place to place are Kalandars. Groups of Darjis cut and sew cloth. Those who weave the *newārs* [large cords used in making rope-cots]

are named Beṇaṭā. Those who work with spades are called Hālān. Those who sell the meat of cows are named Kasāi; for this reason they have no place in Yamapura [heaven].[23]

In the late sixteenth century, the population of lesser *ashraf* and non-*ashraf* Muslims continued to grow, suggesting that a Muslim identity was one among a number of important identities such as class and caste identity. The new rulers, the Mughals, did not take an interest in Bengali culture. Thus, the separate Arabic and Persian literary trend was further reinforced by efforts of these newer *ashraf* while a lesser *ashraf* community continued to flourish.

But in addition to the *ashraf* literature written in Arabic and Persian, *ashraf*, lesser *ashraf*, and non-*ashraf* authors composed literature in the local language for the non-*ashraf*. These genres differed from those written in Persian and Arabic, as did the intended audience. Composed in Bengali with Islamic topics, this other literature was aimed at an indigenous audience. As will be discussed later in the chapter, Bengali literature with Islamic topics included popular Muslim stories and religious instructional works that rarely represented the Islamic normative literary tradition found in the Middle East. Much of this literature introduced Islam to the indigenous people in such a way that Bengal and Bengali culture became situated within a general Islamic historical framework and thus was incorporated into the history of Islam. The literature included histories of the Islamic world in a Bengal-centered view. It was preceded, however, by literature patronized by the ruling elite in urban centers in South Asia from Sind to Sylhet.

Royal Patronage of Arabic, Persian, and Bengali Literature

As early as the eighth century, subcontinental Muslim scholars from Sind traveled to and from Baghdad, engaging in religious scholarly work exclusively in Arabic and Persian.[24] Islamic works included hadith collections, Hanafi jurisprudence, and *tafsir*. For example, one of the first authors of *maghazi* literature (histories of the Prophet's military battles), Abu Ma'shar (d. 786), was from Sind. In the twelfth century, 'Ali al-Kufi, from Ucch, translated an Arabic work on the history of Sind. Razi al-din Hasan al-Ṣaghani (d. 1252) rearranged al-Bukhari and Muslim's hadith collections in his *Mashariq al-anwar*. Al-Minhaj al-Siraj (d. ca. 1270), first principal of the Delhi Nasiriyya madrassa, composed the chronicle *Tabaqat-i nasiri* in 1256. Qadi Shihabuddin Daulatabadi (d. 1445) wrote a Persian commentary on the Qur'an dealing mostly with problems of *fiqh*. He also wrote a commentary on Hanafi law in Persian.[25] Other topics of literary interest included poetry, medicine, history, geography, and biography. This trend continued for centuries, with a significant increase in literature after the 1200s, with contributions by subcontinental authors to the Arabic and Persian bodies of literature.[26]

This trend was evidenced, though not as strongly, as far east as Bengal, where, at rulers' courts, the mystical poetry of Jalaluddin Rumi and other Persian poets was recited.[27] The Muslim Turks who conquered Bengal in the thirteenth century introduced Persian as the court language.[28] A Persian inscription on a mosque built by Zafar Khan in 1298 in southwestern Bengal demonstrates the Turkish conquerors' desire publicly to celebrate elements of their foreign culture as well as Zafar Khan's benevolence as a ruler:

> Zafar Khan, the lion of lions, has appeared
> By conquering the towns of India in every expedition, and
>   by restoring
> The decayed charitable institutions.
> And he has destroyed the obdurate among the infidels with
>   his sword and
> Spear, and lavished the treasures of his wealth in [helping]
>   the miserable.[29]

During Turkish rule in the thirteenth and fourteenth centuries, a substantial number of Muslim scholars and artists visited and then settled in Bengal, promoting Arabic and Persian scholarship in Muslim capitals. Scholars included such famous Persian poets as Amir Khusrau (d. 1284), and Hafiz (d. 1389) of Shiraz, who accepted an offer by Sultan Ghiyathuddin (r. 1389–1410) of Bengal to visit his court, though Hafiz never actually reached the court.[30] Qadi Ruknuddin (d. 1218), who served in the court of Ali Mardan Khilji as a *qadi* (judge), authored the *Kitab al-irshad*. The Hanbali Abu Taw'ama al-Bukhari (d. 1300) settled in Sonargaon, where he established an Islamic institution of learning.

Sonargaon became widely known for the prominence of traditionists (scholars on hadith). There the Sufi saint Shaikh Sharafuddin Yahya Maneri studied with Abu Taw'ama al-Bukhari,[31] and his students in turn traveled throughout the Muslim world in search of hadith.[32] Numerous works in Arabic and especially in Persian were also written in other centers of study in Bengal, including Gaur and Pandua, Darasbari, Rangpur, Dhaka, Bagha, Sylhet, and Chittagong.

During the sultanate period, in 1502, Sultan Husayn Shah erected a madrassa at Gaur where the religious sciences were taught, and he later established a college at Pandua, with the aid of a land grant, in honor of the politically prominent Chisti saint Nur Qutb-i-Alam. In time, both Pandua and Gaur became important Muslim religious centers and pilgrimage sites.[33] At Sonargaon, Sharafuddin Abu Taw'ama wrote on mysticism in his Arabic work, *Maqamat*, and composed a religious guidebook in Persian, *Nam-i-haq*. Makhdum Sharafuddin Yahya Maneri is known for his works on theology, hagiography, and *fiqh*, and there is even evidence of Persian *tafsir* from Mir Abu'l Ma'ali on *Sura-i-ikhlas*.[34]

Muslim rulers were also patrons of Bengali texts on Hindu subjects and, in rare cases, of works with Islamic topics. Poet Shah Muhammad Saghir dedicated his Bengali version of *Yusuf-zulaikha* to his patron, Sultan Ghiyathuddin Azam Shah (r. 1389–1409).[35] In the Ilyas Shahi period, Sultan Jalaluddin is remembered for his generous patronage of local Hindu scholarship, though he invoked the Muslim creed on his coinage and insisted he was the caliph of Allah.[36] During the Husayn Shahi period, Hindu authors continued to enjoy a great deal of royal patronage as a function of the rulers' attempts to gain widespread support and therefore legitimacy in the eyes of the Bengali population. Later sultans also continued their patronage of the indigenous high culture, and by the fifteenth century, many *ashraf* Muslims spoke Bengali.[37] According to Eaton, "By the second half of the same century, the court was patronizing Bengali literary works as well as Persian romance literature. Sultan Rukn al-Din Barbak (r. 1459–74) patronized the writing of the *Śrī Kṛṣṇa-Vijaya* by Maladhara Basu, and under 'Ala al-Din Husain Shah (1493–1519) and Nasir al-Din Nusrat Shah (1519–32), the court patronized the writing of the *Manasā-Vijaya* by Vipra Das, the *Padma-Purāṇa* by Vijaya Gupta, the *Kṛṣṇa-Maṅgala* by

Yasoraj Khan, and translations (from Sanskrit) of portions of the great epic *Mahābhārata* by Vijaya Pandita and Kavindra Parameśvara."[38] Thus, the sultanate rulers articulated their power through the patronage of Persian, Arabic, and even Bengali literature and material arts. Patrons supported Bengali translations of literature on Hindu or indigenous topics but rarely on Islam. The members of the ruling elite saw themselves as a clearly distinct community with their own language and culture and likely criticized those who authored texts about Islam in Bengali.

The Other Literature: The Religious Gentry and Bengali Literature with Islamic Topics

Bengali literature on Islamic topics was composed primarily in verse. It dates back to the sultanate and Mughal periods. Arabic and Persian themes and stories were appropriated into Bengali literature and composed in Bengali meter. For example, Shah Muhammad Saghir's fifteenth-century Bengali version of *Yusuf-zulaikha* is one of the oldest Bengali versions of this Persian tale based loosely on the story of the prophet Yusuf (Joseph) in the Qur'an. The tale of *Laili-majnun*, adopted from the Persian by many authors writing in Bengali, also has Arabic poetic origins. While explicitly concerned with human love, works such as these are laden with esoteric Sufi themes on the subject of the ultimate type of devotional love of God. This literature contained Islamic themes and stories that conveyed basic tenets of Islam as well as more arcane ideas. Āli Rajā's *Agama*, an excerpt from which opened this chapter, offers a sophisticated articulation of Sufi ideas. Literary developments continued throughout the Mughal period (1576–1757), which was marked by the influence of Persian and ultimately Urdu as well as by the appearance of new types of literature. Indeed, as Mughal efforts to cultivate the forest hinterland expanded, more rural mosques, shrines, and schools were constructed, and the literature, a likely product of this expansion, further diversified, as is described later in this chapter.[39]

The Bengali literature of this period on Islamic topics falls into three categories: *risālas* (Muslim tales), *yoga-kalandar* (love poetry), and *marsiās* (Imam Husayn elegies).[40] The *risālas* are religious pamphlets describing duties of the believer. Some titles included under this category are *Nasīhat nāmā* (admonitions and instruction on religious duties and obligations), *Namazer kitab* (on the usefulness of prayer), *Musar-sawal* (a dialogue between Moses and God), *Shariat nāmā* (a work on Islamic prescriptions and prohibitions), *Kifāyat al-muṣallīn* (manual on prayer, fasting, almsgiving, and so forth), *Hidayat al-islām* (advice to Muslims to abstain from un-Islamic activities), and *Namaz-mahatamya* (on the usefulness of prayer).[41] Muslim tales include stories about the life of the Prophet and his military exploits and the biographies and battles of other well-known figures in Islamic history. Such tales include *Nabi baṃsa* (a history of the prophets from Adam to Muhammad), *Rasul bijay* (accounts of the miracles of the Prophet), *Nurnama* (story of the creation of light and Muhammad's subsequent emanation from it), *Shab-i-miraj* (about the Prophet's ascent to heaven), *Ofat-i-rasul* (on the death of the Prophet), *Iblīs-nāmā* (a work on Satan), *Amir hamza* (about the exploits of an uncle of the Prophet),[42] and *Janganāmā* (about the death of a grandson of the Prophet).[43] The *Nabi baṃsa* typifies the religious literature that embraced and incorporated the Bengali cultural milieu. Rafiuddin Ahmed characterized Syed Abdus Sultan's version of the story as representing "what may be called a localized version of popular Islam, with Brahma, Vishnu, Maheswar, Jesus, and finally Prophet Muhammad, all having their due places in it."[44] Most of the premodern Sufi poetry transformed the Islamic message into a mixed assembly of popular stories and narratives with folkloristic elements and esoteric Sufi concepts. In South Asia, Sufis took up the challenging task of employing local languages such as Sindhi, Punjabi, Hindi, Urdu, Bengali, and Tamil to write about Sufi mystical themes.[45]

The *yoga-kalandars* are interesting examples of the way Sufi philosophy was introduced. It was not, as previous authors have argued, a mixed assembly of Sufi with yogic practices. Like the *yoga-kalandars*, the *Tālib nāmā* is a dialogue on mystical doctrine between a teacher and a disciple. As in the sultanate period, romantic tales continued to flourish in the Mughal period, including the popular *Yusuf-zulaikha* tale, with numerous authors composing versions. The *marsiās* represent a direct result of Shi'i Muslim settlement in Bengal. These stories primarily concerned the Shi'i martyr Husayn and the Battle of Karbalā.[46]

As these various styles and genres of poetry became firmly established, an extraordinary growth of Bengali literature by Muslims occurred. This literary trend continued into the eighteenth century during the religious reform movements of Muhammad ibn 'Abd al-Wahhab (1703–87) in Arabia and Shah Wali Allah (1703–62) in India.

Initially in Bengal, Islamic cosmology was incorporated within the local belief system, and Islamic ideas and concepts were presented using familiar indigenous terms. Thus, the Prophet Muhammad was called an avatar and Allah was referred to as *prabhu, gosai,* and *nirañjan,* Bengali words used to refer to a god.[47] These terms gradually were replaced by Arabic words in the normative Islamic literature of Bengal. This allowed the Sufi *pirs* and the general petty religious class to introduce Islam to local rural residents in terms they could comprehend through varying levels of correlation. Many scholars theorize that this literature represented the authors' syncretic tendencies.[48] Tony K. Stewart uses translation theory to demonstrate the flaws of this argument, insightfully suggesting that the style of this literature indicates the authors' efforts to communicate Islamic ideas by finding some kind of "terms of equivalence" in the local language and culture to convey Sufi concepts: "Translation in this context defines a way that religious practitioners seek 'equivalence' among their counterparts. . . . [I]t is this act of translation that offers an alternative interpretive strategy for conceptualizing the way these various Sufi communities formulated their understandings of the contours of power in Bengal."[49] Given the fact that language structures conceptual worlds to the extent that "certain thoughts cannot be entertained," to communicate a Sufi conception of God and the purpose of life, the author must necessarily employ the vocabulary at hand in the target language. That vocabulary will of course be associated only with philosophical concepts already known to that linguistic community. Therefore, as in the example opening this chapter, Āli Rajā's Sufi cosmology is introduced by appropriating, approximating, and expanding the vocabulary used for Samkhya philosophy.[50] Thus, Stewart's work definitively demonstrates that the "religious encounter" was not understood or experienced in terms of conflict between Hinduism and Islam in Bengal, despite assumptions in nineteenth- and twentieth-century scholarship that religious conflict is inevitable.[51] In the late nineteenth and twentieth centuries, reformers targeted all practices, customs, and rituals they deemed un-Islamic and made every effort to convince all Muslims to reject these phenomena.

An examination of a representative tract from the premodern period will show the flavor of this literature and illustrate the ways in which Islamic terminology and concepts were introduced. The earliest evidence of a *nasīhat nāmā* (Book of advice), a kind of work that deals with religious duties, was composed by the sixteenth-century Sufi poet Afzal Ali.[52] The *nasīhat nāmās* continued in their popularity and were composed until well into the nineteenth century. This typical example was written in the seventeenth century by Muhammad Niyaj. It is only four pages long but discusses the topic of faith in God and the benefits of such faith.

Niyaj first and foremost warns that those who criticize their master will be punished. According to the author, critics suffer in several manners. First, they forget all that they learn from their Lord. Second, they lack the means to sustain themselves, and as a result, their lives are ruined. The author goes on to tell the story of a woman of the *jahiliyya* period (period of ignorance) who had faith in the one God. When she dies, her lips darken (the poet employs the Bengali term *kālimābaran*). Seeing her, her son, filled with grief and pain, falls asleep and subsequently dreams that a person approaches his mother adorned in beautifully perfumed cloth and wraps her in it. The son asks the man why he was doing this, and he replies,

I am God's [Allah's, Ar.] angel [Per.].
I take everything according to the order of Allah
This woman read the Prophet's [*nabi*, Ar.] book
Always this woman was devoted [*bhāb*, Ben.] to Allah
For that reason I give fragrance to every part of her body
Her whole face has light [*nur*, Ar.] because I gave it
   luster [*jutirmay*, Ben.][53]

Not everything about this story is what one would expect, such as the son falling asleep when he sees his dead mother. However, the point of this excerpt is to demonstrate the benefits that can accrue to those who believe in God. Heaven and an afterlife await the believer. In another part of the tract, the poet tells a story about a hypocritical man (*munafiq*, Ar.) and his faithful wife. To find an excuse to beat her, he takes a coin he has previously stolen and places it in his wife's view. The next day, he secretly removes the coin and requests that she retrieve it. The faithful wife, who performs every task in the name of God, reaches out for the coin, and it miraculously appears. Amazed, the husband confesses his sin and becomes a believer.

> A wealthy person [mahājan] became a Muslim
> when he confessed his sin [aparādh] to the woman
> He came to love his wife tremendously,
> In happiness, worshipping [cap] the Lord [prabhu] all the time
> Whoever reads Your Word [kalima, Ar.] faithfully [ekmane],
> What can the hypocrites do?[54]

In another excerpt from this tract, the poet advises his readers to pray sincerely.

> The merit that is gained through pain is the best of all merit.
> Without pain one cannot earn wealth
> Doing good works, you will gain peace and happiness.
> If you pray, you will not feel sorrow.[55]

The tract uses some Arabic and Persian vocabulary, but the majority of the terms are indigenous. Islamic concepts were introduced through the use of these familiar indigenous terms. For example, when the poet describes the woman who believed in one God, he uses Bengali terms such as *bhāgyabartī*, *puṇya*, and *nirañjan*. *Bhāgyabartī* is a fortunate woman. *Puṇya* (merit) is an important term in Hindu tradition. It refers specifically to merit that is gained through good deeds. In a Hindu interpretation, these good deeds lead toward a better birth in the next life. Here, good deeds result in peace and happiness. *Nirañjan* is a Sanskrit word that means "one without qualities or color," a conception of God that can easily be comprehended as Islamic. It is a god that cannot be depicted in images.

Stewart argues that language, like religion, communicates and sustains cultural values. Cultural values and conceptions of the world are deeply connected and articulated through the language of a given culture.[56] The challenging task, therefore, to the writer who wishes to teach Islam in a new environment is translating those cultural values into the new language, and these premodern authors faced precisely this challenge. Niyaj makes an identification between the Islamic terms and Bengali indigenous terms. The limitations of the author's use of the term *pun.ya* lie in the fact that in an Islamic worldview there is no rebirth but rather a hereafter. After this description, the poet employs the Arabic terms such as *nur* for light, *Allah* for God, and *nabi* for prophet. By replacing the Bengali terms such as *nirañjan* whenever possible with the Arabic "Allah," the poet introduces Islamic concepts that are understood as distinct from terms already existent in the target language. In this way, new cultural concepts and values are introduced, thereby expanding the meaning of terminology in the target language.[57]

As mentioned earlier, Rafiuddin Ahmed characterized Syed Abdus Sultan's *Nabi baṃsa* as "what may be called a localized version of popular Islam, with Brahma, Vishnu, Maheswar, Jesus, and finally Prophet Muhammad, all having their due places in it."[58] In fact, this genre of literature, *Nabi baṃsa*, plays a more significant role in the Islamization process than this characterization indicates. The Bengali experience of land cultivation in formerly dense forest constitutes a central element of this Bengali Islamic literature. The literature provides a myth of origin for Bengali Muslims and places their experience and that of their ancestors in an Islamic historical context. The Angel Gabriel gives Adam a plow and Eve fire and then explains that Adam will farm the land while Eve will perform the domestic chores. The *Nabi baṃsa* incorporates Bengal into Islamic history in two ways. First it includes Brahma, Maheswar (Shiva), and Vishnu in this history, thus suggesting some kind of parallel with the local culture. Second, it introduces and then explains the roles of Adam and Eve in terms of the Bengali experience of bringing dense forest under cultivation. It is God's command that they do so, designating a station for humans in the cosmic order.

Numerous stories tell of holy men and even women who arrive in Bengal from the Middle East, bringing Islam to Bengal while also making connections to agrarian society. For example, manuscripts dating from the seventeenth century tell the story of the famous saint Shah Jalal of Sylhet. In one version Shah Jalal is identified as a Yemeni Arab whose spiritual guide sends him with a clump of soil in hand to search out and settle in a region that has similar soil. Shah Jalal travels through the subcontinent, making his way east, where he defeats the Hindu raja. Only after Shah Jalal's victory does he notice that the soil is of the same quality as the soil his spiritual guide had given him in Yemen. Shah Jalal then constructs his Sufi hospice on those grounds. This and other accounts of Sufi saints remain vivid in the memory of the agrarian society through the oral tradition of storytelling. Shaikh Tabrizi's life story also reveals his connection with the land, the construction of a mosque, and the king who provided the land.[59]

Along with Shah Jalal, Bayazid Bistami, and Khan Jahan Ali are the most important saints associated with introducing Islam to Eastern Bengal. Bistami (d. 874) likely never visited Bengal. Enshrined in the tomb dedicated to him is Shah Sultan Balkhi, who people believed arrived in Chittagong on a fish. Khan Jahan Ali's arrival is equally fantastic, as he is believed to have arrived in Khulna riding on the backs of two crocodiles. These arrivals in Bengal are associated directly with the introduction of Islam and civilization building. As chapter 4 will demonstrate, the veneration of these and many other saints also reaffirms Bangladesh's place in Islamic history and Islamic identity.

In another manuscript dating to the early seventeenth century, a writer named Tamiji composed a work about his patron, the *zamīndār* of Lalmati, 'Ali Husayn. Tamiji makes numerous references to Muslim prophets and at one point states that the angel Jibril (Gabriel) told Solomon that God had requested that the son of the king of Lalmati marry the daughter of the East.[60] Perhaps this story serves to demonstrate that according to divine authority, Bengal is supposed to come under the influence of Islam. The Muslim king's son represents Islam, and his bride represents both the Bengal region and its people.

Further evidence of the link between the petty religious class and the land can be found in the authors' biographical materials sometimes included in the prefaces or in the main texts of these tracts, many of which indicate that the authors were Sufis and that their works were commissioned by *zamīndārs*. For example, in *Tatimaina*, a religious instructional work, Muhammad Naqi states that he wrote the text under the patronage of Trahiram Chowdhury, a Hindu landlord of Charamba village in Chittagong. *Zamīndārs* such as Asad Ali Chowdhury of Husainabad authored works as well.[61] Another *zamīndār*, Wahid Muhammad of Chittagong, patronized Fazil Nasir Muhammad's *Ragmala*. Muslim writer Nawajish Khan received the patronage of Hindu *zamīndār* Baidyanath Roy.[62] Poet Afzal Ali was born in a village in Chittagong, and his father was known by the name Banga Fakir (Bengali Faqir). Afzal Ali was regarded as a Muslim saint and a disciple of Shah Rustam.[63] Another celebrated poet of the sixteenth century, Sabirid Khan, was the son of a man said to have founded the village Nanupur in Chittagong.[64] These numerous examples testify to the roles played by the petty religious class and the *zamīndārs*. Many of the *zamīndārs* were in fact Hindu, while most of the members of the petty religious class were Muslims, which indicates that religious affiliation was inconsequential to the success of these arrangements. These poets sometimes created fictional or fantastic accounts of the lives of the religious gentry, filling them with magic and miracles to illustrate and legitimate the process of change that was presented as civilization building in the region.

Conclusion

The birth of Bengali literature dealing with Islamic topics and Muslim heroes and heroines during the sultanate period and its subsequent and dramatic growth during the Mughal period was not primarily a function of direct patronage. These rulers had no interest in introducing Islam to the Bengali population. On the contrary, the Mughals were even less interested in the local culture than were the sultans and were not concerned with patronage as a way of gaining legitimacy as rulers. Yet Islam's influence grew in this time, and the landscape became increasingly populated with mosques and shrines. Bengali literature on Islamic topics also flourished. The growth of this new literature resulted indirectly from an interest in increasing agrarian output as the economic frontier continued to move eastward. The petty religious class, which led the people in cultivating the land, built simple rural mosques, shrines, and learning centers where many of these tracts and poems were written, as evidenced in their prefaces and texts.

Much of Bengali literature, as indicated by its content, was intended for a Bengali population that had no access to Arabic and Persian literature. These works were authored by members of the Muslim religious gentry who had knowledge of the local language and familiarity with some Arabic and Persian literature. Some Bengali works, such as the *Yusuf-zulaikha* and *Laili-majnun* poems, were patronized by lower-level administrators. Being born in Bengal or having exposure to the local language through intermarriage would make it possible to transmit this religious knowledge in a foreign language. In addition, the sultanate period featured urbanite local individuals called *kalandars* (the Persian term for holy men); this category of individuals may at one time have claimed *ashraf* descent or may have descended from people who did so, but having settled and intermarried with local women, they gradually identified themselves or were identified by the "newer *ashraf*" as local or Bengali. Sultan Husayn Shah (r. 1494–1519), of Arab origin, married a Bengali woman, as did other sultans. The *ashraf*/non-*ashraf* classifications clearly became increasingly complicated over time. The *ashraf* or those who claimed *ashraf* descent would likely have had the requisite knowledge and understanding of Islam to teach its basic tenets. Finally, as the *ashraf*/non-*ashraf* distinction became further obscured, *ashraf* literary production diminished.

Because the indigenous population had virtually no knowledge of Arabic, the language of the sacred text, very little in the way of the Islamic sciences was transmitted. In fact, no evidence indicates that the traditional science of *tafsir* existed before the nineteenth century in Bengal. The rural population had even less direct access to the Qur'an itself.

The rural religious institutions were not well endowed. Therefore, the benefactors of these institutions confined their religious instructional efforts to whatever they could teach about Islam in the Bengali language. The important figures in the Qur'an and the identification of their place in Islamic history, Islamic morality, ethics, duties of the faithful, and a great deal of Sufi philosophy are well represented in all of the literature of the premodern period. This literature also depicted in metaphorical terms the historical change experienced in Bengal at the time, such as the introduction of Islam and the settlement of the forest hinterland. These compositions linked Islam with agrarian development by a literary affirmation of the benevolence of Islamic superhuman agencies. By their nature, these works written in Bengali had to employ Bengali terms to convey the meaning of Islamic concepts expressed in Arabic. These writings paved the way for the modern Bengali commentary on the Qur'an. By the eighteenth century, however, the way that the Bengali Muslim rural population demonstrated its Muslimness through customs, oral literature, and culture was often at variance with the understanding of the eighteenth-century urban *ashraf*. The religious praxis of rural residents and their means of expressing themselves as Muslims soon came to face criticism from a variety of sources.

two

Nineteenth-Century Religious Reform Movements

As our blessed Lord has required us to pray that his kingdom may come, and his will be done on earth as it is in heaven, it becomes us not only to express our desires of that event by words, but to use every lawful method to spread the knowledge of his name.
—Excerpted from William Carey's *An Enquiry into the Obligations of Christians to Use Means for the Conversion of the Heathens*

The eighteenth century in the Islamic world has often been discussed in terms of decline. The most obvious examples of this decline include the Mughal, Safavid, and Ottoman Empires. This decline occurred simultaneously with the successful British and Dutch economic penetration of South and Southeast Asia. Yet while Muslim authority was deteriorating, signs pointed to increased intellectual growth and activity. The colonial experience directly contributed to this growth in a number of ways that were effected through administrative policies and through the presence of

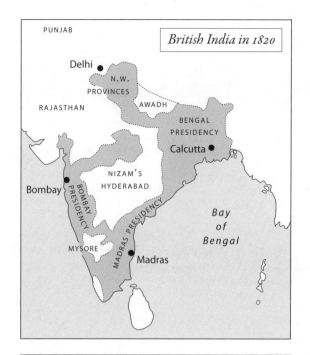

MAP 3. The British Raj, 1820 and 1856. (Adapted from John Keay, *India: A History* [New York: Atlantic Monthly Press, 2000].)

Christian missionaries who, like William Carey, strove to spread the Christian Gospel. Muslims and other colonized peoples met such efforts with a number of creative responses. For one, an abundance of literature about Islam in the vernacular appeared on the frontier of the ever-expanding Muslim world, including in Bengal.[1] Eighteenth-century religious reformers Muhammad ibn 'Abd al-Wahhab (d. 1787) and Shah Wali Allah (d. 1762) would become major influences on the direction of religious and intellectual activities.

In the geographic regions of the Arabian Peninsula and the Indian subcontinent, nineteenth-century reformers made many references to both Muhammad ibn 'Abd al-Wahhab and Shah Wali Allah. Both leaders identified moral decay as the significant ill within Muslim society, and both sought to purge Islam of practices they believed were wrongly associated with Islam. They were therefore termed "revivalist," seeking a return of religious praxis to a pristine Islam. A glorified view of the early Islamic period, when Medina emerged as the home of the *umma* under Muhammad's guidance, is the ideal Islamic society, the pristine Islam to which these and many subsequent reformers refer. This glorified image of the early Islamic community became the model of many reform efforts of the eighteenth and nineteenth centuries. Here I will examine the life of Shah Wali Allah and the elements of his teachings that later generations of reformers in India emphasized.[2]

Shah Wali Allah and Reform in the Indian Subcontinent

Shah Wali Allah began his studies by the age of five, eventually studying hadith, *tafsir, fiqh, kalam*, and the works of Fakhruddin 'Iraqi (d. 1289), Ibn 'Arabi, and Jami (d. 1492). Shah Wali Allah's father and spiritual guide, Shah 'Abd al-Rahim (d. 1719), was a member of three Sufi orders: the Naqshbandiyya, Chistiyya, and Qadiriyya; he taught at the Rahimiyya Madrassa in Delhi. By the age of fifteen, Shah Wali Allah had become a member of the Naqshbandiyya order and had received permission from his father to begin teaching Islam. In 1730, at the age of sixteen, Shah Wali Allah became the principal of the Rahimiyya Madrassa. Shortly thereafter, he went on the hajj and remained for more than a year in the holy cities, where he continued his study of hadith.[3]

During the eighteenth century, hadith studies were viewed as an avenue of reform in Muslim society and became a main occupation of reformers; modernist Islamic reformers criticized the amount of attention hadith studies received over the following century, suggesting that the true focus should be the Qur'an.[4] Many Muslims who believed that loss of Muslim political authority was tied to deteriorating and corrupt religious practice and weak faith also believed that a time had existed when Islam was practiced with near perfection. Some religious reformers and leaders believed that during the lifetime of the Prophet Muhammad and the early Medinan community, Islam was practiced more correctly than at any time since. Holding onto this early period as the golden age of Islamic faith and practice, reformers attempted to retrieve those early practices and rid society of any innovative practices. According to reformers, the best example for Muslims is the life of the Prophet Muhammad: his actions and words as well as those of his companions represent the most central illustrations of "true Islam." Thus, the intensified study of hadith became one of eighteenth-century religious reformers' main occupations.

Coincidentally, in the Hijaz (the Arabian Peninsula), Shah Wali Allah had some of the same teachers as Muhammad ibn ʿAbd al-Wahhab. Although the two men had great differences in their views on aspects of Islam such as Sufi practices, both desired to establish a normative Islam. Shah Wali Allah became a prolific religious scholar in both Arabic and Persian, writing, for example, Persian and Arabic commentaries on Malik ibn Anas's (d. 795) *Muwatta'*, one of the first compilations of Islamic law. He also wrote an Arabic work on principles of Qur'anic exegesis, *al-Fawz al-kabir*. Having been greatly moved by his year of study in the Haramayn, he came to believe that Arab Muslims were superior to all other religious communities. Shah Wali Allah affirmed that all Muslims should learn Arabic and adopt Arab customs, which he saw as essential elements to living an authentic Islamic way of life. Islam had arisen in an Arab cultural environment, so many reformers found it impossible to distinguish between Arab and Islamic customs.

During Shah Wali Allah's lifetime, significant political instability occurred in Delhi. The Mughal government had been drastically weakened, and ten rulers had sat in a span of sixty years.[5] Shah Wali Allah was aware of the increasing threat to Muslim authority and power from the Marathas in the south and the Sikhs in the Punjab. In reaction to these increasingly unstable political circumstances, he wrote to Muslim rulers expressing his concern about this internal threat.[6] These political circumstances may have influenced his teachings and his desire for religious change in Muslim society in the subcontinent.

Shah Wali Allah also adamantly opposed Shi'i beliefs and rituals, such as the extensive and elaborate commemoration of 'Ashura'[7] as well as many popular Sufi practices, such as veneration of saints and worship at their tombs.[8] Yet he saw the benefits of Sufi beliefs. In fact, he argued that no one *tariqa* was superior to another; this view, meant that he, like his father, was eventually initiated into three orders: the Naqshbandiyya, Qadiriyya, and Chishtiyya.[9] Shah Wali Allah, like many reformers before him, wanted only to reform Sufi practices, not to denounce Sufism.

In terms of Islamic law and jurisprudence, prior to his trip to the Hijaz, Shah Wali Allah rejected the notion that one must accept, to the exclusion of all others, the rulings of one school of law. Although Shah Wali Allah disagreed with some Hanafi school rulings, over time he accepted them and the notion of *taqlid*.[10] His main dilemma was that he preferred the analytical principles of the Shafi'i school, which, according to Shah Wali Allah, allowed a higher level of *ijtihad* (independent reasoning).[11] He felt that the Hanafi school, unlike the Shafi'i school, no longer engaged in a rigorous analysis of hadith. But like many Indian Muslims, Shah Wali Allah in the end abided by Hanafi law.[12] Still, the next generation of reformers widely accepted Shah Wali Allah's initial rejection of *taqlid* and his rationale for doing so.

In the nineteenth century, Islamic reformers extensively debated adherence to one school of law, or *taqlid*. Some reformers regarded *taqlid* as blind adherence to centuries of legal rulings, highlighting the fact that during the lifetime of the Prophet Muhammad, no schools of law existed. Therefore, these reformers saw no need for the four Sunni schools of law in modern times and instead proposed that Muslims needed to look further back in Islamic history, to the time of the Prophet, and needed to make rulings based on how the first community of Muslims lived. To do so would be to return to true Islam. In the Indian subcontinent of the nineteenth century, the highly contested issue of *taqlīd* was debated in *munāzara* and *bāhās*.[13]

Shah Wali Allah believed that religious reform and the reestablishment of a powerful Muslim authority in the subcontinent were necessarily intertwined. In political terms, having witnessed the disintegration of the Mughal Empire's power, he desired the reestablishment of a strong Muslim authority. He therefore sought a religious reform that would result in the Muslims of India identifying with their Muslim brethren in the Middle East, seeking also to disassociate and distinguish Islamic praxis from anything indigenous or from what he perceived as Hindu. He believed that Muslims would again gain God's favor, which they had lost as a result of the lack of correct performance of religious obligations.

Later Bengali reformers such as Sayyid Ahmad (d. 1831) of the Tariqah-i-Muhammadiyah movement, who was a disciple of Shah Wali Allah's son, Shah 'Abd al-'Aziz, and Haji Shariatullah of the Faraizi movement continued to address the problems identified by Shah Wali Allah.[14] Nineteenth-century reformers interpreted his teachings in a variety of ways ; however, many reformers fondly and respectfully recalled these teachings but held different opinions on exactly what those teachings were. Many reformers often quoted the works of Shah Wali Allah. Indeed, even the Ahl-i-Hadith reform movement claimed to have been influenced by Shah Wali Allah's teachings. Members of this movement rejected the four schools of law, as did Shah Wali Allah in his early years. Like the Tariqah-i-Muhammadiyah, Ahl-i-Hadith emphasized the role of the Prophet, the Sunna, and the Qur'an. According to Annemarie Schimmel, "The depth of [Shah Wali Allah's] influence is only slowly coming to light. It shaped not only the members of his family, who continued his work by translating the Koran into Urdu and who were influential in supporting some of the most important religio-political leaders of the early 19th century, but is visible—though in a different style—also in Sir Sayyid Ahmad Khan, and in Iqbal."[15] The nineteenth-century religious reformers thus essentially worked to eradicate the problems identified by their eighteenth-century predecessors, especially Shah Wali Allah, but did so in a number of different ways. These nineteenth-century reformers claimed many of the same influences, focusing on the meaning of the Qur'an and Sunna, but ultimately found a variety of meanings. They too, believed that Muslim political authority could be regained by a return to a purer Islamic way of life. Doing so meant examining current practices in light of the Qur'an and Sunna.

All of this creative activity increased tremendously in the nineteenth century, when the British became fully entrenched in governing the subcontinent. At the same time, a growing population of Christian missionaries was working to convert the indigenous people to Christianity. The missionaries' presence, activity, and interaction with indigenous people marked a reenvisioning of community in terms of a religion that would remain dominant in the twentieth and twenty-first centuries.

British Colonial Policies

The missionaries believed that Islam could not be a true Abrahamic tradition because Muhammad was not a true prophet of God. Similarly, the missionaries saw Hindus as idolaters and children of the devil. Consequently, the missionaries' sought to spread the Gospel among members of those two groups. Not surprisingly, such efforts and representations of Islam and Hinduism encountered defensive responses from Muslim and Hindu thinkers.[16] Reformers then adopted the missionaries' vital tool, the print medium, which became the primary means for shaping the manner in which communities were imagined. Muslim and Hindu reformers employed print to address members of the public willing to read about what they believed were the needed reforms of their respective communities.

In their rule over India, the British administrators categorized people primarily based on religious affiliation. Historians have demonstrated that colonial classifications differed from the classifications that existed in the precolonial period.[17] The most influential tool the British used was the census. Arjun Appadurai suggests that the census as used in British India served purposes quite different from the British census at home. In the eighteenth century, the British learned the utility of census and data gathering in England to assess needs of individual towns and communities and to determine land tax revenue. Appadurai declares that "the idea had become firmly implanted that a powerful state could not survive without making enumeration a central technique of social control."[18] To a great extent, the census proved a useful tool in England. India's cultures and religious traditions were so different, and the census there thus came to include questions that aided the British in categorizing people by religion and caste, information that was not included in the censuses of England. The numbers and statistics thus conveyed the nature of this vast region under colonial rule in terms that higher-level bureaucrats could comprehend.[19] Through a complex process explicated by Appadurai, data collection increasingly focused on identifying groups. Group identity initially focused on caste, but the census led to the broader categorization of religious identity. The census questionnaires sought information on literacy, education, profession, wealth, religious affiliation, and caste. The reports based on the censuses categorized people by religion and compared the relative levels of literacy, education, profession, and wealth among Muslims, Hindus, British Christians, Anglo-Indians, Indian Christians, and so forth.[20]

From the beginning of British rule in India, British administrators were often concerned about the possible threat "Muslims" posed to British rule.[21] By the 1890s, the British viewed Muslims and Hindus as two separate communities with distinct political interests. Further reinforcing this notion were the interactions between missionaries and the colonized people. Missionaries developed different strategies for converting members of the two religious communities. Government policies on education, the establishment of separate electorates, and civil service positions exemplified the ways in which the British emphasized and assumed that religious communities comprised separate body politics. By the late nineteenth century, indigenous leaders were using the same language, claiming to represent Muslim or Hindu interests and often referring to their own communities with the term "nation."

Orientalist writing, missionary critique, British governing policy, and the use of print technology to address reform shed light on how religion came to inform ideas about the "nation" in South Asia in the twentieth century. Beginning in 1765, the British East India Company maintained a policy banning missionary activity in India as a consequence of the belief that doing so would minimize the potential for violent disruptions and political instability caused by interference in indigenous cultural life. By 1813, the missionaries had swayed British public opinion and policy, convincing Parliament to include an education clause that obligated the government to spend a minimum of one hundred thousand rupees on education. The 1833 ruling subsequently granted missionaries the right to reside in India. The missionaries' efforts to change policy met with such success as a result of their ability to convince the British public that providing Hindus and Muslims with Western education would make them better consumers of British products, and William Carey and other missionaries included religious education in this category. Significantly, these missionaries equated Christianity with modernization. Thus, by becoming modernized, the Indian subjects would likely become consumers of British goods, thus fulfilling the company's original mission.

Missionaries, Orientalist Scholarship, and the Civilizing Mission

It is difficult and disingenuous to separate out Orientalist scholarship from missionary efforts, as they sometimes overlapped. Missionary efforts to convert—to influence the values and cultural norms of colonized peoples of South Asia—directly shaped the development of modern language, vernacular literature, the reform of Islam in India, and the construction of modern Hinduism. Missionaries eagerly learned Indian languages and then wrote theological tracts in these languages, justifying the superiority of Christianity over "Muhammadanism" and "heathen" traditions. One of the most important early Christian missionary figures to come to Bengal was William Carey (1761–1834). Written works by Carey and others inevitably opened the door to response. Indigenous response soon turned to internal communal debate about religious life and values. Thus, the printing press became reformers' and intellectuals' dominant medium for communicating views on proper Muslim ritual practice and behavior. Printers used the lithographic press to publish low-cost books and magazines written and edited by Muslim reformers and intellectuals as a complement to other means of responding to these critiques. In 1792, while still in

England, Carey wrote *An Enquiry into the Obligations of Christians to Use Means for the Conversion of the Heathens* under the patronage of Thomas Potts, a businessman who had been to the American colonies and so had had firsthand contact with "heathens," thereby justifying his patronage of missionary efforts. Carey's short tract presents theological justifications for carrying out conversion efforts around the world. The tract was reprinted four times and provides an excellent example of the pietistic views that inspired missionaries abroad. Carey explains that Christians' role is to spread the Gospel and civilize the world, providing proof texts from Isaiah 1:9: "Surely the Isles shall wait for me; the ships of Tarshish first, to bring my sons from far, their silver, and their gold with them, unto the name of the Lord, thy God." He comments that this verse "seems to imply that in the time of the glorious increase of the church, in the latter days (of which the whole chapter is undoubtedly a prophecy) commerce shall subserve the spread of the gospel." Carey clearly equated the civilizing mission with spreading the Gospel, asking readers, "Would not the spread of the gospel be the most effectual means of their civilization?" Carey believed that Christians had a duty to support the missionary effort, either directly, by embarking to the land of the non-Christians, or indirectly, by providing financing. In 1793, Carey and his wife set out for India to achieve his missionary goals. To support his family, he took a job managing an indigo factory, where he began learning Bengali and, against East India Company regulations, preaching Christianity. The indigo factory eventually collapsed, forcing Carey to leave Calcutta.

In 1800 Carey and his family relocated to Serampore, a Danish colony north of Calcutta. At the request of the Danish governor, Carey, William Ward, John Fountain, D. Brunslow, and J. Marshman founded the Serampore Mission on 10 January 1800.[22] The mission received the protection of the Danish king, Frederick VI. Unlike the British merchants who formed the East India Company, Frederick VI wanted missionaries to propagate the Gospel in India. At Serampore, Carey and his like-minded colleagues believed that much of the success of their work depended on translating and communicating the virtues of Christianity in literary form. The missionaries of Serampore and elsewhere, intent on converting the local people, quickly learned the Bengali language. Soon after arriving in Serampore, Carey set up a printing press and by 1801 was able to publish his translation of the New Testament, the first version in any South Asian language and the first book of Bengali prose. In the same year, Carey printed a Bengali grammar book and was appointed professor of Bengali at the newly established Fort Williams College at Calcutta for the training of East India Company employees. The salary from this job provided the much-needed funds to support his ongoing mission. To complement their effort in publications, the missionaries at Serampore also opened schools for Bengali boys in 1800; by 1818, they opened their first Bengali girls' school. By 1817, the missionaries operated forty-five schools for boys; by 1824, six schools for girls were in operation. Carey's effort, the establishment of the Serampore press under the protection of the Danish government, and the work of Orientalists at Fort Williams College constituted important factors in the growth of modern Bengali literature until the beginning of the 1830s, when a printing press became available in Calcutta.[23] After a long, hard battle at home led by pietists in 1813, the British Parliament passed a law allowing missionaries to preach freely in settlements under British authority, further expanding the region in which missionary activity took place.

The prose style of the translations and missionaries' essays on the advantages of Christianity over other religions were new to the Bengali language. As more Bengali writers became familiar with the prose style, it grew in popularity, particularly among Hindus. In his work on missionary literature, William A. Smalley has stated that "the infusion of Serampore publications became model and catalyst to the development of modern Bengali prose."[24] The printing press had never before been so widely used in South Asia. Carey worked furiously to oversee the translation of the Bible into more than thirty-four Indian languages, including Sanskrit. Carey also wrote dictionaries, grammar books, and language instruction books for the study of Punjabi, Sanskrit, and other South Asian languages.[25] The Serampore Mission also became the first to publish a weekly newspaper in a vernacular language, *Samachar Darpan*, which met with the approval of the East India Company.

In addition to the Bible translations, the missionaries wrote tracts on the benefits of Christian life. They also wrote books and tracts criticizing Islam and the Hindu tradition, including *Prophet's Testimony of Christ* (1830), *Gods and Idols* (1833), *Praises of the Self Existent* (1833),

God's Punishment of Sin (1833), *Krishna and Christ Compared* (1802), and *Jagannath Worship* (1812), which concerns "the folly of such worship."[26] Most of the initial written works addressed Hindu religious practices and beliefs, but the missionaries gradually increased their publications that criticized Islam. Much of the debate with Muslims took place on missionary visits to villages where Muslims resided. The missionaries attempted to convince Muslims that Muhammad's many wives provided evidence that he was not a prophet, that he did not die for the sins of others, and that he was a murderer and adulterer. These and many other accusations against Islam and Muhammad outraged rather than converted many Muslims.[27] The missionaries at Serampore published a tract in Persian, *An Address to Mussulmuns with an Appendix Containing Some Account of Mahomet*, that accuses Muslims of perverting God's commandments: a section on the life of Muhammad states that "it is clear that no wise man will believe in his Creed which is only the source of mental darkness." The work declares Islam a "lying religion" and advises Muslims to convert to Christianity.[28] Christian missionaries began translating hadith and biographies of the Prophet Muhammad to use in essays and books explicitly attacking Islam, and by the end of the nineteenth century the missionaries began writing Bengali translations of the Qur'an. In 1823, the Reverend William Goldsack printed the first Mussalmani Bengali-English dictionary as well as other works such as his hadith collection and his biography of the Prophet.

Missionary efforts inadvertently elicited a backlash from Muslims and Hindus. The missionaries and by extension the colonial rulers were contesting and giving great significance to people's religious selves through the pen and public policy. The British identified and classified people by religious belief, and in the manner of response and debate, these contested identities became most important and defended by Muslims and Hindus. People responded in writing as Muslims and Hindus, thus reaffirming the preeminence of religious identity over any other identity, regardless of common bonds among members of the two groups and regardless of any differences in class, gender, ethnicity, language, or local customs among people of the same religious community that had existed and been acknowledged prior to the colonial period. The colonized people's religious identities had come under attack, becoming one of the most important markers for guiding British administrative policies. The tensions, debate, and policies thus led to greater divisions between these religious communities.

Literary activity initially took the form of short pamphlets on appropriate practice, and newspapers were directed at a Muslim audience. The literature on religious community expanded, and new, inventive genres in regional languages were created. The literary endeavors culminated with the introduction of high genres such as *tafsir* scholarship in regional languages, written more for the popular audience than for traditional scholars. All of this productivity became possible only after religious reformers initially led movements and debated these questions first in oral debates and later in print.

The Significance of the Nineteenth-Century Reform Movements

Although the nineteenth-century Islamic reform movements may have been inspired by the decay of Muslim authority on the Indian subcontinent, they were simultaneously a product of colonial experience—Orientalist enterprise, Christian evangelism, and colonial domination. Although the stated goal of all these movements was religious reformation, many were in essence political movements. Reformers, the elite, and the British inaccurately assumed distinctive political interests for each religious community. Religious reformers were eager to contend with the growing imposition of Western cultural, legal, and political influence on the South Asian Muslim way of life. Muslim reformers and leaders claimed that the loss of Muslim authority and Islamic ideals demanded a reevaluation of South Asian Islamic societal norms. South Asian Muslim leaders concluded that their community's major ill was that their practices had become "misguided" or inaccurate. They did not believe that what they saw of agrarian Muslim practices was in fact Islamic. To the *ashraf,* these practices and the literature described in chapter 1 rather reflected some local syncretic belief system. Therefore, according to the *ashraf,* the agrarian people—the majority of the Muslim population—needed to reform their practices to be more like the practices of the *ashraf.* This also meant that the non-*ashraf* should embrace the language of the *ashraf.* Only then might Muslims regain political authority. This was particularly true in Bengal, where the 1872 census demonstrated the existence of one of the largest Muslim communities on the subcontinent. There, these movements served as the impetus for some of the more popular forms of modern Bengali religious literature, which was regarded as a means of teaching the people proper and normative Islamic praxis. However, this literature also inadvertently created the distinct Bengali Muslim identity that would in the twentieth century call into question previously held notions of Islamic nationhood for South Asia.

In the first half of the nineteenth century, the most prominent movements were the Faraizi movement of Haji Shariatullah (d. 1840), the Tariqah-i-Muhammadiyah of Sayyid Ahmad (d. 1831), and the Ta'aiyuni movement of Karamat Ali (d. 1873). The Faraizi movement, which emphasized the political and economic problems of the rural poor, rapidly gained support against the Hindu landlords and British rulers. Under its founder, Haji Shariatullah, the movement took a socioreligious form, emphasizing the importance of performing obligatory duties.

Haji Shariatullah was originally from Faridpur in East Bengal and spent twenty years studying in the Hijaz. In 1821 he returned to Bengal, where he saw great differences in Muslims' worship and practices. He took this difference to mean that Muslims of Bengal did not properly practice Islam and began preaching the ideals of his movement. It took the name Faraizi from *fara'id*, or "obligatory duties." He adamantly opposed pirism in all its forms. He considered India *dar al-harb* but did not go so far as to promote jihad against the British.[29] In his understanding of *dar al-harb*, *'id* (two Islamic high holy days) and *jum'a* prayers (Friday congregational prayers) could not be performed in India because no Muslim ruler resided there. Reformers had no consensus about what constituted *dar al-harb* or the status of India. Although India still had a Muslim community, it was now under the rule of Christians. Those who believed India now to be in the sphere of *dar al-harb* could legitimate jihad against the British.

After the death of Haji Shariatullah, his son, Dudu Miyan (1819–62), took over leadership of the movement. Under his guidance, the movement gained a more politicoeconomic character. Unlike his father, Dudu Miyan supported anti-British activities with the general backing of the Muslim *ryots* (land tenants). He established a system in each village of Muslim arbitrators known as *khalifas*, from whom members of the reform movement were expected to seek arbitration in all matters, rather than relying on British courts. Dudu Miyan made the exploitation of Muslim *ryots* by Hindu landlords, British authority, and indigo planters the main agenda of the movement, arguing that if Muslim *ryots* took up jihad and Muslim rule was restored, the *ryots* would hold land rent free. The movement became violent at times, with riots instigated by Dudu Miyan in 1838, 1841, 1844, and 1846. However, when Dudu Miyan died in 1862, this movement lost its momentum.[30]

The Tariqah-i-Muhammadiya movement was also openly involved in political struggle and in the jihad against the British and Sikhs on the northwest frontier.[31] Most of those involved in the movement were *ryots*, mullahs, and skilled artisans.[32] This movement sought to achieve the two goals of purging Islamic practice of innovations and defending Islam on the subcontinent in hopes of returning it to Muslim rule.[33] The founder of the movement, Sayyid Ahmad of Barelwi, studied with Shah 'Abd al-'Aziz and was inducted into the same three Sufi orders as Shah Wali Allah—the Naqshbandiyya, Qadiriyya, and Chishtiyya.[34] Another reformer, Maulana Ahmad Riza Khan Barelwi, accused Shah Muhammad Isma'il, a prominent leader of the Tariqah-i-Muhammadiya, of introducing Wahhabi practice and doctrine to India.[35] For example, the Tariqah-i-Muhammadiya did not adhere to the rulings of any one particular school of law. However, a major distinction between this movement and the Wahhabis was the Tariqah's acceptance of Sufi thought. Sayyid Ahmad of Barelwi attempted to reform Sufi practices in India but did not explicitly condemn them. In 1831 he and Shah Muhammad Isma'il died in battle on the northwest frontier.

Karamat Ali (d. 1873) founded the Taiyuni movement. Born in Jaunpur, Uttar Pradesh, he was influenced by the teachings of Sayyid Ahmad of Barelwi. Karamat Ali traveled throughout Bengal and parts of northern India, where he gained a wide following. Unlike Sayyid Ahmad, Karamat Ali did not join the jihad on the northwest frontier. Some of the main targets of Karamat Ali's reforms included Muslim customs that he viewed as Hindu, such as maintaining vegetarian diets, frowning on widow remarriage, attending Hindu festivals, visiting the tombs of saints, and consulting astrologers. He addresses these issues in his *Radd al-bid'a*. The other major target of his criticism was Muslims of other sects, whom he regarded as heterodox and whose practices he attacks in *Hidayat al-rafidin*. Curiously, although his movement was essentially a grassroots movement with followers in villages throughout Bengal, he wrote predominantly in Urdu.[36] His public preaching activities targeted the poor, but his writings seem to have been directed at other Muslim reformers.

Another interesting though less influential movement, the Ahl-i-Hadith, represented moderation and criticized some of the more radical approaches of the Faraizi and Taiyuni movements. The Ahl-i-Hadith's founders, Siddiq Hasan (d. 1890) and Saiyid Nazir Husain (d. 1902), relied nearly exclusively on Qur'an and hadith. Thus, like the Tariqah-i-Muhammadiya, they opposed *taqlid* and in fact all the schools of law (*madhahib*).

In the latter half of the nineteenth century, Mirza Ghulam Ahmad (d. 1908) established the Ahmadiyya movement in the Punjab. Ahmad claimed to receive divine inspiration as a *zillin-abi* (shadow prophet) of God.[37] He also claimed to be the *masih* (messiah) and mahdi who would unite Muslims in worship and practice throughout the world. His claims and his acceptance of disciples led to serious controversy in India among the Muslim *'ulama'* and vocal Muslim leaders. The movement and its leader subsequently became the target of many fatwas and the subject of many *munāẓara* and *bāhās*. In Bengal they gained little foothold.

While all of these reformers propagated a revival of "pure Islam," their methods to achieve that goal differed, as did their notions of "pure Islam," even though they were based on the same model—the life of Muhammad and the first *umma*. These differences of opinion led to ad hominem attacks and counteraccusations. Indeed, in attempting to recruit Muslims of the subcontinent to their particular movements, members of these groups criticized each other's doctrines and practices. This competition took many forms, including the issuance and publication of fatwas, the holding of *bāhās* and *munāẓara*, and the publication of journals, newspapers, and books for Muslims and religious schools.

Tools for Religious Reformation

The Role of Fatwas and Bāhās *in Reshaping and Redefining Muslim Visions of Community*

For Indian Muslims, much of what occurred in nineteenth-century British India centered on the question of how the Muslim community defined itself. Reformers utilized fatwas, *bāhās, waz mahfil,* the publication of *nasīhat nāmās,* journals, newspapers, and, specifically in the Bengal region, Islamic high scholarship in Bengali to communicate reform ideas. Some reformers or reformist movements utilized fatwas, *bāhās,* and *waz mahfil,* while others were more likely to utilize publications.

By issuing fatwas, reformers articulated the directions in which they envisioned the *umma* moving. Typically, a mufti issued fatwas concerning *'aqā'id* (beliefs), customs particularly related to Sufism, and *'ibadat* (acts of worship), with a particular focus on reprehensible innovation.[38] Peter Hardy's *The Muslims of British India* provides specific examples of fatwa topics of the nineteenth century, such as whether it was lawful to learn English if there was no danger to religion, to collect interest from a Christian, or to use money orders and bills of exchange on which interest was charged.[39]

Many fatwas also dealt with the various religious reform movements and their levels of orthodoxy, raising questions about whether an individual reformer was truly orthodox or a *kafir.*[40] For example, Maulana Ahmad Riza Khan Barelwi (d. 1921), who considered himself vehemently anti-Wahhabi, issued fatwas naming several prominent South Asian Muslims *kafirs* because in his view they were Indian Wahhabis.[41] And in India, being a Wahhabi was synonymous with being a *kafir.* Maulana Ahmad Riza Khan Barelwi thus devised several categories of Wahhabis. He denounced those who believed there are six or seven prophets like Muhammad, calling them *Wahhabiyya Amthaliyya.* Those who believed there is a last prophet appointed to each of the other levels of the earth were accused of being *Wahhabiyya Khawatimiyya.* In this category, for example, Maulana Ahmad Riza Khan Barelwi included Maulana Qasim Nanutawi (1833–79), a Sufi and founder of the Dar al-'Ulum at Deoband. Maulana Ahmad Riza Khan Barelwi found problematic Maulana Nanutawi's contention that prophetic superiority had nothing to do with being the last prophet.[42] Those who claimed that Allah could lie, Maulana Ahmad Riza Khan Barelwi designated as *Wahhabiyya Kadhdhabiyya*. Those who affirmed God's ability to lie included the founder of the Tariqah-i-Muhammadiya and Rashid Ahmad Gangohi (d. 1905), a Deobandi patron and founder. Maulana Ahmad Riza Khan Barelwi even accused some of following the path of Satan, designating them *Wahhabiyya Shaytaniyya*.[43] This group included anyone who seemed to question the extent of the Prophet's knowledge, such as Gangohi and two Deobandi *'ulama'*, Khalil Ahmad Ambethwi and Ashraf 'Ali Thanawi.[44] Maulana Ahmad Riza Khan Barelwi found *kufr* in Ambethwi's refusal to believe that the Prophet Muhammad had knowledge of the unseen. At the time, Ambethwi was in the Haramayn, and because some Hijazi muftis supported this fatwa, he was subsequently forced to leave.

Maulana Ahmad Riza Khan Barelwi employed the term "Wahhabi" in a manner that had little if any connection to eighteenth-century reformer Muhammad ibn 'Abd al-Wahhab. Maulana Ahmad Riza Khan Barelwi essentialized the name "Wahhabi" to designate anyone who, in his view, denigrated the status of Muhammad as the seal of the Prophets. On the Indian subcontinent, anyone accused of being a Wahhabi was seen as politically disruptive.[45] According to Usha Sanyal, "Indian Muslim hostility to 'Wahhabis' was largely a response to the Muwahhiduns' record of uncompromising opposition to popular practice, especially in connection with their demolition of the tomb over the Prophet's grave at Medina. Additionally, in the aftermath of 1857, the term came to be associated in British circles with 'sedition.'"[46] The Tariqah-i-Muhammadiya, whom Maulana Ahmad Riza Khan Barelwi accused of being Wahhabis, also fell under British suspicion for its jihad activities on the frontier.

As a consequence of these fatwa accusations, the fatwa war[47] impacted the changing Muslim identity on the Indian subcontinent. Many potential leaders of the Indian Muslim community attempted to exert their influence and introduce reform measures through widespread publication of fatwas. In nineteenth-century British India, designating someone a *kafir* represented a common strategy for blacklisting targeted Muslims whose views and practices the denouncer wanted to call into question and to suggest lay outside the pale of

Islam.[48] The fatwa war inevitably turned into a debate about what constitutes Islamic belief and Muslim identity.

The success of such publications was possible, ironically, because the fatwas were, by this time, written in the vernacular, Urdu.[49] In 1837 Persian was abolished as the court language. The British colonial powers instead instituted vernacular languages for government administration. For the regions of Bihar, Oudh, the northwestern provinces, and Punjab, Urdu was considered the regional language and therefore became the language of governance in much of the North. Even though non-Muslims as well as Muslims spoke Urdu, the language increasingly became identified with Muslims because of its dramatically increased use in writings on Islamic religious reform.

By the late nineteenth century, the Deoband issued all fatwas in straightforward, easy-to-read Urdu. Muslim scholars and educators wrote many works in Urdu. For example, Sir Syed Ahmed Khan published a bilingual journal in Urdu and English. Urdu would become a cultural symbol, crucial in Muslim identity reformation in much of the British Raj. In "Two Fatwas on Hajj in British India," Barbara D. Metcalf has written, "The move to Urdu as the vernacular—and increasingly, by the end of the century, a specifically Muslim vernacular—was a result of the colonial framework of both formal decisions and implicit practice interacting with indigenous strategies of cultural reproduction. It was precisely the deployment of Urdu in texts like this that was crucial in creating community and in identifying Urdu as a cultural symbol."[50] Urdu's success as a cultural symbol resulted in large part from the reformers' ability to produce inexpensive print material in that language.

Many Muslim reformers took advantage of the printing press and began to do a great deal of translation work. They wanted to provide their own versions of Islamic religious works rather than rely on Christian translations, which were intentionally antagonistic toward Islam.[51] The Qur'an and many of the great Arabic and Persian works were translated into Urdu; there were many translations of the Qur'an, representing the interpretations of the various reformers. Metcalf notes that by the end of the nineteenth century, the Bohras of western India began to use Urdu over Gujarati, and Tamil Muslims soon followed suit. The combination of low-cost printing and the accessibility of printing presses for production of religious materials also led Hindus in turn to promote the Hindi language. Thus, Metcalf has concluded that Urdu became the "preeminent symbol of Muslim identity."[52]

While Urdu became a pivotal cultural symbol that inspired a common religious identity for a majority of Muslims on the subcontinent, it met with only limited success in Bengal. In Bengal, only the urban *ashraf* Muslims knew Urdu; most people, who lived in rural areas, could not read texts written in Urdu. Unlike those in other regions of India, Bengal's Muslims were mostly poor, rural, and uneducated. Muslim religious scholars and reformers in Bengal therefore began to write fatwas and other works in Bengali. One well-known example of a Bengali fatwa concerned the writings of a Muslim novelist, Mir Mosharraf Hussain. In his novel *Go-jiban*, Hussain dealt with Hindu-Muslim communal problems, criticizing India's Muslims for sacrificing and eating cows. In response, Maulana Mohammad Naīmuddīn issued a fatwa calling Hussain a *kafir*. Unfortunately for Hussain, most prominent Muslims of the time backed the maulana, and he could not find support. The tone and type of questions raised in fatwas was affected by the reform climate and became one of the most effective ways of envisioning and reshaping group identity around religion. The fatwas additionally helped define the Muslim community by its denouncements of actions considered un-Islamic.

That so many religious reformers arose simultaneously with the same objectives on the subcontinent in general and in Bengal in particular suggests that these movements contributed, however inadvertently, to the formation of a specifically religioethnic way of envisioning community. Out of necessity rather than desire, Bengali vernacular language, an ethnic marker, became a medium for communicating ideas about membership in a wider religious community. The development of a specifically Bengali Muslim notion of community was most affected by the printing press and by scholars' growing willingness to publish in Bengali vernacular. Yet paradoxically, scholars intended not to reinforce identification with the Bengali language but instead to share more with the Islamic Middle East than with their Hindu neighbors closer to home. Despite this concern, changing the religious practices of Bengal's Muslims required the reformers to contend with religious praxis issues using the vernacular Bengali.

In contrast to the reformist forces, the traditionalists, or mullahs, and the *zamīndārs* wanted to maintain the status quo for political and economic reasons. The rural mullahs and *maulvis* were not as well educated as their urban counterparts who attended the prominent madrassas of Calcutta, Dhaka, Bogra, and Rajshahi, so these rural mullahs and *maulvis* could therefore provide only rudimentary religious instruction. These teachers not only provided the rural people with religious guidance but also commanded some influence over the people—for example, through the perception that the teachers could exorcise evil spirits. As Rafiuddin Ahmed has explained, "Their clientele went to them as they still do for talismans, charms and amulets, incantations, divination, astrology and various other occult aids."[53]

Mullahs in the rural areas often made their living by exploiting the rural people's fears and ignorance. These traditionalists did not seek religious reform. They claimed to refer only to the Qur'an and the Sunna for religious guidance. In some cases this meant that they performed, accepted, or turned a blind eye to unorthodox religious praxis in the rural areas where they gave guidance. Many of the religious reform movements essentially threatened the traditionalists' rural power base. Along with the debates among the educated urban religious scholars and the movements they represented, the interaction of reformist and traditionalist forces in rural Bengal led to further disputes and to the need for the traditionalists to defend their position in polemical literature and later in *bāhās*.[54] In this socioreligious environment, mullahs and *maulvis* became compelled to participate in religious reform dialogue as a way of protecting and preserving their interests as religious leaders and guides in the rural areas.

Public debates on religious questions, known as *bāhās* or *munāzara*, were an interesting phenomenon of the late-nineteenth-century Indian subcontinent, but they were neither unique to this region nor a nineteenth-century innovation. *Munāzara* can be defined as oral theological disputes. Traditionally, in the classical period, *munāzara* were held before an audience and arbitrated by a *wazir* or caliph in a question-and-answer format. The *munāzara* was later adapted to a literary format.[55] This tradition continued in a somewhat altered fashion in the non-Arabic-speaking Muslim world, where respected individuals acted as arbitrators. Sanyal has confirmed that *munāzarāt* were common in the nineteenth century, noting that as "with other groups of 'ulama', they [debate participants] supplemented the written word with the oral, holding debates (*munāzara*) on theological issues that were attended by great numbers of local people."[56] These debates helped reformers increase their influence, allowing them to reach a wider and more diversified audience. Moreover, the holding of *bāhās* or *munāzara* represented an effective way of reaching the Muslims whose practices had come under close scrutiny.

In Bengal, these debates were known as *bāhās*. The various religious reform groups and traditionalists held these debates in villages, dealing with controversial religious questions such as whether it is legal to hold *jum'a* or *'id* prayers in Bengal,[57] the distinction between believers and nonbelievers, and the observance of *taqlid*. For example, in 1867 Karamat Ali of the Taiyuni movement debated Abdul Jabbar of the Faraizi movement on the question of prayers. In 1879 Karamat Ali debated the Faraizis again in Madaripur on the same question.[58] The issues debated, the debaters might argue, concerned all Muslims and addressed aspects of worship, just as the fatwas did. Other debates involved Christians and Muslims, with Muslims defending themselves and Islam from attacks by Christian missionaries. By the end of the nineteenth century, these debates had become common Muslim social events, a source of entertainment that involved whole villages.

Rural illiterate people's participation in these events evinced for some their desire to better understand their own religious traditions. *Bāhās* also took on a festive atmosphere, often lasting three days and being attended by thousands of Muslims.[59] *Bāhās* forums allowed members of the community to ask questions and forward opinions without fear of reprimand regarding issues concerning all Muslims. Ahmed contends that the majority of *bāhās* observers did not understand the legal arguments and the legal hairsplitting.[60] Yet because these *bāhās* focused on issues relevant to the life of every Muslim of Bengal, such as whether *jum'a* or *'id* prayers should be given in Bengal, whether jihad was necessary, and what distinguished Muslims and non-Muslims, they were well attended. In any case, regardless of the difficulty in understanding the dialogue and subsequent debate on such issues as the indispensability of observing *taqlid*, the *bāhās* provided an excellent forum for mobilizing Bengal's Muslims on questions of correct Muslim practice, involving in reform people from all walks of life and all social classes.

Less dramatic but also an important tool of the religious reformers were the *waz mahfil* events (religious meetings), which also took place in villages and were attended by thousands of Muslims. They remain a part of Bengali life today. The goal of the *waz mahfil* was not to debate issues but rather to encourage proper praxis as defined by a particular religious reform group. The organizers of such events also attempted to assist in building needed religious institutions such as *masjids* (mosques) and *maktabs* (Islamic schools). These *waz mahfils* impacted Muslim communities both positively and negatively. Negatively, the *waz mahfils* often alienated non-Muslim village residents by initiating boycotts of Hindu *zamīndārs* and Hindu-owned businesses. More positively, the *waz mahfils* inspired more dedicated worship, reinvigorated communities, and strengthened people's participation in the Muslim *umma*.[61]

The Nineteenth-Century Literary Milieu in Bengal:
Writing the Transition from Muslims of Bengal to Bengali Muslims

These notions of correct practice, in all their variety, were conveyed in local languages in part through public debate but soon thereafter via the print medium. Increasing amounts of scholarship and literature began to appear for public consumption in Urdu for the many educated Muslims. But by the mid–nineteenth century, reformers in Bengal determined that a need existed for magazines and newspapers in Bengali. They realized that to reach a Muslim population that knew Bengali but not Urdu, the publications had to be in Bengali. In fact, in the introductions of many Bengali books about Islam written by Muslims, the authors expressed their apologies for having resorted to the local language. Even the monthly and weekly journals and newspapers often declared that their agenda was to teach Muslims about Islam, its glorious past, and proper Muslim practices. Authors in these publications stated that they had been forced to write in Bengali because so many Muslims in Bengal were unfamiliar with Islamic languages— specifically Arabic, Persian, and even Urdu.

These writings collectively provide an important indicator of the nineteenth-century transformation in communal self-consciousness. Muslim intellectuals and reformers worked primarily to reconstitute communal association by religious affiliation rather than class, ethnicity, or caste. Their public debates, *bāhās*, fatwas, and publications aimed to make less educated rural Bengali Muslims more conscious of their membership in a larger Muslim community. Furthermore, reformers sought to encourage a deeper bond among members of the greater religious community by way of encouraging practices the reformers deemed orthodox while eliminating anything they interpreted as "Hindu" accretions. In other words, the reformers attempted to make practices uniform across South Asia.

The effect of print technology on community identity has been noted in other areas of the world, most notably in the work of Benedict Anderson, who has explained the transformative impact of print technology on national consciousness in Western Europe. First, he has suggested that "the coalition between Protestantism and print-capitalism" expanded the reading publics to include those members of society who did not know Latin.[62] Common language became the basis of national communities. In the European context, there was a resistance to the language of the church hierarchy in favor of vernaculars. However, a close examination of the South Asian context reveals that national consciousness was based in large part on religious affiliation, for which Anderson's theory does not account. Peter van der Veer suggests that Anderson relies on a modern-traditional dichotomy that does not allow him to see how in another context these innovations in communications might enhance the importance of some religious languages.[63] Veer argues that Arabic and Urdu gained prominence among Muslims, while Hindi gained prominence among Hindus.[64] To a large extent, Veer is correct, but Urdu does have its limitations. In South Asia, not only did a community choose to use a common vernacular language, but the content of published scholarship also shaped national consciousness. Print technology provided the means of widening the audience, while the choice of language was a pragmatic one for the Muslims of Bengal. This concern for reform sprouted directly from the colonial encounter. Islamic history has numerous examples of reform efforts to bring practice in conformity with what reformers have argued is the intent of the Qur'an as further demonstrated in the Prophet Muhammad's life. The Islamic notion of a *mujaddid* (a renewer of the age) affirms the importance of internal discourse about "orthodoxy." In the eighteenth century, the most influential reformers were Muhammad ibn 'Abd al-Wahhab (d. 1787) and Shah Wali Allah (d. 1762). The nineteenth century saw many reformers, and what is unique about this time period is that reformers were also reacting to the new British social, economic, and political domination in South Asia.

Muslim Reform Literature in Bengal

Prior to missionary-printed works, no urgent need for the printing press existed. In the Mughal period, books were reproduced by hand in small numbers. Francis Robinson has suggested that publications by Muslims increased under colonial rule: "Where Muslims were under some form of colonial rule, and the threat of the West was more evident, the response was much more rapid, much more urgent."[65] Robinson has crucially observed that Muslim reservations about the use of print for the publication of religious scholarship lie in the challenge print posed to traditional forms of transmission of knowledge: print "attacked what was understood to make knowledge trustworthy, what gave it value, what gave it authority."[66] The learned memorized their knowledge and communicated it orally, a process viewed as more reliable than written transmission.[67] The central model for oral transmission of knowledge in the Muslim world is the Qur'an. Nineteenth-century Muslim reformers dramatically changed their attitudes about the appropriate use of print technology because of the urgent need to respond in kind to critiques of their religious beliefs. Robinson has asserted that the shift in Muslim attitudes regarding the use of print technology resulted from Muslim loss of power: their use of print technology "interacted with a context in which Muslims were beginning to realize that they were a minority, about 25 per cent, in a majority Hindu population. It interacted with a context of Islamic revival in which there were calls to renew Islam being expressed both inside and outside the region. It interacted with the rapid social, economic and political changes set off by British rule. But most important of all it interacted with Muslim attempts, after six hundred years of political domination on the subcontinent, to find answers to the questions of how to be good Muslims, and how to enable the Muslim community to survive under foreign Christian power."[68]

Because of the British strategies of categorization and enumeration, notions of majority and minority became equated with dominance and disenfranchisement.[69] The Muslim elite rather than the lower classes or women subsequently became concerned with their loss of power. Because those groups had no power to begin with, their voices were never heard in the public sphere. Muslim reformers were interested in modifying the practices of this now-quantifiable Muslim community. Muslim reformers' attempts to modify Muslims' religious practices also constituted a response to missionary critiques. These responses to the new colonial environment also extended to Hindu reformers. The Muslim elite began to look at all Muslims in India as a community with common interests based primarily on religious affiliation. This growing perspective was certainly reinforced by the British administrators as well as missionaries, who, in their efforts to rule and control and to convert a large and diverse population, categorized and interacted with the local population primarily by their caste and religious affiliation, ignoring often conflicting economic interests with particular religious communities. Evidence in literature by the British clearly indicates an understanding of the populations as either Muslim or Hindu. The terms "religion," "nation," and "sect" were not clearly distinguished, so religious communities were also referred to as "nations."[70] This led to the conscious privileging of religious self-perception not only by the British but also by colonized people, who were responding to British criticism and governing policies. Class, caste, ethnicity, and gender were other categories, but the overarching groupings were "Hindu" and "Muhammadan," from which sprang "majority" and "minority."

Print technology first became important because it was the tool employed by the missionaries to publish works in Bengali and other indigenous languages as a way of reaching local populations. Upper-class intellectuals and the educated defended or modified their religious beliefs and communicated their responses to the locals via the same technology. Print technology was not new among Muslims, but it became more than ever before a means of communicating religious reform.[71] Print technology served a fresh purpose. This written discourse led to a growth in Bengali prose writing. Second, by virtue of the literature's subject matter, it gave religious communal identity unprecedented prominence. This latter point necessitates a more detailed consideration.

Having swiftly acknowledged the language and authority of the new British rulers, Hindus preceded the Muslims in accepting English and Bengali education; accordingly, Hindus began to write in modern Bengali prose. Not surprisingly, much of this literature defended Hindu tradition and dealt with issues concerning religious "reform."[72] Some central figures of this important movement included Ram Mohan Roy, Debendranath Tagore, Keshab Chandra Sen, and M. G. Ranade. Compelled to respond to the attacks on Islam and even to counterattack the Hindu and Christian ways of life, Muslims eventually joined the new literary movement. In her examination of Urdu works, Metcalf has noted the dramatic increase in religious writings by Muslims in the nineteenth and early twentieth centuries, quoting Murray Kempson, the director of public instruction for the Northwestern Provinces, as declaring, "Unusual energy has been shown by the Mahomedans in providing for their educational wants in their own way."[73]

Muslim scholars in Bengal continued to write some traditional Arabic and Persian works during this period of Muslim religious reform. According to Schimmel, in the nineteenth century, "the poet Nassah from Calcutta is mentioned among the better writers of Persian, whereas the classical tradition was maintained, into the [twentieth] century, by the Suhrawardi family whose most noted member 'Ubaidullah Suhrawardi (d. 1885) wrote Persian poetry and encouraged Islamic studies."[74] Conversely, by the second half of the nineteenth century, Bengal's Muslims were expressing themselves in the prose of modern Bengali literature and publishing journals about Islam at an unprecedented rate.

The *Nasīhat Nāmās*

By the mid–nineteenth century, mullahs and *maulvis* began to carry out the changes propagated by the reformers. According to Ahmed, religious leaders "fought a rearguard action against the reformists, and confronted them in numerous *bāhās*, in order to defend the traditional system, but were now quick to perceive the urgent need for reform from within."[75] Many mullahs and *maulvis* guided the debates of the *bāhās*, which allowed these officials to maintain participation and a leadership role in the community. They also maintained their power base by distributing and sometimes writing *nasīhat nāmās.*[76] Mindful of these religious pamphlets' purpose, the mullahs and *maulvis* struggled with the question of the appropriate language to use to discuss Islam. The authors of these pamphlets firmly opposed writing *nasīhat nāmās* in the older style discussed in chapter 1, which they regarded as confused, syncretic theology. The later *nasīhat nāmās* became, in Ahmed's words, "more rigid and orthodox both in their approach and presentation, including the language."[77] Referring to the older *nasīhat nāmā* literature, Ahmed has written that "there was a vast corpus of Muslim religious literature in medieval Bengal, dealing with the faith of the ordinary believer. Their aim, too, was to transmit to the Bengali-speaking Muslim a basic knowledge of the laws and principles of Islam. But, unlike the later literature, most pre-reformist works gave the impression of confused religious thinking, much of which would appear sacrilegious to the orthodox Muslims."[78] In Ahmed's depiction, the premodern literature is syncretic, based on the evident blending of Islamic and Hindu terminology. This is certainly how nineteenth-century reformers interpreted these earlier writings in Bengali about Islam. As discussed in chapter 1, however, Tony Stewart has demonstrated the limitations of a depiction of this literature as syncretic based simply on an examination of its language and terms. He has instead proposed a study of the "process of production" of this early literature. Employing translation theory, Stewart asserts that the authors of the prereform *nasīhat nāmās* often adopted terms associated with Hindu deities and Vaishnava concepts in their search for "the closest terms of equivalence" for Islamic ideas and concepts.[79] Doing so allowed the writers of premodern *nasīhat nāmās* to convey Islamic ideas, which were new to Bengali language and culture, using terms already known in the local language. These writers wanted Bengali speakers to gain an appreciation and understanding of the benefits of the basic Islamic ideas. However, nineteenth-century reformers and scholars alike lacked understanding of the premodern authors' efforts to convey Islamic ideas, viewing these early writings as aberrations that contained value to neither Islamic nor Hindu traditions. Reformers thus rejected this style and these writings when in fact they provide evidence of their particular cultural context and value, as Stewart has demonstrated. The reformers' misunderstanding was based in large part on the fact that by the time they were writing, they did not have to resort to as many—if any—Sanskrit terms because Islamic vocabulary had become more established as part of the Bengali language. The language of nineteenth-century writers came to be known as Dobhashi, or Mussalmani Bengali.

In the premodern period, those who spread Islam in Bengal sought to introduce Islam to the rural people, whereas in the later period the goal was to bring practices in line with some "orthodox" ideal propagated by the self-proclaimed *ashraf* Muslims. In light of the nature of premodern religious literature and the misunderstanding of it in the nineteenth century, it is significant that the nineteenth-century language became a critical sticking point for conveying messages of "orthodox" practice. The reformers attempted to break from this early style primarily by deliberate attention to language usage. They were concerned with reforming behavior and even language usage (Muslim reformers considered Bengali a Hindu language) that could be interpreted as Hindu and therefore un-Islamic. So the authors' language therefore reflected an effort to distinguish Islam from Hinduism. For the British and Muslim elite too, "Islam" was the religion of a people primarily of foreign descent, so why should Muslims resort to using what they regarded as a Hindu language?

To resolve this dilemma, authors of reform period *nasīhat nāmās* initially authored Urdu *nasīhat nāmās*. But because the rural Muslim population did not know the "Islamic" languages, the pamphlets written in Urdu lacked readership. As these pamphlets were not intended for the *ashraf* but rather for the less educated rural and urban Muslim population, the publications had to be written in Bengali. The reformers, thus formulated and employed Mussalmani (or Musalmani) Bengali.

Mussalmani Bengali, otherwise known as *Dobhāṣī Bangla*, was a literary style that had roots in the mid–eighteenth century but became prevalent in nineteenth-century Bengali literature written by Muslims.[80] Mussalmani Bengali represents an attempt by writers to Islamize Bengali by introducing Arabic and Persian terms into simply written Bengali religious tracts. The Mussalmani texts, including the *nasīhat nāmās*, were written predominantly in verse and in Bengali script, in a simple style for an audience with limited schooling.[81] In poetic style and simple syntax, these works hearken back to medieval Bengali literature. But distinguishing these Mussalmani Bengali texts from the earlier style was the extensive use of foreign words appropriated from the Islamic languages (Arabic, Persian, and Urdu) and a simultaneous lack of ostensibly Hindu or Vaishnava religious terms. In the introduction to his Mussalmani Bengali–English dictionary, William Goldsack states that the importance of Mussalmani Bengali "may be gauged by the fact that the Bible Society finds it necessary to publish the Christian Scriptures in this dialect for the exclusive use of Muslims; whilst hundreds of books and papers are published by Muhammadans themselves in the same dialect."[82]

Muslim reformers wanted to do away with "popular" (and what they regarded as localized) interpretations of Islam, which they condemned as "un-Islamic" praxis. The final objective of these works was to assist in creating and reinforcing a Muslim identity that was orthodox (in line with the Muslim elites), an identity that clearly distinguished between what was and was not Islamic—that is, an Islam that was more uniform. In other words, the authors of these later *nasīhat nāmās* sought to bring practice in line with an ideal universal notion of an Islamic life. These writers and their patrons had become convinced that Muslims were suffering and had lost power as a consequence of un-Islamic practices and that Muslims needed to be purified of the tainting influences of other cultures. Ahmed cites *Tuhfat al-mubtadi o akbar al-salat*, a *nasīhat nāmā* published in 1878 by Muhammad Khatir:

> The first obligation is to recite *kalema* with honest intentions.
> The *kalema* should be said in Arabic. . . .
> Secondly, offer *namaz* regularly. This will count on the
> day of judgment.
> Thirdly, *roza* is very important. It is obligatory on all adults. . . .
> Fourthly, *zakat* must be paid on wealth. . . . *Zakat* is obligatory
> on all men of wealth. But no one is exempted from *kalema*,
> *namaz*, and *roza*. . . .

Fifthly, it is obligatory to go on pilgrimage to *bait al-ka'ba*
on those who can afford to pay for their passage and
maintenance. . . .
Anyone who abides by these five injunctions is truly a
Muslim according to the *kitab*.[83]

This sample piece exemplifies the politicized nature of language. Significantly, wherever there is mention of Islamic ritual practice, Bengali
terms are not used: these authors consider only Arabic and Persian
terms suitable. Arabizing language is equated with the Islamizing goal.

Journals and Newspapers

Along with the growth of *nasīhat nāmā* literature came the populariza-
tion of journals and newspapers. In the second half of the nineteenth
century, educated Muslims and the *'ulama'* published religious materials in modern Bengali for an audience that was predominantly Muslim,
educated, and male. Numerous daily, weekly, and monthly journals
focused on Islamic topics, including religious teachings, history, biographies of famous Muslims, and events affecting Muslims in Bengal
and India, thus affirming ties with other Muslims in India. These journals sought to inform the Bengali Muslim public of Islamic history
while playing the role of the voice of the community by responding to
Christian and Hindu critiques and by suggesting normative practices
and beliefs. For example, remarking on the goal of the monthly journal
Islām-Prachārak, whose publication commenced in 1891, the editor,
Mohammad Riazuddin Ahmed, stated, "The object of the periodical
is the spread and reformation of Muhammadanism. The Christians
and Brahmos are making their influence felt among the lower class
Musalmans of Bengal, whose priests, owing to their ignorance cannot
cope with the intelligent and educated preachers of other religions,
and the fakirs of Bengal have brought Islam into contempt. The editor
wants to counteract the influence of these men by making the vernacular the medium of transmitting instructions to Musalmans."[84]

The editors of numerous other papers and journals targeting a Muslim audience shared Mohammad Riazuddin Ahmed's mission. The

monthly paper edited by Mohammad Naīmuddīn, which commenced publication in 1895, stated its goals as first and foremost to discuss Islam as well as to discuss any criticisms of the religion.[85]

The publications pursued these goals in several ways. Some of the first journals, such as the *Samācar sabhārājendra* and the *Jāduddīpak bhāskar*, were multilingual, never excluding Bengali. These papers had little success. As one critic pointed out, "[it] is a polyglott Newspaper, consisting at present of ten folio pages of ample breadth and length, and intended ere long to be enlarged to sixteen pages. Each page consists of five parallel columns in five different languages, viz, Persian, Hindi, English, Bengali and Urdu or Hindustani. [The editor's] Persian is too much Arabicized, his Urdu too much Persianized, and his Bengali too much Sanskritized, to be easily, if at all, intelligible to the great mass of readers."[86] Editors were constrained by their efforts to force a certain character on these languages. For these editors, eloquent Persian relied heavily on Arabic terms, as Bengali did on Sanskrit. Moreover, the editors could not easily break with their assumptions that Arabic was associated with Islam while Bengali was associated only with Hinduism. Thus, they continued to struggle with the role of Bengali in communicating Islamic religious ideas and Bengali's relation to Muslim identity.

These monthlies and weeklies addressed numerous issues that both explicitly and implicitly define orthodoxy. Some papers, such as *Hitakarī*, edited by Mir Mosharraf Hussein, attempted to diminish tensions between religious communities by addressing the issue of Hindu-Muslim relations. Other publications, including *Hāphej*, did not allow Mussalmani Bengali to disappear but published poetry in Mussalmani Bengali as well as articles in modern Bengali prose. Throughout the nineteenth century, several dozen Bengali journals and newspapers were directed at a Muslim audience. Many of them did not survive more than a few years. Some ceased publication but were later revived, such as *Hitakarī*. Table 1 provides a list of the widely available journals from this period.

The production and consumption of these journals demonstrated the developing sense of community based on religious affiliation among Bengal's Muslims by drawing attention to issues concerning the Muslim world, emphasizing the value of a common religious heritage

TABLE 1. Muslim Journals of the Nineteenth Century

	Year Publication Commenced	Journal	Editor	Circulation
1	1831	*Samacar sabharajendra*	Sheikh Alimullah	Weekly
2	1846	*Jāduddīpak bhāskar*	Maullavi Rajaba Ali	Weekly
3	1861	*Pharidpur darpaṇ*	Allahadad Khan	Biweekly
4	1874	*Ājijan nehār*	Mir Mosharraf Hossein	Monthly
5	1874	*Pa-rila ba-rtta-baha*	Anisuddin Ahmed	Biweekly
6	1877	*Mahāmmadi ākhbār*	Kazi Abdul Khalique	Biweekly
7	1878	*Mahāmmadi ākhbār*	Kazi Abdul Khalique	Weekly
8	1884	*Ākhabāre islāmīyā*	Muhammad Naimuddin	Monthly
9	1884	*Musalmān*	Muhammad Riazuddin Ahmed	Weekly
10	1885	*Musalmān-bandhu*	?	Monthly
11	1885	*Islām*	Akinuddin Ahmed	Monthly
12	1886	*Naba-sudhākar*	Muhammad Riazuddin Ahmed	Weekly
13	1886	*Āhmadī*	Abdul Hamid Khan Yusufzai	Biweekly
14	1887	*Hindu-mosalmān sammilanī*	Munshi Golam Kader	Monthly
15	1889	*Sudhākar*	Sheikh Abdur Rahim	Weekly
16	1889	*Bhārater bhram nibāriṇī traimāshika Patrikā*	Muhammad Abidin	Trimonthly
17	1890	*Hitakarī*	Mir Mosharraf Hossain	Biweekly
18	1891	*Bhishak-darpaṇ*	Mohammad Jahiruddin Ahmed	Monthly
19	1891	*Islām-pracārak*	Mohammed Riazuddin Ahmed	Monthly
20	1892	*Mihir*	Sheikh Abdur Rahim	Monthly
21	1892	*Hāphej*	Sheikh Abdur Rahim	Biweekly
22	1892	*Ṭāṇgāil hitakarī*	Moslemuddin Khan	Weekly
23	1895	*Mihir o sudhākar*	Sheikh Abdur Rahim	Weekly
24	1895	*Ākhbāre islāmīyā*	Muhammed Naīmuddīn	Monthly
25	1897	*Hāphej*	Sheikh Abdur Rahim	Monthly
26	1898	*Kohinur*	S. K. M. Muhammed Roushan Ali	Monthly
27	1899	*Pracārak*	Modhu Miya	Monthly
28	1899	*Hitakarī*	Mir Mosharraf Hossain & S. K. M. Muhammed Roushan Ali	Biweekly
29	1899	*Islām*	Abdur Rashid	Monthly
30	1899	*Islām- pracārak*	Muhammad Riazuddin Ahmed	Monthly

SOURCE: *Banglar Śāmayik Patra.*

NOTE: For further information on these publications, see Anisuzzaman, *Muslim baṅglar samiyikapatra (1831–1930)* (Dhaka: Phajale Rabbi, 1969).

as well as other issues relevant specifically to these Muslims. The unitive and cohesive element is evident in the effort to bring these issues into a public forum. In addition, the oral debates of the *bāhās* extended to the print medium. Many of the resulting newspapers and journals served as mouthpieces for different reform movements, becoming in many respects the literary voices of a newly imagined community that began to identify itself as both Muslim and Bengali. These publications marked the beginning of a new and distinctly Bengali Muslim literature that emphasized correct Islamic behavior as narrowly defined by individual writers and reformers. The reformers viewed women's and rural Muslim practices as syncretic. Numerous journals represented differing viewpoints were self-conscious and ambivalent about writing in Bengali.[87] Nevertheless, such journals provided an important forum for encouraging intellectual growth and discourse on religious issues among Muslims of Bengal as well as for defending against outside attacks on Islam. With print culture, the audience grew. However, the reformers' audience was not clearly defined beyond being what may be regarded as Muslim and Bengali-speaking. In a sense, this audience constituted what Anderson has called an "imagined community," as it had no official membership but instead comprised an amorphous and growing group of readers and writers increasingly unified by linguistic and religious identity.[88]

Conclusion

The influence of Shah Wali Allah of Delhi can be measured by the fact that reformers as far east as Bengal in the nineteenth century claimed to be advocating the changes of their predecessor. Twentieth- and twenty-first-century thinkers remember him and even Wahhab in a variety of contesting ways to serve normative agendas. The nineteenth-century reform movements shared Shah Wali Allah's vision to the extent that they too suggested that reform was needed to universalize Islamic practice on the subcontinent. Yet the many reform movements often disagreed about doctrine and ritual and thus competed with one another in an effort to increase membership.

As we have seen, in the latter half of the nineteenth century, one

way that Muslims encouraged a normative Islamic practice in South
Asia was by adopting modern Bengali for the composition of books,
pamphlets, and journals on Islamic history; discussions regarding contemporary religious issues; religious polemics; and instruction. Unlike
their precolonial predecessors, authors hesitated to write about Islam
in Bengali because of its association with Hindu culture. These authors made every effort to distinguish their literary acts from the prereform literature by self-consciously avoiding ostensibly Hindu terms.
However, Muslims' and Hindus' adoption of the modern Bengali
language to debate religious issues was inevitable, as the Christian critiques of Islam and Hindu tradition drew Muslims into dialogue to
defend their religious praxis.

Such strategies as issuing fatwas, debating religious practices at
bāhās, and publishing journals on religious reform issues contributed
to the reformation effort. As Muslim communities in many regions of
the subcontinent came to accept Urdu, the language became a Muslim
cultural symbol. Subsequently, in the eastern region of Bengal, out of
necessity rather than desire, the Bengali language became the medium
of communication in both written and oral form. Urdu would never
replace Bengali regardless of cultural status. Urdu represented an ideal
whose impracticality would be fully realized only in the early years of
a united Pakistan. Language constituted a crucial factor in this process because any measures the reformers sought could be achieved only
through the Bengali medium. Mussalmani Bengali was developed and
employed to communicate to Muslims of the rural areas, while the well
educated increasingly employed modern Bengali to discuss and debate
religious reform. Thus, though it was not part of the grand design of
the reformers, religious reformation by necessity took place in the
Bengali vernacular.

To convey their message of reform, nineteenth-century reformers
took advantage of both old and new methods of communication. They
revived the *bāhās*, a tradition that has its roots in the medieval period
in the Middle East, to publicly debate religious issues in an effort to
win over Muslims to their reformist ways. Reformers also confronted
Christians' written and oral criticisms of Islam. All of these activities
constituted crucial factors in the continued development and wider

use of Bengali for Islamic scholarship. The move from the publication of religious journals to exegetical work in Bengali was made possible by the publication of entire original books in Bengali, the first of which also addressed religious practice. These books were written for an audience educated in modern Bengali—not Arabic, Persian, or even Urdu.

three

Breaking New Ground & Transgressing Boundaries

After all, we were born in Bengal. Most people do not understand Arabic or Persian. That is why I write this *kalam* [holy book] in Bengali. Muslims! Try to learn the principles of Islam in Bengali and manage to learn the truth about God and Prophet somehow.
—From the preface of Maleh Muhammad,
　Ketab shah ahkam-i-jumah

The Composition of Bengali Books on Islam

Urdu was the first South Asian language in which the *'ulama'* wrote interpretations of the Qur'an in the late eighteenth century. At that time, other classical religious works were also being translated into Urdu. Some of those early Urdu translations of the Qur'an were written at Fort Williams College in Bengal, and in 1844 the American Presbyterian missionaries sponsored an Urdu translation of the Qur'an.[1]

By the late nineteenth century, the production of religious books printed by Muslims had dramatically increased. Religious books became the most widely read genre of literature all over the subcontinent.[2] Also in this period, more than fifteen authors translated the Qur'an into Urdu. According to Barbara Metcalf, religious scholars seized the opportunity to compete with their religious opponents in a new arena. These scholars were prompted in part by the desire to make the Qur'an available in a language more natural and idiomatic than that of the earlier versions: less attention was now given to maintaining Arabic word order and style. The competing translations also represented the fruit of rivalries among religious leaders, for the 'ulama' of each school produced their own translations. Among the early Deobandis, 'Ashiq Illahi Mirathi, Ashraf Ali Thanawi, and Mahmud Hasan did translations, as did their rival, Ahmad Riza Khan Barelwi. Sayyid Ahmad Khan began a translation and commentary, and Nazir Ahmad, his associate, wrote an almost conversational translation accompanied by a glossary and index.[3]

Members of the public snapped up these translations. Many religious reformers writing in Urdu began to believe that making the Qur'an more accessible lay at the heart of successful reform, and Bengali reformers soon followed this lead. In villages throughout Bengal, people bought copies of books written in Bengali on Islamic topics. Though the majority of Muslims in rural Bengal had little to no schooling, people gathered in groups, where someone read aloud to an audience. Because of the reform climate, new literary genres flourished in the Bengali language. In this new prose style, reformers began to compose entire books dedicated to Islamic religious life. One of the first examples of this new literature was Mohammed Naīmuddīn's *Jobdātal masāyel* (Essence of the issues).

In subject matter, *Jobdātal masāyel* resembles the *nasīhat nāmās*. It provides instruction on all aspects of ritual observances and duties of the individual as well as the community. These instructions included Naīmuddīn's views on a wide range of Islamic issues, including purification, prayer, the call to prayer, proper prayer attire (at home and in the mosque), fasting, breaking fast, 'id prayers, marriage, the type of women who are prohibited from marrying, divorce, Judgment Day, and *waqf* properties. What distinguishes this work from the mullahs' *nasīhat nāmās* is that *Jobdātal masāyel* is written in simple, standard colloquial Bengali prose. In his preface, Naīmuddīn explains that he wrote *Jobdātal masāyel* at the request of *zamīndār* Hafiz Mahmud Ali Khan, who believed that a great need for such a book existed. In fact, many authors of Islamic religious texts included explanations for the production of such works in Bengali.

A *zamīndār* from Mymensingh, Khan recognized Naīmuddīn's potential as both a writer and teacher of Islam and therefore provided the financial backing for his first book on Islam, which was tailored to a wider Muslim audience literate in Bengali.[4] This endeavor represented a novel approach. Indeed, at the time, virtually no books were written with this kind of audience in mind. While Hindu Bengalis had taken the lead in modern Bengali prose writing, predominantly in fiction, Muslims of Bengal remained more attached to old literary styles and traditions. Thus, Muslims who did not know Persian or Urdu were familiar with older styles of Bengali poetry, while the educated Muslim elite clung to Persian and Urdu literature, though efforts were being made in Bengali, as evidenced in journal publications and *nasīhat nāmās*. Their commitment to these works remained steadfast, notwithstanding the fact that a growing population was becoming less familiar with these languages.

With his patronage in place, Naīmuddīn agreed to write a book in modern prose on a religious topic. In 1873, at the age of forty-one, he published his first book, *Jobdātal masāyel*. Muslims' hesitation to write in Bengali illustrates that in the 1800s, educated Muslims commonly believed that their coreligionists were of foreign descent and knew Urdu and Persian but not Bengali. As chapter 2 discussed, Bengali in this period was associated with Hindu Bengal, yet the educated Muslims had to acknowledge that many Muslims of Bengal spoke Bengali.

Jobdātal masāyel is written in question-and-answer format, with questions posed by a student and responses provided by a teacher, a pedagogical format that has been typical in the Islamic world for centuries. This book was so widely read that more than fifteen editions were published. In the preface, Naīmuddīn indicates that the book answers questions posed by an observant, educated Muslim. First, he states that although earlier writings on shari'a exist, many educated Bengalis object to the books' language and style. *Jobdātal masāyel*, however, is written in standard colloquial Bengali and is therefore accessible to far

more readers. This book is also so innovative because it is not a translation of an earlier Arabic book but instead represents the author's personal understanding of the main points of Islamic law pertinent to the
lives of Muslims in nineteenth-century Bengal. He requests, therefore,
that his readers seek the guidance of a Hanafi *faqih* (jurist) if they question the responses in the book. Finally, he implores the readers not to
desert their *madhhab* (school of law), which he concludes would be a
grave mistake.

Biographical information gathered from these writings indicates
that Naīmuddīn's ancestors immigrated to Delhi from Baghdad during the Mughal period.[5] The family ultimately settled in Bengal, in
the district of Tangail, where Mohammad Naīmuddīn was born. He
was tutored at home by his father prior to formally commencing his
education in school. Around 1846–47 he began his traditional Islamic
education with an *'alim*, studying Persian, Arabic, Urdu, hadith, *tafsir*,
fiqh, and logic. He then furthered his religious education by traveling
throughout the Indian subcontinent to various cities to study with
other famous *'ulama'* and *walis*. Sources indicate that these travels included visits to regional centers of Islamic learning such as Murshidabad,
Bihar, Allahabad, Jaunpur, Gazipur, Agra, and Delhi. The subject matter of all of Naīmuddīn's works strongly suggests his concern for those
Muslims of Bengal who abandoned *taqlid* and in particular the *Hanafi
madhhab*, a controversial issue at the time. Naīmuddīn was a staunch
Hanafi who warned Muslims against abandoning the Hanafi school.
In his view, disregarding the laws of one particular school of law would
lead Muslims to observe practices only when they proved convenient.

Most Bengali Muslims were Hanafi, yet the Tariqah-i-Muham-
madiyas, Ahl-i-Hadith, and Rafi-yadayns all argued that they were not
bound to obey the rulings of one particular school of law. Their reasoning was based on an attempt to live a religious life that replicated, as
much as possible, the Prophet's first *umma*. Members of these movements opposed adherence to a single legal school, arguing that during
the Prophet's life no single school existed and that they should not be
so constrained by centuries of human interpretation of the law.

Naīmuddīn vehemently disapproved of the *la-majhābis*, as they were
commonly called,[6] and he demonstrated his dislike of them through his
writings. For example, *Ākher johar* centers on the debate between the

la-majhābis and the Hanafis regarding the latest possible time for *jum'a* prayers. In the preface to his book, *Ādellāye hānifiy*, he states, "Reader! If you read this book which is about the people without a *madhhab*, you cannot help but laugh and feel pity for them as the book discloses their ways. In this edition, the last part of the book reveals their fraud. I hope that readers of the previous edition are now satisfied and that they are gaining fruits from performing religious works."[7] As a staunch Hanafi, Naïmuddīn devoted a great deal of his writing to the highly charged issue of *taqlid* to the Hanafi school. *Ādellāye hānifiy* refers to a *bāhās* where the issue being discussed was whether one must recognize and abide by the laws of a particular *madhhab*. As expected, the adjudicator of the *bāhās* found in favor of *madhhabs*; as Naïmuddīn put it, the misdirection of the *la-majhābis* was revealed, and many returned to the Hanafi *madhhab*.[8] This victory may not have actually occurred, but it was customary in such works to insist that victory in the debate had been achieved and to claim that those on the losing side had been dissuaded from their prior convictions.

Naïmuddīn stood at the epicenter of many controversial issues in the Muslim community of Bengal. He issued opinions on a variety of matters. Because of the numerous religious reform movements that arose in nineteenth-century Bengal, such as the Tariqah-i-Muhammadiya, Faraizi (Faraidi), Ahl-i-Hadis (Ahl-i-Hadith), and Taiyuni, debate at the *bāhās* was directed at the question of whether particular reforms were orthodox. Because Faraizi and other reformers considered India *dar al-harb*, one of the most controversial issues debated at the *bāhās* was whether *'id* and *jum'a* prayers could be given in India.

Naïmuddīn issued fatwas and evaluated the methods and practices of the various reform movements.[9] He took it upon himself to defend many of the practices of the Muslim community that were the targets of critics. For example, Mir Musharraf Hussain, one of the pioneer Bengali writers of the nineteenth century, wrote *Go-jiban* (1888), a novel in which he articulated a point of view that did not go over well with Muslims such as Naïmuddīn, who saw himself as a protector of Islam and its correct practice. When Naïmuddīn read the published excerpt of *Go-jiban*, he accused the author of being a *kafir*.[10] Naïmuddīn criticized Musharraf for suggesting that Indian Muslims should neither sacrifice cows nor consume beef as a demonstration of their respect for their Hindu neighbors. For Hussain, cow sacrifice was one clear cause of communal violence and growing tensions between Muslims and Hindus. Naīmuddīn subsequently issued a famous fatwa naming Hussain a *kafir*. Writing as a Muslim had certain consequences. The contrast between the two writers is striking. While Mir Musharraf Hussain hoped to defuse communalism through his works of fiction, Naīmuddīn was more concerned with articulating obligations of the Muslim community of Bengal and with protecting practices he deemed properly orthodox and in unquestionable contrast to Hindu customs. In the end, Naīmuddīn was victorious. Even the Sudhakar group, the literary organization to which Mir Musharraf Hussain belonged, eventually supported Naīmuddīn's fatwa.[11]

In the midst of these literary efforts among Muslims, a small but growing group of Brahman reformers and intellectuals in Bengal came to serve as an important catalyst in Bengali Muslim literary productions. In their efforts to reform Hindu practices, they became interested in Islam despite trends that would later contribute to growing communalism. This group was the Brahma Samaj, whose leader, Keshab Chandra Sen, sponsored Girish Chandra Sen's translation and commentary on the Qur'an, the first ever in the Bengali language.

The Brahma Samaj and *Tafsir* Scholarship

To understand non-Muslim Girish Chandra Sen's (d. 1910) lifelong interest in Islam and his resulting publications on the subject first requires some knowledge regarding the Brahma Samaj reform movement, of which he was a member, and related sectarian developments. Sen found in the Brahma Samaj answers to the problems of intensifying communalism during the colonial period. Sen's membership in the Brahma Samaj, founded by Ram Mohan Roy, was the main impetus for Sen's later writings on Islam.

Roy was born into a wealthy Brahman family at the end of the eighteenth century. He accepted many British critiques of Indian society and consequently became a prominent social, religious, and educational reformer who addressed the social evils and aspects of Indian culture and religion that the British depicted as deplorable. Not surprisingly, one of his main preoccupations was with the monotheistic traditions, which he came to view as more credible, a typical modernist response to Christian and Muslim critiques of Hindu beliefs. His studies began with Islam and the languages associated with the study of Islam, Persian and Arabic. Like many Orientalists, he became particularly attracted to the Sufi tradition in Islam, which led him to write *Tuhfat al-muwahhidin* (*Gift of the monotheists*) in Persian with an Arabic preface. The book celebrates monotheism and criticizes the worship of the many deities of the Hindu pantheon. Roy argued that polytheism did not reflect the religion of the Vedas. A few years later, his monotheistic beliefs led to "The Precepts of Jesus," which the Christian missionaries at Serampore in West Bengal severely criticized. In "The Precepts of Jesus," Roy took a unitarian approach that opposed the Christian trinity.[12] Roy distinguished between the words of Jesus as presented in the Gospels and the precepts of Christianity as interpreted in other parts of the New Testament. The missionaries, however, took offense at Roy's distinction. By 1828, Roy had organized a universalist monotheistic service in Calcutta that welcomed people from all religious traditions. In his later years, he endeavored to create unity among India's three dominant religious communities, Islamic, Christian, and Hindu.

Roy's idealistic goals for this universalist movement began to lose momentum with his death in 1833. Eventually, however, Debendranath Tagore took over and revived the movement. Tagore was a philosopher as well as a social and religious reformer who joined the Brahma Samaj in 1838. Like Roy, Tagore was attracted to the monotheistic conception of the divine. Also like his predecessor, Tagore was intellectually shaped by British criticisms of Indian society. Setting out to prove that monotheism was not alien to the Hindu tradition, Tagore found evidence in Vedantic literature. The British critics of Hinduism applauded these views, and some believed that Tagore might effectively "reform" the Hindu tradition, ridding it of "idolatry."[13]

The British made a basic assumption that Hindu tradition had over time become tainted by polytheism and ritualism. This view presupposed the existence of some "original" monotheistic Hinduism. Because of the Protestant West's emphasis on Scripture, these early scholars looked to texts to understand Hinduism—what Veena Das has called the Semitification of Hinduism.[14] These Orientalists and reformers turned primarily to Vedantic philosophy, the Upanishads, and epics such as the *Bhagavad Gita* for evidence of early and, in their view, original monotheistic tendencies.[15]

As evidenced here and in their response to Roy's "The Precepts of Jesus," the British paid close attention to religious activities and made public their opinions of those activities. In 1857, a visionary named Keshab Chandra Sen joined the movement and soon became one of its central charismatic leaders. Sen, a non-Brahman-educated Calcuttan, was attracted to Tagore's monotheistic ideas, and by 1859 Keshab had formed the Sangat Sabha for the discussion of religion and social reform. He and other younger members of the Brahma Samaj became increasingly interested in social action as a vehicle through which to bring about needed reform in India. Keshab was part of a growing group within the Brahma Samaj that supported intercaste marriage, and by discarding the Brahman *'upavita* (a sacred thread worn over the right shoulder by male members of the Brahman caste), he hoped that the spiritual leadership would thereby break out of the traditional caste mold, which had come under fire from missionaries and Muslims.[16]

Keshab also founded several journals and newspapers, including the English *Indian Mirror* in 1861 and the Bengali daily *Dharmatattva* (*Religious thought*). Keshab Chandra's journals sought to establish a written forum for the discussion of monotheism as found in Islam and Christianity and in monotheistic interpretations of Brahmanical texts such as the Vedas, Upanishads, and Puranas. While Tagore was more interested in reform of the Hindu tradition, Keshab Chandra became increasingly drawn toward universal teachings. The result of these growing differences and divergences in worldview was an 1866 split in the Brahma Samaj. Tagore led the older group, now known as the Adi Brahma Samaj, while Keshab Chandra Sen led the new group, the Brahma Samaj of India. At that time, Keshab moved even further toward universalist monotheistic teachings, while Tagore's older cadre attempted to reform Hindu teachings to align with Christian thought and to stem the number of Hindus converting to Christianity. Tagore firmly believed that to propagate the tenets of the Brahma Samaj, the group could not break with Hindu tradition, as the younger group sought. To do so, he believed, would condemn the Brahma Samaj to a fate similar to that of the Buddhist tradition, which had long ago virtually disappeared in India.[17]

In 1870, Keshab Chandra Sen made a historic journey to England, where he met with Queen Victoria and gave lectures on the Brahma Samaj movement and his group's religious beliefs. At his historic meeting with the queen, he established the limits of his ideas for social reform, expressing his acceptance of British rule over and above Indian nationhood. While the British were pleased with his efforts and his acceptance of British rule, his stand against Indian nationalism made Keshab the target of tremendous criticism at home. Nevertheless, he accepted British criticism of Indian religious traditions and practices. Perceiving Christianity as a model tradition from which the Indians could learn, Keshab became convinced that the British presence in India served a purpose for the Indian people.

In 1872, Keshab founded the Bharat Ashram on Calcutta's Mirjapur Street, where he, his family, his preachers, and their families lived in a communal setting. He reportedly said that there was no institution like a "middle-class English home" and believed that such an environment would be an ideal place for spiritual growth and for the development of a religious community.[18] The ashram was subsequently relocated outside the city, first in a farmhouse in Belgharia and later in Kankurgachi. At the ashram, Keshab Chandra Sen continued to redefine religious practices and rituals.

In nineteenth-century India, the idea of nation and religious communities as fixed categories began to take shape through interaction with missionaries and British administration. In this social and political climate marked by transition and transformation, Keshab Chandra Sen transgressed the boundaries of "religion" and "nation" being asserted by his fellow citizens of the British Raj through his interest in other religious traditions and his wish to incorporate into the Brahma Samaj rituals and beliefs from these other traditions and then endow them with new meaning. Sen fully accepted the romantic Orientalist image that all religions are similar at their core. His goal was to adopt religious elements from other traditions that would contribute to molding monotheistic belief and practices in Brahma worship. This endeavor demonstrated how Sen adopted British scholars' and missionaries' notions of religion and religious sources. Sen focused on Scripture as a source of authentic religious knowledge. Thus, it is no surprise that K. C. Sen sought to distance the religious life and the activities of his group from "Hinduism." Sen was instrumental in passing a national legislative document that recognized Brahma marriages and in effect recognized the Brahma Samaj as a religious community with an identity separate from the Hindu community of India, which was associated with polytheism, a clear example of the transformations taking place in this modern milieu.

In 1881, Keshab Chandra Sen inaugurated the Naba Bidhan (New Dispensation) sect, which propagated universalistic ideals. Many close watchers of the Brahma Samaj were confused by this move. Some British critics charged Sen with abandoning some of the basic Christian doctrines and returning to the fold of the mainstream Hindu community. In his book *The Brahmo Samaj*, David Kopf suggests that Sen actually abandoned the missionaries, whom he now viewed merely as a vehicle for British imperialism.[19]

In general, Keshab Chandra Sen was interested in creating traditions that had specific meaning for Indians. This goal led him to pursue a continual search as well as an inventive process that sometimes alienated his followers. His spiritual exploration in the years following the founding of the Naba Bidhan centered on acts invoking imaginative empathy, bringing together for liturgical purposes within an Indian cultural framework ideas attributed to several prophets and social reformers from all parts of the world. An example of this eclectic practice occurred when he began a meditation on saints whereby Brahma members studied the lives of important philosophers and reform figures from Socrates to Moses and Muhammad. Based on this study, Brahma members played the roles of the prophets and reformers, answering questions posed by other participants. Keshab Chandra Sen also adopted ritual and symbolic elements, such as the Christian baptism and Eucharist, and gave them new meanings.[20]

All of these changes in ritual practice emerged as a result of studies that K. C. Sen requested five of his followers to conduct. Approximately three years after establishing the ashram, he became interested in the teachings of Scripture and the earliest prophetic and reformist articulations of Islamic, Christian, Hindu, Buddhist, and Sikh traditions. Choosing five of the most qualified Brahma members to pursue studies in these traditions, Keshab Chandra Sen endeavored to make knowledge of the traditions readily accessible so that he and his intellectual cadre would be able to incorporate various sectarian elements into Brahma worship, belief, and practices. Keshab Chandra Sen made the Brahma Samaj an innovative movement among Bengal's middle-class intellectuals. The lack of its long-term influence over the people of India might result in part from its transgressive nature. It did not clearly demarcate boundaries between Hindu, Muslim, and Christian at a time when communal lines were being highlighted.[21]

Girish Chandra Sen and the Brahma Samaj

K. C. Sen requested that Girish Chandra Sen, who had extensive knowledge of Persian, study the Qur'an, and in 1881 he published the first volume of his translation and commentary. This work was widely accepted and applauded not just by the Brahmas but also by Bengal's Muslims, who viewed it as a pioneering contribution to Islam that benefited their religious community.

Girish Chandra Sen further studied Islam with Muslim scholars before writing his translation. Knowing that Urdu and Persian were not enough, in 1876 he went to Lucknow to study Arabic, Islamic history, and religious literature with Muslim scholars. Sen became a prolific Bengali writer on Islam, but he also wrote about the Naba Bidhan sect of the Brahma Samaj and penned an autobiography. In addition, his writings include translations of works by famous Muslims, including a version of Sa'di's *Gulistan*, which he dedicated to Keshab Chandra Sen. Girish Sen also wrote biographies of central Islamic figures such as the Prophet Muhammad; his wives, Khadija and 'A'isha; his daughter, Fatima; and his grandsons, the Imams Hasan and Husayn. All of these works were produced at Keshab Chandra Sen's request. Other leaders in Girish Sen's repertoire included Abraham, Moses, David, and Rabi'a, a Sufi. Girish Sen's translations into Bengali of the works of al-Ghazali and Rumi reflect his particular interest in Sufism. Girish Sen also wrote an original piece about Sufism and translated into Bengali a hadith collection with commentary. His works on Islam demonstrated his appreciation for many of its theological concepts.

Girish Chandra Sen's works on the Naba Bidhan sect include biographies of central figures such as Sri Ramkrishna. Sen also wrote commentaries on Roy's monotheistic theology. Many of Sen's literary efforts were directed toward Brahma religion and the influences of other religions on it, the life of a preacher, and the politics of the Brahma Samaj. Sen's commitment to women's issues eventually led him to edit and publish a Bengali magazine for women. Although Girish Chandra Sen was not a central figure in Brahma Samaj leadership, he was one of the main literary instruments for Keshab Chandra Sen's religious ideas, spreading the teachings of the Brahma Samaj through publications.

Passionate about the universalist vision articulated in the Brahma Samaj, Girish Chandra Sen also endeavored to make Islam familiar to Hindu Indians, presenting Islam and its intellectual and religious heritage in a positive light at a time when differences between religious communities were being emphasized. The religious synthesis attempted by the Brahma Samaj made sense to many Bengali intellectuals such as Girish Chandra Sen, whose scholarship on Islam and the Qur'an in particular reflected the Brahma vision but lacked broader appeal.

Sen was the first person to write a translation and commentary on the Qur'an in Bengali. He published the initial volume of this pioneering work anonymously because he was keenly aware of the reasons why Muslims of this period had not already translated it. Yet to the surprise of many, the publishers received several letters from Islamic organizations expressing their gratitude for the production of a translation and commentary. One such letter, written by the Arabic senior scholar of the Calcutta Madrassa and signed by other *maulvis*, stated, "As we are Mahommedans by faith and birth, our best and hearty thanks are due to the author for his disinterested and patriotic effort and the great troubles he has taken to diffuse the deep meaning of our holy and sacred religious book, the Koran, to the public. The version of the Koran above quoted has been such a wonderful success that we would wish the author would publish his name to the public, to whom he has done such a valuable service, and thus gain a personal regard from the public."[22] Heartened by this response, Sen eventually released his name and continued his translation and *tafsir* of the Qur'an. Most Muslims were shocked to learn that the author was not even a Muslim.

The production of a work such as the translation and commentary of the Qur'an had a much greater effect than Girish Chandra Sen ever imagined. As a result, the Muslims of Bengal granted Sen the titles of *bhai* (older brother) and *maulana* (reserved for learned scholars), an illustration of their admiration for him and their approval of his work. Furthermore, Sen inspired Muslims to write their own translations and commentaries by taking the initial risk of criticism. The timing of Sen's book also played a key role in its success in the Muslim community. In a climate of religious reform among Muslims and Hindus, Sen made the Qur'an accessible to a Bengali audience when many reformers debated correct practice. Sen also unwittingly provided yet another tool for Muslim scholars' reform efforts. Even today, Bengali Muslim scholars continue to write commentaries in Bengali, and Sen's translation remains widely available in Bangladesh's markets although other early translations written by Muslims do not.

Girish Chandra Sen's *Korān Śarīph*

In the short preface to his *Korān śarīph*, Sen provides some information about the methods he employs and his approach toward interpreting the Qur'an. Sen begins by mentioning that although many English translations of the Qur'an existed, few were widely available in India. Those that were available had limited value, because most Indians at the time had only a rudimentary command of the English language. The introduction does not mention Keshab Chandra Sen or any other specific individual who might have encouraged Girish Chandra Sen to write the book; instead, he emphasized that his translation sought to make the Qur'an accessible to Bengali speakers who might otherwise be precluded from fully understanding its timeless teachings. Sen employs a great amount of "imaginative empathy" throughout his *tafsir*, leaving the reader to assume, as many did at the time, that the *mufassir* (exegete) of this *tafsir* was indeed a Muslim. For example, in his preface, Sen offered a definition of the term "Qur'an": "The meaning of the word 'Qur'an' is Word of God or *kalāmāllāh* (*īśvar-bānī*). From time to time, a prophet, Muhammad, transmitted it for the benefit of the world. It was collected and put together in this book and became the Qur'an. Muslims revere the Qur'an as the word of God."[23]

He also describes how one begins recitation. "I am immersed in the clear meaning of the Qur'an. Firstly, 'In God I seek refuge' and 'In the name of God' (I am immersed in the name of God), these are said humbly with an open heart and in a pure form that the reader reads correctly. When engaged in the study and before every sura, save sura *Tauba*, one must say 'In the name of God—*Bismillah*' and if at the time of study he utters another word, he should say *Bismillah* and it will be as if he is seeing God and God is seeing him."[24] Girish Chandra Sen goes on to explain that if one is interrupted in his or her recitation, the individual is required to recite these phrases again. Sen treats this ritual recitation method as the only way to recite the Qur'an. Sen then directs his discussion of the term "Qur'an" to the topic of Muslim piety and reverence for the word of God. Thus he states, "It is written that if someone listens to and studies the Qur'an, he gains much merit. Every Muslim must speak according to the doctrines of the Qur'an. If anyone transgresses what is in the Qur'an in any way, he is a great sinner. When reading the Qur'an, the reader should obey the following rules and regulations: for example, when brushing his teeth, performing ablutions (scrubbing hands, feet, and face according to certain prescriptions) the student should sit on pure ground with pure intent. It is best if he sits in a mosque, properly facing west."[25] This statement provides evidence that Sen was familiar with private acts of piety and reverence for the Qur'an as interpreted in parts of the Indian subcontinent, particularly in Bengal. *Sharīf* (noble) is one of the many reverent adjectival terms used to refer to the Qur'an by Muslims, especially Bengali Muslims and even Sen.

To transmit the essence of the Qur'anic meaning, Sen explains, each word must be separately translated. Because Bengali, an Indic sub-branch of the Indo-European language group, and Arabic, a Semitic language, differ vastly, Sen explains at length Arabic word order and the difficulty of literal translation, informing the reader that in many cases his translation method demands lengthy Bengali paraphrasing to achieve a nuanced meaning.

Sen's last point in his preface concerns the need for commentary because translations are often insufficient to accurately convey intended Qur'anic meanings. Although his commentary is derived from only three sources, *Taphsir hosenī* (*Tafsir husayni*, Ar.), *Taphsir phāẏda* (*Tafsir fa'ida*, Ar.), and *Taphsir jalalin* (*Tafsir jalalayn*, Ar.), he relies most heavily on the first two.[26] *Tafsir husayni*, written by Husayn al-Wa'iz al-Kashifi (d. 1504–5),[27] is a Persian commentary well known on the Indian subcontinent. *Tafsir fa'ida*, an Urdu work, was written by Shah 'Abdul Qadir, a son of Shah Wali Allah. Only in the second edition of his *tafsir* did Sen include *Tafsir jalalayn*.

Beginning with the title of each sura, Sen wrote his entire *tafsir* in Bengali. It is likely that he worked from Persian, of which he had an excellent command, rather than Arabic, with which he had limited experience. As the illustration shows, below the title and the sura's number, the total sum of verses in that sura is indicated. In parentheses below the statement of the number of verses is the *basmala*, given in Bengali. After each verse, Sen provides the verse number. Exclusion of the Arabic text of the Qur'an is highly unusual in the *tafsir* tradition. Commentators commonly include the text of the Qur'an, providing a verse-by-verse commentary. Yet Sen chose not to include the Arabic text, perhaps because of his belief that his readers, particularly the scholars of the Brahma Samaj, were unfamiliar with Arabic and therefore that the inclusion of Arabic would have served little purpose for Sen's readers. His format, excluding the Arabic, indicates his interest in simply conveying the text's underlying meaning.

Another divergence from the *tafsir* tradition was Sen's use of the Western footnote system. Although Sen cites all sources, his citations are brief. For example, the first time he cites a particular author, he names the source as follows: *Tafsir husayni*, *Tafsir fa'ida*, *Tafsir jalalayn*. Thereafter, Sen uses an abbreviation system to refer to these sources, such as t, f for *Tafsir fa'ida*. Perhaps believing that his reader is either familiar with the original sources or would not refer to them, Sen provides only the author's initials. To refer to the original texts, the reader would have to be familiar with *Tafsir jalalayn*, *Tafsir husayni*, and *Tafsir fa'ida* and have sufficient knowledge to find the relevant information.

Commonly known as *Tafsir husayni*, the Persian commentary *Mawahib-i-'aliyyah* was composed by Husayn al-Wa'iz al-Kashifi from 1492 to 1494. Mir 'Ali Shir requested that al-Kashifi write a commentary on the Qur'an. Al-Kashifi wrote the first volume, the lengthy *Jawahir-altafsir li tuhfat-alamir*, which consisted of commentary on the first three suras and on the first part of the fourth, with a detailed introduction on Qur'anic exegesis. He then decided to write the much

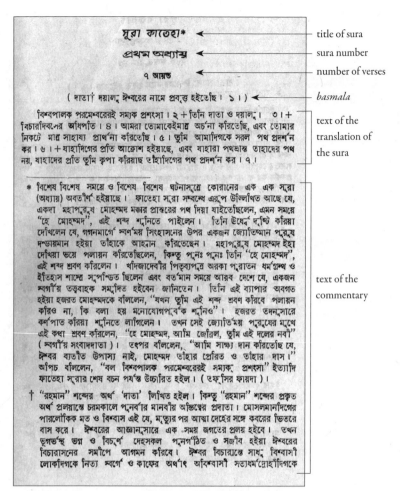

A sample page from Sen's *Korān śarīph,* first published in 1881.
The arrows point to the main elements of this commentary and translation.

shorter *Tafsir husayni,* which became one of the most widely read *tafsir* works on the Indian subcontinent.[28]

The version of *Tafsir husayni* on which Sen relied was published in India with Urdu commentary by Shah 'Abd al-'Aziz (d. 1823), son of famous religious reformer Shah Wali Allah of Delhi. Shah 'Abd al-'Aziz followed in his father's footsteps, actively engaging in religious reform. According to Peter Hardy and Rafiuddin Ahmed, Shah 'Abd al-'Aziz declared India *dar al-harb.* Barbara Metcalf has refuted this point, however, observing that his intentional ambiguity on that point intimates his possible opposition to jihad on the frontier.[29] Shah 'Abd al-'Aziz unquestionably opposed British interference in internal Indian legal matters as well as in shari'a, with the imposition of British penalties and offenses effectively replacing Islamic religious law.[30] He was also one of many religious scholars who employed fatwas to disseminate his reform ideas, which included discussions regarding the proper conduct at saints' tombs, homeopathic medicine, and the conditions under which a Muslim might accept a job with Christians or the British.

Tafsir fa'ida (Tafsir for benefit) was written by Shah 'Abd al-Qadir (d. 1827), another son of Shah Wali Allah. Before writing this commentary, in 1790–91 he wrote a highly regarded Urdu translation of the Qur'an known by two titles, Muzih al-Qur'an and A'inah-i-Qur'an. Like his brother Shah 'Abd al-'Aziz, 'Abd al-Qadir was actively involved in religious reform, teaching, writing, and issuing fatwas. A third brother, Shah Rafi'al-Din (d. 1833–34), also wrote and published an Urdu translation of the Qur'an under the title al-An'am. Why each brother wrote a separate Urdu translation is unclear. There is no evidence of either personal animosity or theological disagreement among them. On the contrary, copies of al-An'am contain notes from Muzih al-Qur'an.[31]

The third tafsir source for Sen's commentary is Tafsir al-jalalayn, authored by Jalal al-Din al-Mahalli (d. 1459) and Jalal al-Din al-Suyuti (d. 1505). Al-Mahalli was al-Suyuti's teacher, and according to al-Suyuti, al-Mahalli commented on surat al-Fatiha (1) and on al-Kahf (18) through al-Nas (114); al-Suyuti completed the work, which is predominantly philological. Al-Suyuti was, among many other things, a philologist and a scholar of the Qur'an, on which he wrote twenty works. However, because Tafsir al-jalalayn deals predominantly with clarifying Arabic grammar, word usage, origin, and syntax, it had limited utility for Sen's work. Tafsir al-jalalayn is directed to an audience that knows Arabic and is interested in grammatical and syntactical questions. It is therefore often employed as an "orthodox" teaching text in madrassas. For those less familiar with Arabic, Tafsir al-jalalayn might serve as a reference on difficult points of grammar. Having studied Arabic for only a short period, Sen was certainly not as comfortable with Arabic as he was with Persian and Urdu. Furthermore, his audience was likely unfamiliar with Arabic. Perhaps Sen chose this work for its legitimizing and authoritative function, but without the accompanying Arabic verse, it makes little sense. Therefore, the only possible value of employing such a text was to demonstrate his familiarity with subcontinental Islamic standard *tafsir*.

Of 1,818 individual verse explanations, only 131 (7.2 percent) are not explicit quotations and may thus be Sen's own commentary. Of those, 61 state only whether the sura is considered Meccan or Medinan. This kind of information is based primarily on the *asbab al-nuzul* (occasions for revelations) and *al-nasikh wa 'l-mansukh* (abrogating and abrogated) literature. Generally, however, Sen prefers to defer to the Muslim *mufassirun* (exegetes) when, after providing his own translations, he nevertheless determines that a particular verse needs additional explanation.

Sen's employment of the three *tafsirs* is also unique. Traditionally, when exegetes provide interpretations of a word, phrase, or an entire verse, they typically include within their interpretations the opinions of other exegetes. This inclusion is often introduced by the phrases "It is said" or "According to." Unlike these classical exegetes, however, Sen does not provide commentary as a means of supporting his opinions or interpretations. Nor does he provide, like al-Tabari (d. 923), other commentary to demonstrate varying interpretations. What distinguishes Sen's style from this classical tradition is that the opinions of other exegetes are not a mere element of his explanation; instead, they often constitute the only explanation of the verse in question. Thus, Sen's *tafsir* provides a monovalent reading of the Qur'an, a method more in line with the more conservative approaches to the Qur'an taken by scholars such as Ibn Kathir.

The only aspect of the commentary that is authentically Sen's is his translation of the Qur'anic Arabic into Bengali. Sen claimed that unlike many nineteenth-century Urdu translators and commentators of the Qur'an, he did not rely on Persian translations of the Qur'an. Sen states in his preface that he translated directly from Arabic to Bengali and did not rely on a Persian translation to distinguish his work from those of other subcontinental religious scholars. This claim is dubious, and he clearly relied on Persian and Urdu works in the commentary section of the *tafsir*. We do not know for certain whether he used a Persian translation of *Tafsir al-jalalayn*. His choice of commentators is not unusual in that he selected those who were highly regarded and well known on the subcontinent, at least by scholars who would be judging the value of his contribution. Sen's commentary is marked by his unique style and by his goal of explaining the Qur'an to non-Muslims and to those unfamiliar with its content.

Sen's style is consistent throughout his *tafsir*. He struggles with translation of particular Arabic terms such as Allah, *qiyama*, and *kafir* as well as the names of the suras and even the term "sura." The problem of achieving a literal translation is evident throughout his work. For example, Sen never uses the Arabic term "Allah" to refer to God. Instead he chooses to employ Bengali terms such as *iśvar, parameśar*, and *adhipati*. Sen's attempt to be both universalist and true to the original Arabic in his translation renders it inconsistent: some terms are not translated from Arabic and are left unexplained, while numerous other terms receive Bengali translations. This might suggest that Sen viewed some Arabic/Islamic terms as having equivalent terms in Bengali, while others did not. Thus, Sen's explanation of the term *rahman*, a name of God, was not intended as a literal translation but rather constituted a doctrinal elaboration. His struggle with literal translation provides an understanding of Islamic doctrine and practice and suggests his desire to provide his Bengali readers with a basic understanding of the text in an effort to make Islam accord with transcendent monotheism. By demystifying Islam, Sen strove to break down stereotypes of Indian Muslims and to identify elements of their beliefs shared by the Brahma Samaj. Bengali translation of the Qur'an would therefore create a vehicle by which the Brahma Samaj could adopt Muslim concepts, doctrines, beliefs, and practices originally spelled out in the Qur'anic Arabic.

Many people may be surprised or even shocked to discover that a Hindu-derived religious movement would go to such lengths to borrow ideas from Islam, of all religions. A modern informed view of the Hindu-Muslim dichotomy would suggest that such boundary transgressions do not, should not, and have not occurred and that these two worldviews have always existed in opposition.[32] Understanding the circumstances of Sen's borrowings requires breaking with twentieth-century monolithic conceptions of "Hindu" and "Muslim" and from the assumption that a conflictual relationship has always existed between the two. As demonstrated in chapter 1, the two groups have a history of religious exchange in which the emphasis on religious difference was not always pronounced. In this light, it becomes less surprising that Bengali Hindu intellectuals would look to their Bengali Muslim neighbors for monotheistic sources of inspiration. In the 1800s, Sen and the Brahma Samaj exemplified the continued exchange across religious boundaries. Nevertheless, during the same period, communal affiliation increasingly became based first on religious affiliation by reformers, the elite, and the British. As this social and administrative environment demonstrates, a great deal of the way religious life changed resulted in part from colonial encounter. This privileging of religious communal affiliation and its publicly manifested nature arises from systems—both structured (governing policy) and unstructured (internal communal discourse)—of exchange and engagement among colonial administrators, colonized subjects, and missionaries.

In such a fertile religious and intellectual environment, Muslims published *tafsir* in Bengali. Naimuddīn (d. 1908) was the first Muslim to do so, and his objectives contrasted with Sen's lofty goals. Naimuddīn, the second Bengali *mufassir*, sought to normalize and unify Muslim practices in Bengal. He had opinions on all reform issues, as evidenced in his journal, editorial writings, fatwas, and his first book-length publication, and he was concerned about what he believed was the "correct" understanding of Islam. These attitudes are reflected in his books as well. Unlike Sen's work, Naimuddīn's *tafsir* was directed specifically at a Muslim audience whose primary language of communication was Bengali.

Naimuddīn's *Korān Šarīph*

Mohammad Naimuddīn went on to publish the first part of his *tafsir* in 1891, ten years after the publication of Sen's Qur'an translation and *tafsir*. Naimuddīn received the financial backing for this work from the *zamīndār* Mahmud Ali Khan. Naimuddīn died in 1908, having completed the translation and *tafsir* for the first nine *paras* of the Qur'an.[33] The first volume contains commentary on *surat al-Fatiha* (1) and *al-Baqara* (2) through verse 203. The second volume, which he completed a few years later, ends with *surat al-nisa'* (4) verse 76. Nowhere in his *tafsir* does Naīmuddīn indicate whether he was influenced by Sen's *tafsir*. However, while Sen was working on his *tafsir*, Naīmuddīn had already published *Jobdātal masāyel* in 1873. Like Sen, in these early works Naīmuddīn began to employ a modern Bengali prose style. His patron urged him to write this book for a growing population of Muslims who read Bengali. Thereafter, he frequently published works on a variety of religious topics, all in Bengali. It seems likely that Naīmuddīn, a scholar cognizant of contemporary religious debates, was aware of Sen's writings on Islam; only after Sen published his *tafsir* did Naīmuddīn begin work on his version. He may have wanted to counter Sen's universalizing mission or simply to provide Bengali-speaking Muslims with a *tafsir* written by a Muslim. Having broken the barrier to writing a *tafsir* in Bengali, Sen cleared the way for Naīmuddīn's project.

Unlike Sen, Naīmuddīn does not provide an extensive introduction to his *tafsir*. The first page, for example, contains an advertisement for his other books. The next page is an introductory prayer, followed by a one-paragraph preface stating only that the work is a Bengali translation of the Qur'an with explanations. Naīmuddīn concludes his preface by indicating matter-of-factly his intention to publish a second volume of this work in the near future. The preface to the first volume provides no information on methodology but only very generally indicates the purpose of the work: to help all Muslims and serve as a teaching guide for the entire Bengali-speaking Muslim public; it is not intended just for scholars and teachers. Naīmuddīn published a second volume a few years later but never completed a *tafsir* of the remaining suras, although his sons finished the task many years later.

As the three illustrations show, at the beginning of each sura, Naīmuddīn's *tafsir* states the ordinal number, the title of each sura in Bengali, and the number of verses for that sura, followed by the *basmala* written in both Arabic and Bengali. Naīmuddīn's work differs in form and content from Sen's work in several ways. First, although Bengali is written from left to right, in an attempt to make Bengali more like Arabic and therefore to make the text more authentically Islamic, Naīmuddīn innovates on this tradition by commencing the book from the right leaf.[34] Naīmuddīn indicates that he struggles with defining a new style that targets a Muslim audience and tries to maintain a distinctly Islamic appearance. He resists employing a Bengali that relies little on Perso-Arabic terms common in the Bengali spoken by Muslims. His struggle over the use of language highlights the politics associated with language.

A second major difference between the two authors is that Naīmuddīn, unlike Sen, provides the Arabic text at the core of his commentary before the Bengali, furnishing a line-by-line translation of the sura. As is the case today in much of the Islamic world, many non-Arab Muslims in Bengal learned at least to read or recite Qur'anic Arabic, though they may have been unfamiliar with the exact meaning of what was being recited. Naīmuddīn likely included the Arabic verses so that he could provide readers with translations and interpretations. His inclusion of the Arabic constitutes perhaps just one indication of the difference between his intended audience and that of Sen. That is, by including the Arabic, Naīmuddīn acknowledges the readers' probable basic familiarity with the Arabic script and its pronunciation and their simultaneous familiarity with both the Arabic and Bengali languages.

Naīmuddīn's commentary is more traditional than Sen's. Naīmuddīn does not, for example, use Sen's footnote system. Rather, Naīmuddīn provides his commentary after translating each verse, a method more in line with the practice of traditional exegetes. He does, however, use footnotes to explain tangential matters—for example, to explain an Arabic grammatical point or the appropriate honorific appellation recited when referring to a prophet by name or a companion of the Prophet Muhammad. Naīmuddīn also uses footnotes as an instructional tool, explaining, for example, why one should always say "Peace be upon him" in Arabic after mentioning the Prophet Muhammad.

Finally, like traditional exegetes, Naīmuddīn includes the comments of *mufassirun* who have written in Arabic, Persian, and Urdu. Traditional *mufassirun*, when referring to works of other authors, state simply that "X stated that . . ." or "in Y's work it is written. . . ." Naīmuddīn usually does not name his source but instead makes statements such as "An ancient learned person stated. . . ." Thus, it is difficult to determine clearly Naīmuddīn's sources. Those he names in this commentary include the hadith collections of al-Bukhari and Muslim, *Tafsir ahmadi*, Ibn Maja, Abu Da'ud, Shah Abdul Aziz, Darmi Sharif, and Nishai Sharif. Naīmuddīn delves more deeply into the meaning of the text than does Sen, who is satisfied with providing other *mu-*

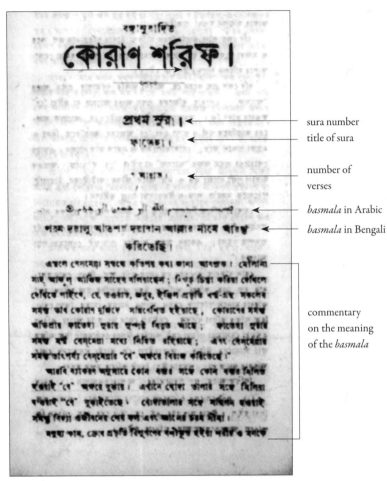

A sample page from Naīmuddīn's *Korān śarīph,* first published in 1891.
The arrows point to the main elements of this commentary and translation.

The labels on the sample page read:
- sura number
- title of sura
- number of verses
- *basmala* in Arabic
- *basmala* in Bengali
- commentary on the meaning of the *basmala*

fassirun's interpretations without contextualizing or further explaining them. Thus, Naīmuddīn renders a much lengthier *tafsir* than does Sen. By the time of his death, Naīmuddīn had completed his *tafsir* only from *surat al-Fatiha* to the fortieth verse of *surat al-Anfal*—that is, the first nine *paras.*

A brief look at some of Naīmuddīn's *tafsir* of *surat al-Fatiha* reveals his general viewpoint on acceptable Islamic belief and practice. He defines and explains the esoteric (numerological) significance of the

too, describes Gabriel with the phrase *joʼtirmaẏ purush*. However, he inserts in parentheses the word *nurrānī*, an Arabic derivative of the noun *nūr* (light) combined with a Bengali suffix to form a noun of person. To describe Muhammad's venture into the "wilderness" to meditate, Sen uses the term *prāntarer path*, while Naīmuddīn uses the term *māṭhe*, which is more appropriately translated as "field." He describes the occasion for this revelation and delivers a line-by-line translation, providing detailed explanations of all the phrases and words he believes are unclear. The phraseology is significant, not only because the terms suggest different images but also, and perhaps more importantly, because the terms introduced by Naīmuddīn were derived from Arabic, a language somewhat familiar to many educated Muslims in Bengal, and thus remain within the Islamic semantic universe.

Naīmuddīn introduces Arabic and Persian terminology throughout this work. For example, in his *tafsir* of the verse *malik yawm al-din* (Lord of the Day of Judgment) he says that the day referred to in this verse is called *keẏāmat*, the Arabic term (*qiyama*) for the resurrection. Later in the explanation of this verse Naīmuddīn introduces the Persian term *beheśt* and two other Arabic terms, *kāpher* and *mośrekgan*. He states that those who have lived well on earth will live thereafter in heaven—that is, *beheśt*—while the *kāpher* and *mośrekgan* will be banished to hell. *Beheśt* is the Persian term for heaven commonly used in Bengali. *Kāpher* (the Arabic term *kafir*) is usually translated as unbeliever or infidel. The term *mośrekgan* is a Banglicized form (by the addition of the Bengali plural suffix *-gan*) of the Arabic term *mushrik*, which can be translated as "polytheist." Naīmuddīn uses these Arabic and Persian terms interchangeably to facilitate the reader's recognition and to further common employment of them in what Naīmuddīn would regard as the appropriate context.

Naīmuddīn's commentary seeks to explain basic Islamic teachings. For example, to provide a more in-depth understanding of the verse *iyyaka naʻbudu wa iyyakanastaʻin* (Thee do we worship, and thine aid we seek), he separates the verse into two segments, *iyyāka naʻbudu* and *wa iyyāka nastaʻin*. He suggests that the first part means that God and only God deserves to be worshipped. To emphasize this point he introduces in parentheses the Arabic term *maʻbud*, which means "the Worshipped," or "God" or "Godhead." Naīmuddīn explains that as

God is worshipped, knowledge increases, eyes open, and hearts are illuminated. To be voluntarily humble to someone else with great devotion is called worship and adoration. Muslims call this *ebādat*, from the Arabic term *'ibadat*, which is a technical term in Islamic law referring to the acts of worship. Naīmuddīn also states that the one who worships God is called *bāndā*, a Persian term meaning "servant." In metaphoric terms, he suggests that we worship God with our entire being, including our eyes, ears, tongue, hands, and feet. One form of *'ibadat* he calls *etekāph* (*i'tikāf*, "withdrawal," Ar.) with one's feet, which he explains in a footnote as living in a mosque for a specified period of time at the end of Ramadan for the purpose of performing acts of devotion.

A great deal of Naīmuddīn's commentary takes on the tone of a teaching guide, explaining in detail the precepts, rituals, and attitude of the believer. This is the major distinction between his work and those of traditional scholars writing in Arabic in the premodern period. Scholars wrote *tafsir* for other scholars; in the modern period, scholars began to write *tafsir* and other specialized genres for a wider South Asian audience. Naīmuddīn often refers to stories and explanations that can be found in other *tafsirs*, but his commentary also includes lengthy digressions that would not necessarily appear in the earlier, more scholarly versions.

Naīmuddīn first gives the text of verse 7 of *surat al-Baqara*:

God hath set a seal
On their hearts and on their hearing,
And on their eyes is a veil;
Great is the penalty they [incur].

He then explains in detail the plight of the *kafir*, or sinner.

There is a mark or seal in their hearts and so truth cannot enter into their hearts. There is a mark or seal in their ears so they cannot hear, and their eyes are veiled so they are blinded from seeing the right path. It is very difficult for them to be religious. A severe punishment is waiting for them in the next world. If anyone asks how will they have faith if God [*khadātālā*] made a seal in their hearts, ears, and eyes? How will they believe the truth? How will they listen to the truth? How will they accept the right path?

And how will they become sinners? What is the reason for their punishment? Fault cannot lie with them if God closed the door, not allowing them to enter. These objections of the *kafir* will not be accepted because God did not seal the door before. Had he sealed it before, then no words could enter their hearts. They would not be able to listen or see anything. They would have been born deaf and blind. They can understand everything but the truth. They can listen to everything but the truth. They can see everything but the right path. Therefore, they are the enemies of the Muslims; they are Satan. They are nothing but *kafirs*. After seeing their evil activities, God sealed off their hearts and ears. They are blind because their eyes are veiled. They will be banished because of their envy, enmity, and satanic activities. Their objections [will not be heard], nor their requests be granted. Those who are born blind, born deaf, they are not answerable. They do not need to answer for their deeds, and there is hope for their redemption on the Last Day.

Naīmuddīn's explanation of this verse amounts to a theological discussion. This commentary on verse 7 leads smoothly into his commentary on verse 8, where he defines faith, the Last Day, the faithful Muslims, and the hypocrites. His discussion of the hypocrites (*munafiqun*) is the predominant theme of the commentary on verses 8–21.

Naīmuddīn's commentary on verse 22 reflects a localized understanding of the verse. The text of the verse reads,

Who has made the earth your couch,
And the heavens your canopy;
And sent down rain from the heavens;
And brought forth therewith
Fruits for your sustenance;
Then set not up rivals unto God
When ye know [the truth].[37]

Naīmuddīn translates this verse somewhat differently:

Because of you, God gave this earth to you as your bed and the sky or heaven as your shelter. He makes rain fall from the sky, and with that he makes various crops grow, such as fruit. So do not consider anything as your God's or anyone God's equal [partner] *sarik*. You are informed of this.

His translation is loose yet well suited to a predominantly agricultural community. The commentary that follows is again indicative of a more localized understanding of this particular Qur'anic verse.

That means that God [*khadātālā*] is saying, "O People! For your happiness I created this earth as your bed, for your happiness I made this heaven as your home. For your food I have made rain fall from the sky, and after the ground was wet I created a variety of tasty vegetables, delicious fruits, and for fragrance various flowers, and for medicine various trees and vines. You are informed of this, also that no one else other than I created you or your ancestors and that you should not consider anyone my equal [partner]—that is, do not believe in more than one God."

No matter what religion you follow, if you think it over carefully, it will be evident to everyone that God is all-powerful and is one, and no one is able to deny this. But many deluded people in the world believe in many gods.

A group of people called Majusi[38] believe that there is a creator of good and also there is a creator of evil.

Another group of people called Chaẏebīn[39] believe first of all that God is omnipotent, but they believe all good and bad deeds lies in the stars and so they worship the stars.

Hindus believe that there are many gods and they make many idols with gold and silver and then they worship these idols.

Another group of people, the *Pīr* worshippers[40] (Guru worshippers) find any person who cannot really speak [the truth], and they worship him when he dies. They even worship his tomb.

Ignorant people see anything bright or surprising and worship it. Some of them worship fire. Some worship the Ganges River, or a type of basil plant [*tulsī*]. Some worship beasts and some worship mountains. So in this way they worship many gods. They will not be saved until they refrain from this blind faith.

Thus, Naīmuddīn employs Qur'anic verses that he broadly understands as a critique of the kinds of worship he wants to criticize in his society.

Verse 22 essentially describes God as creator of all living things and asserts that one should not associate other beings with the one God. Naīmuddīn then elaborates with specific examples from his audience in Bengal, which include the Hindu community, the taking on of a *pir* or guru, and visits to tombs of saints or *pirs*. He criticizes veneration of saints and visiting of tombs but not Sufism. He refers to the Hindus as "ignorant people" and defines their ignorance by their worship of fire, the Ganges, and the *tulsī* plant.

The final example of Naīmuddīn's commentary included here illustrates his affirmation of the apotropaic power associated with its recitation to avert danger. In addition to his use of numerology and other esoteric commentary, his commentary on verse 5 of the second sura discusses the protective power of the recitation of verses. The verse reads,

> They are on [true] guidance,
> From their Lord, and it is
> Those people who will prosper.

In his first example he states that Ibn Mas'ud mentioned that if *surat al-Baqara* is read from evening until morning, Satan will not enter the home in which it is recited. Naīmuddīn also cites Ibn 'Umar, who heard Muhammad say, "If someone dies among you, do not keep the body in the home; bury him as soon as possible and read *surat al-Baqara* over him." Naīmuddīn then refers to a hadith reported by al-Bukhari that relates the story of someone who pitched a tent near a river. Area inhabitants warned that the tent might be looted at night, but only one person remained in the tent that evening while the others ventured into the city. The person who was left behind recalled hearing from Ibn 'Umar that the Prophet had said, "If one recites thirty-three verses from the Qur'an until the morning, then he will be protected." The man did just that.[41] The next day, as the group departed the campsite, they met an old man who asked if they were men or angels. The man who spent the night reciting Qur'anic verses replied that they were indeed men. The old man claimed that when he and his men attempted to attack the campsite, they were confronted by a wall of iron. And so the man who had recited the verses from the Qur'an conveyed the relevant hadith suggesting that one should recite Qur'anic verses for protection. For Naīmuddīn, reciting the Qur'an had divine power, and he conveyed this belief throughout his *tafsir*, which is filled with stories from hadith.

Jobdātal masāyel, along with Naīmuddīn's *tafsir*, journals, fatwas, and the *tafsir* work of Girish Chandra Sen, led the way for Muslims to begin a discourse on religious questions in standard colloquial Bengali. This simple but profound maneuver addressed the cultural milieu not only specific to the people of the subcontinent but also particular to the people of Bengal. Other books by Mohammad Naīmuddīn addressing this concern include *Phatuja ālaṃgiri* (1884),[42] *Insāph* (Justice) (1886), *Dhokā bhañjhan* (Dispelling deception) (1889), *Kalamātula kufaru* (The words of the nonbeliever) (1890), *Ākher johar* (Last possible time for midday prayer) (1892), *Reter* (1894),[43] *Ādellāye hānifiy* (The Hanafi legal school) (1894), *Molud śarīph* (The noble birth) (1895), *Raphāijadahana* (The Rafi-yadayns) (1896),[44] *Chahi bukharī* (Bukhari sahih) (1898), and *Dharmer lāṭi* (Religion's fighting stick) (1903). He also edited the monthly journal *Ākhabāre islāmīyā*, which focused on issues related to shari'a.

Other Muslims soon followed in the literary footsteps of Girish Chandra Sen and Mohammad Naīmuddīn. These successors included Shaikh Abdur Rahim, who wrote *Hajrat Muhammader jiban carit o dharmanīti* (Hazrat Muhammad's life, character, and religious principles) (1887), *Islam* (1896), *Nāmāj tattva* (The essence of prayer) (1898), and *Hāj bidhi* (The procedures for performing hajj) (1903); Yaqinuddin Ahmad, who published *Islām dharmaniti* (The religious principles of Islam) (1900); Samiruddin Ahmad, who published *Muhammadiya dharmasopān* (Muhammadan religious steps) (1902); and Syed Nawab Ali Chaudhuri, who published *Id al-ājhā* ('I-d al-aḍḥā) (1900).[45]

Sen and Naīmuddīn's *tafsir* works were the first in the Bengali language, having a ripple effect on Muslim authors writing in modern Bengali prose about Islam generally and more specifically about the Islamic sciences. Shortly after Sen's and Naīmuddīn's *tafsirs* were published, other writers began publishing their own *tafsirs* in Bengali. In the one hundred years after Sen and Naīmuddīn wrote, more than a hundred *tafsir* works have been written in Bengali (see the appendix).

Mohammad Naīmuddīn did not merely translate Arabic texts but also wrote original works about Islam. Naīmuddīn's Bengali Islamic scholarship may have been inspired by Girish Chandra Sen, whose profound impact on Bengali Muslim scholarship should not be underestimated. His publication elevated the status of this vernacular and therefore legitimized its use for Islamic scholarship, inspiring a profound shift in Bengali Muslim identification with the Bengali language. Through this process, the culture of Islam was acknowledged as tied to the culture of the Bengal region.

Benedict Anderson's work is useful here in highlighting the role of language and its relation to national consciousness raising. Anderson has persuasively argued that Protestantism and print capitalism combined to exploit inexpensive print technology, which first created vast reading publics in Europe. In his discussion of Europe and the way print languages became the source of national consciousness, Anderson has written, "Speakers of the huge variety of Frenches, Englishes, or Spanishes, who might find it difficult or even impossible to understand one another in conversation, became capable of comprehending one another via print and paper. In the process, they gradually became aware of the hundreds of thousands, even millions, of people in their particular language-field, and at the same time that *only those* hundreds of thousands, or millions, so belonged. These fellow-readers, to whom they were connected through print, formed, in their secular, particular, visible invisibility, the embryo of the nationally imagined community."[46]

The language of printed materials was always based on pragmatic, un-self-conscious choices.[47] In India, after the 1837 government decision to replace Persian with Urdu (also written in Arabic script) as the court language in North India, and with Urdu being taught in schools, Urdu became the language of the Muslim elite throughout the subcontinent. Metcalf has suggested that by the late nineteenth century, Deoband and other Islamic schools incorporated Urdu language into the curriculum. Muslims all over the subcontinent, including South India, began to communicate in Urdu.[48] As Muslims increasingly identified with Urdu as a consequence of the enormous publication of religious material in that language, Hindus began to disassociate with the language and to associate more with its Devanagiri-scripted Hindi version with vocabulary derived predominantly from Sanskrit. While the employment of Urdu led to the creation of a vast reading public, it did not gain ground among the rural and uneducated Bengali-speaking Muslims. In fact, the cultural divide between Urdu-speaking and Bengali-speaking Muslims was further reinforced by the growth of a diverse Islamic literature in both languages. Though Bengali Muslims widely viewed Urdu as an Islamic language of the subcontinent, out of necessity they increasingly communicated their beliefs and practices in Bengali. As a result, Bengali Muslims, unlike other Muslims of the subcontinent, became less attached to Urdu culture. Thus, to the dismay of reformers and activists such as Muhammad Akram Khan, although Urdu became a cultural symbol for Muslims, its lack of popularity in Bengal simultaneously alienated Bengali Muslims.

Khan (1868–1968), a religious scholar, writer, and publisher turned political activist (a leader of the provincial Muslim League), bore witness to the first translations of the Qur'an into Bengali and other subcontinental languages. He found this acceptance of Qur'anic translation crucial for the reform he believed that South Asian Muslim society needed to undertake. He wrote in both Bengali and Urdu but saw a practical need only for Bengali. As a Muslim modernist, he hoped that the greater access to the Qur'an afforded by translations and interpretations would lead to the necessary reforms. For example, he argued that rights afforded Muslim women were being ignored. He also criticized many Muslim scholars for being superstitious and ignorant. By the beginning of the twentieth century, translations and exegetical work in subcontinental languages was replaced by a new interest in the translations of Arabic and Persian legal texts. Khan criticized this shift in a 1929 article, "Back to the Qur'an": "Owing to the widespread neglect of exegesis of the Qur'an, up to this day Shaukani's exegesis has not yet been printed. As a result, knowledge of the Qur'an and its stories is overshadowed by the stories compiled in *Jaygun Hanifa* [an eighteenth-century Bengali romance]. If you do not read *Hidaya* and Bukhari, you cannot become a maulavi. But it is heartrending to note that to be a *maulavi* does not require study of the Qur'an. In our society in the modern world, how many *maulavis* are able to say with sincerity that their study of the Qur'an is a tenth of their study of jurisprudence, *hadith*, and the principles of jurisprudence? The last chance to remedy the situation is now."[49]

Translation work had begun to take a new direction in the early twentieth century. In many respects, it was logical to move from translations of sacred texts to the translation of texts that South Asian Muslim scholars considered authoritative and classic. Nevertheless, this new direction of scholarship would have its own impact on twentieth-century ways of thinking about Muslim community not foreseeable in the 1880s.

Conclusion

An examination of excerpts from these two authors' translations and interpretations reveals the difficulties of doing translations and interpretations. They faced the forbidding challenge of demonstrating to the public the need for Qur'anic translations. For Sen, to render the Qur'an in Bengali was not a personal religious dilemma. He perceived the merit of such an undertaking for his religious community and perhaps for all people living in Bengal—Hindu, Muslim, and Christian alike. He did not believe, as did many Muslims at the time, that such a work was irreverent. He never apologized for having written it, although he did publish it anonymously. Second, Sen sought to make the Qur'an accessible to all Bengali readers, irrespective of religious affiliation.

One of the main challenges of the Bengali *tafsir* project is exemplified in Sen's initial anonymous publication of this work, a decision that suggests that he feared Muslims' criticism for rendering their sacred text in the Bengali language.[50] It is true that, on the subcontinent, the Qur'an had been translated into Urdu, but unlike Bengali, Urdu had earned the status of an "Islamic language." Not only did Sen write about Islam in Bengali, but he chose the most important text for translation, a potentially explosive choice. Nevertheless, Sen chose the Qur'an for several possible reasons—because the Qur'an is the central text from which Muslims derive their worldview and praxis, because of the influential impact of Protestant valuing of sacred text over ritual, or because of some combination of these two factors. Because of the Semitic origins of the sacred texts of Christians and Muslims, the similarities between the way sacred texts are employed among these Abrahamic traditions is not surprising. Sen may also have chosen the Qur'an because nineteenth-century Orientalists believed in the need to study religious texts to understand a religious community. Not surprisingly, therefore,

Sen, who was clearly influenced by the Christian and colonial presence in South Asia, thought the Qur'an was the ideal place to initiate a better understanding of Islam.

Sen's introduction acknowledges his desire to provide a literal translation of the Qur'an. In so doing, he rarely employed Perso-Arabic words that were part of the Bengali language spoken by Muslims. Sen's employment of Sanskritized Bengali terms for "God," for example, is reminiscent of the *puthi* literature of the Sufi *pirs* discussed in chapter 1. A clear difference exists, however: Sen wrote for an audience educated in modern nineteenth-century writing styles, which include a Sanskritized Bengali, the language of modern Hindu writers, with only sparse Islamic terms. His *tafsir* was clearly influenced by the social, political, and religious climate in which he wrote. It was a time when writers self-consciously associated languages with particular cultures and religions, a trend quite different from the precolonial period. Furthermore, observers perceived no overlap between these religious traditions/cultures and thus believed it obvious that Bengali should be highly Sanskritized and Urdu highly Persianized. Where Sen translated the Qur'an to allow readers to retrieve already familiar concepts and beliefs, Sufi *pirs* of the premodern period saw themselves as introducing beliefs to the audience. Thus, the *pirs* were compelled to employ Bengali terms (clearly derived from Sanskrit) to aid in conveying the message. These terms, though limited, made possible the introduction of new cosmological concepts into the Bengali semantic world, an important distinction between the writings of the two periods. Sen also limited commentary, opting instead to rely on the opinions of Muslim *mufassirun* at points where he felt that clarification was necessary. Although Sen could have provided his own explanations, he chose not to cross a line he delineated.

Sen clearly distinguishes himself from the Muslim *mufassirun*. As I discussed at the beginning of this chapter, one of the Brahma Samaj's most interesting teachings is the sense of imaginative empathy when trying to comprehend the doctrines of other religious traditions. Sen held an unusual appreciation of the long scholarly tradition in the Islamic world. Unlike the Orientalists of his time and more akin to the Western universalist approaches, Sen studied Islam with Muslim scholars in Lucknow. He consequently demonstrated his appreciation and respect for their knowledge by deferring to the Muslim scholars in his explanation of Qur'anic verses. But also significant is that Sen chose to use commentaries held in great esteem by a majority of South Asian Muslim scholars. The Islamic scholars with whom Sen studied in Lucknow likely influenced these choices, which then made his work highly acceptable to most educated Muslims at the time.

In contrast to Sen, Naimuddīn was clearly writing for a Bengali-speaking Muslim audience. He knew that those interested in his work were Muslims, not members of other religious communities. Sen paved the way for Naimuddīn by violating a conservative taboo against rendering the Qur'an in Bengali. It then became up to Naimuddīn to provide his own *tafsir* as a Muslim to Muslims. As a Muslim, he intentionally targeted Muslims as his audience, which is obvious from both his choice of language and the kind of information disseminated in his work. He wrote his *tafsir* in the hope of disseminating what he saw as orthodox teachings to counter the influences of other nineteenth-century Islamic reform movements in Bengal. All of his references are to hadith and to other older *tafsir* works. This examination of Naimuddīn's scholarship reveals that he advocated little change compared to other Muslim reformers. He apparently sought to promote a brand of orthodoxy that included Sufism, recognition of the four Sunni schools, and ridding the Muslim community of practices he associated with Hindu customs and beliefs such as saint veneration. Saint veneration is popular throughout much of the Islamic world; nevertheless, some South Asian Muslims considered and still consider it too closely associated with Hindu customs and rituals.

Naimuddīn used two basic strategies to counter the teachings of other reformers. First, he taught his understanding of Islamic orthodoxy based on the Qur'an and hadith by way of the print medium. Second, he imparted to the reader knowledge of proper Muslim practices and everyday acts, such as what one recites after saying the name of the Prophet Muhammad or when it is appropriate to say the *basmala*. His *tafsir* contains elements of Sufi esotericism. For example, he affirms the power of recitation but condemns visits to shrines and tombs. This attitude toward Sufism was not new but had been held for centuries by some Muslim scholars around the world.[51] Naimuddīn's *tafsir* is clearly pedagogical as, in a sense, all *tafsir* works are, but it is distinctive in that the targeted audience does not comprise other schol-ars. Rather, his audience is ordinary Bengali-speaking Muslims. Unlike Sen's *tafsir*, Naīmuddīn's work is extremely readable—that is, accessible to many—despite its elaborate detail and digressions on creed, dogma and ideology and its general abundance of Arabic terms. He addresses an audience of Muslims educated in Bengali but not necessarily in any other Islamic languages, and by the end of the nineteenth century this segment of the population was growing as fewer Muslims were writing in Urdu. He also explicitly makes this intention clear in his introduc-tion when he states that his *tafsir*, like many of his other works, essen-tially constitutes a how-to guide on Muslim life and praxis.[52]

While Sen was closer than Naīmuddīn to the fringes of the *tafsir* tradition, Naīmuddīn's and Sen's works share a common space on the margins with their similar concern with disseminating to the common people knowledge found in the Qur'an. A reading of Sen's work re-veals that his target audience is clearly middle-class Bengalis. Sen's mar-ginality is demonstrated in several respects. First, he wrote *tafsir* as a non-Muslim who deferred to Muslim *mufassirun*. His translations are literal, and his exclusion of the original text in Arabic clearly distin-guishes him from the dominant tradition. Some contemporary Muslim scholars in Bengal do not regard Sen's work as *tafsir*, specifically because of his exclusion of the Arabic.[53] In this regard, Naīmuddīn's inclusion of the Arabic is more consistent with past practices. Moreover, his use of hadith, which makes his work the first Bengali example of *tafsir bi'l ma'thur*,[54] is more consistent with the dominant *tafsir* tradition.

Yet Naīmuddīn's work lies outside that central *tafsir* tradition in that it is not directed at religious scholars or students of Islam but at those with little knowledge of Arabic and the Islamic sciences. In other words, it is not an example of high Islamic scholarship, like the main *tafsir* tradition, but is directed at the general Bengali Muslim public. Naīmuddīn thus creates a new genre in Bengali that combines ele-ments from a genre of high Islamic scholarship found in Arabic with interpretation suited to an audience unskilled in Islamic religious sci-ences. Bengal's Muslims made the genre more exclusively Islamic than Sen's effort by directing this literature toward a Muslim audience, mak-ing it pedagogical and including the Arabic. Naīmuddīn may not be remembered by many Bengalis today, as his *tafsir* is no longer in print and fewer than a handful of copies are preserved in libraries, but the remarkable contribution of his work was not so much the content of his message but his use of Bengali language. He catered to an audience that was simultaneously Muslim and Bengali. His *tafsir*, unlike Sen's, was not highly Sanskritized but rather reflected Naīmuddīn's comfort with discussing Islamic ideas in a Bengali that more easily borrowed from Arabic, Persian, and Urdu. Thus, the authors, those who provided the funds needed to support such works, and the audience ready for these works enthusiastically embraced the possibility of a *tafsir* in Bengali. These works had greater implications than being the catalyst for the new *tafsir* tradition in Bengali. They had a direct effect on the communal identity of Muslims in Bengal.

Naīmuddīn's contribution to religious reformation in the late nineteenth century represented an attempt to invite Muslims who spoke Bengali to revive orthodox beliefs and avoid changes in religious praxis encouraged by other reformers of the time. Some of his activities, such as issuing fatwas, were political. His opposition to other Muslim reform movements was evident in books, articles, and opinions on issues debated in *bāhās*. Like other reformers of his day, Naīmuddīn's lifelong agenda clearly was to unite the Muslims of Bengal in their worship and practices.

Print technology, religious reform, and a defense of Islam together contributed to newly pronounced visions of community. The act of reading and writing about what it means to be a Muslim, which is the act of developing a discourse about Islamic ritual behavior in a vernacular, further enhanced a regionally informed religious group affiliation. The assertion of this vision of community over others was based on the interactions between those who governed and those who were governed. Missionary activity and the drive to convert Muslims and Hindus to Christianity further reinforced religious identity as a primary form of group affiliation. As a consequence of their effort to convert "heathens," Christian missionaries came to be viewed by both Hindu and Muslim reformers as an unprecedented threat to these religious communities' continued existence and prosperity. Again, viewing a threat from the outside further encouraged defense of religious visions of community.

By the end of the nineteenth century, Bengali was more fully embraced—a modern prose Bengali that reflected the changing times. By accepting Bengali to express theological and ritual concerns, educated Muslims demonstrated a growing association with the language and therefore with Bengali ethnicity. This identification with language was subsumed in religious identity as the content of the authors' writing was about being Muslim, not about being Bengali. Yet paradoxically, these authors did not intend to reinforce a specifically Bengali sense of community but rather sought to make Muslim customs, practices, and beliefs more like those of Muslims in the Middle East than those of Hindus closer to home. Nevertheless, by virtue of the further development of the Bengali language and the creation of new literary genres in Bengali, a significant cultural production arose that enhanced Bengali or, perhaps more specifically, Bengali Muslim culture.

Anderson's argument does not account for the content of the literature, which in South Asia had an equally important role in national consciousness raising. The content (overwhelmingly about Islamic life and reform) and vernacular language worked together to unconsciously and effectively bond Urdu-speaking Muslims while alienating Hindus. Though the literature had a homogenizing effect vis-à-vis the reinforcement of a Muslim vision of community led by educated, *ashraf* Muslims, it simultaneously reified boundaries and constructed a self-image that stood in direct contrast not only to Hindus but also to other Muslim self-images.

Nineteenth-century indigenous peoples had a growing sense that communities were naturally defined primarily by religion; consequently, the elite colonial administrators and missionaries viewed religious communities as having enduring common political interests, as the following chapters will discuss further. This assumption is a crucial factor in the development of religious nationalism. Religion became a public concern through the interaction of several factors: print technology, interreligious debate, and public policy formulated around and directed at religiously defined communities. The public was therefore also political by the fact that British public policy such as separate "Hindu" and "Muhammedan" laws, as discussed in chapter 2, reflected an affirmation of this employment of the categories of religion and caste. After the partition of South Asia into two separate states in 1947, the Muslim populace realized that shared faith would not necessarily translate into the peaceful coexistence of Muslims with diverse views, practices, and most significantly political interests that was the vision of Muslim League leader Muhammad Akram Khan and many others. During this period, a conscious shift occurred in visions of community: the Muslims of Bengal became Bengali Muslims as they asserted their identification with Bengali language and culture without denying religious affiliation.

In this process, religious community for the Muslim elite and reformers came to represent a political (national) community that superficially muted other interests. In the twentieth century, these conflicting interests rose to the surface to produce internal conflict. The experience of Bengali Muslim nineteenth-century reform would eventually undermine the national unity (common religious affiliation) on which Pakistan would be based. When Muslims gained nationhood, ethnic divides emerged between Bengali and Urdu speakers. Bengali Muslims coalesced as a group primarily identifying along the lines of ethnic/linguistic identity, and the sudden utility of a common religious identity faded while Bengaliness gained prominence. Just as religious identity supported the creation of a separate state, so too did linguistic identity later support the creation of a new nation. Yet Bangladesh today continues to find itself in a predicament over competing national visions of community.

four

Bengali or Bangladeshi?
The Conflict between Religious and Ethnic Nationalisms

Can I forget the twenty-first February
Incarnadined by the blood of my brother?
Twenty-first February, built by the tears
Of a hundred mothers robbed of their
 sons,
Can I ever forget it?
Wake up today twenty-first February,
Do wake up, please.
Our heroic boys and girls still languish
In the prisons of the tyrant.
The souls of my martyred brothers still cry.
But today everywhere the somnolent
 strength
Of the people have begun to stir,
And we shall set February ablaze
By the flame of our fierce anger.
How can I ever forget the twenty-first
February?
—Abdul Gaffar Choudhury

As the preceding two chapters discussed, nineteenth-century reformers' and Muslim elites' attempted to create a unified subcontinental Muslim culture and community but inadvertently also reinforced a uniquely Bengali vision of Muslim community. This vision alienated the Bengali Muslims from their coreligionists who identified more closely with the broader subcontinental Muslim culture symbolized in the knowledge and use of Urdu. The alienation became evident only after Pakistan gained independence from the British. This was not merely a Bengali community distinct from Muslim identity but was rather a Bengali-informed Muslim community. In this chapter, I argue that Islam is always regionally informed and that this regionalism constituted a major source of conflict between East and West Pakistan. The suggestion that Islam is regionally informed defies popular assumptions that "Islam" represents a monolithic culture. It also defies arguments that any diversity in global tradition suggests that some members maintain inauthentic practices. Interpretation of Qur'an and Sunna vary by period, as Talal Asad has argued, as well as by region. Second, regional distinctiveness and conception of community, the product of nineteenth-century literary production in the Bengali language, would not be supplanted in the twentieth century by some form of West Pakistani culture that West Pakistanis viewed as more authentically Islamic. Bengali Muslims would not surrender the regional distinctiveness that had been so prolifically articulated in the previous century. Bengali Muslim efforts to keep Bengali culture alive would feed the move to independence from Pakistan. Secularism instead of Islam in addition to Bengali culture would be the basis of nationalism in Bangladesh.

Though Bengali Muslims refused to give up their distinctive customs, indigenous or regional cultures cannot be easily distinguished from religious cultures. If Bengalis had given up Bengali-informed Islam, a northwestern Islam of Pakistan would have replaced it. There are, broadly speaking, cultural traditions that are closely tied to a region and those that are clearly associated with religion. More difficult is the task of decoding more complex rituals and traditions that cut across our assumed religious and regional boundaries (an intellectual construction of modernity) and whose traditions cannot be clearly traced back to some distinctly religious or regional origin. For example, we should not assume that *sajda* performance and the kissing of saints' tombs are innovations influenced by Hinduism. Such statements represent the observations of reformers and serve only as a source of their polemics. Reformers, powerful elites, and scholars often mistake rituals and traditions in Bengal for a seeming blend of Vaishnava or Hindu and Islamic traditions, thereby delegitimizing the religious practices. Richard King's suggestion that the academic study of religion would be better conceived as a form of "cultural studies" is useful here.[1] In this way, the relationship between regional culture and religious culture must be acknowledged.

The regional-religious overlap is evident in all periods of Bengali history. As chapter 1 discussed, the precolonial writers who sought to explain Islam in the Bengali language had to resort to words that they had already associated with Hindu tradition because Islam came much later to the subcontinent. However, just because a text has employed terms associated with pre-Islamic terms in the region, we cannot assume that the text or belief is syncretic, as Tony K. Stewart has pointed out. Words are formulated as needed and so are closely tied to a particular cultural context. However, for new ideas to be absorbed into the target culture, the new ideas have to be conveyed with extant terms that have some kind of equal value.[2] In the colonial period, a struggle occurred over the appropriate terminology for conveying ideas of reform. Reformers explicitly expressed their discomfort with using terms they strongly associated with Hinduism. In a discussion of religious and secular identities, acknowledgment of culture in broader terms as inclusive of "the religious" is central to understanding the politics of religiously constructed imagining of community and the circumstances within which such politics may fail. Muslims of West Pakistan generally frowned on Bengali-informed Muslim culture, ultimately deeming many practices "un-Islamic." Bengali language too was criticized for being foreign to Islam. These attitudes led Bengali Muslims to conclude that the common bond of Islam provided an insufficient basis to believe in the success of a nation. Bengali roots became a source of pride and national fervor that would lead to the creation of Bangladesh. Traditions would be created that celebrated Bengaliness and would, after Mujib's death, be contested by an emphasis on Islamic culture. We will see how secular nationalism came under fire and how it now competes with Islamic nationalism and fundamentalism.

From East Pakistan to Bangladesh

In the twentieth century, as plans were under way for the creation of a united and independent India, the architects and leaders of the independence movement in both the Congress and the Muslim League debated the question of how the independent state should be governed. Of great concern to the Muslim leaders was the protection of their rights as a large but nevertheless "religious" minority community. The final resolution was the creation of two separate states, India and Pakistan, the latter, many people believed, a state created for Muslims but nevertheless a secular democracy like India.

The governing of Pakistan was complicated by the geographical distance between the four provinces in the West and East Bengal, which lay approximately one thousand miles to the east. Within the first few years of independence, Bengali politicians decried major economic, social, and political disparities between the western provinces and East Bengal. However, one of the first conflicts between the two wings occurred in regard to national language. In 1948, Muhammad Ali Jinnah visited East Bengal, where he publicly announced that East Bengalis must learn to speak Urdu, the lingua franca of West Pakistan. He hoped that the country would be united in religion and language. This statement further increased tensions between the two regions. The debate about the place of Bengali language intensified. Students prepared for public protests and demonstrations in February 1952, but officials learned of the students' intentions and banned all public meetings. Students at Dhaka University ignored the ban and consequently clashed violently with police, leaving at least four Bengalis dead and many others injured.

These tragic clashes marked a turning point in the young nation's history and collective memory. Politicians from Bengal would later refer to these events as a pivotal moment for Bengali people. The Bengalis saw their ethnicity as coming under attack by West Pakistanis. Ethnic difference soon became a prominent issue. In the 1950s and 1960s, West Pakistanis viewed customs and traditions observed by Bengali Muslims that were common to Bengali Hindus—such as singing Rabindranath Tagore's songs, wearing *bindis*, and the middle-class custom of having children study the fine arts—as acts of cultural resistance. Bengalis saw central government policies and attitudes that affected Bengali culture as an assault and fought back accordingly.

In 1949, Husain Shaheed Suhrawardy, Ataur Rahman, Maulana Bashani, Shamsul Huq, and Sheikh Mujibur Rahman founded a new political party, the Awami Muslim League, that they hoped would better represent the interests of the East Pakistanis. The organizers hoped that the league, which, as its name indicated, sought to represent Muslims, would advocate the social, political, and economic rights of East Pakistanis and protect their cultural distinctiveness. As tensions continued to escalate, East Pakistanis, regardless of religion, established more of a common bond based on ethnicity. By the late 1950s, a further shift occurred within this new and popular political party, and it changed its name to the Awami League. It declared a more inclusive platform, thus welcoming non-Muslim Bengalis into the party, a marked move away from the bonds of religion and minority status that had supported the creation of Pakistan. The Awami League posed many challenges to the Muslim League, as evidenced by the diminished role granted to political parties by the West Pakistani leaders who dominated the national political scene.[3]

In 1970, Pakistan held its first general elections. The Awami League celebrated a landslide victory in East Pakistan, winning 167 of East Pakistan's 169 National Assembly seats. Part of the victory resulted from the boycott conducted by other parties in the province. In contrast, Zulfiqar Ali Khan Bhutto's Pakistan People's Party won only 83 of the 131 seats allotted to West Pakistan.[4] General Yahya Khan, martial law administrator, postponed the convening of the National Assembly, which led to war. On 16 December 1971, Bangladesh declared independence.

Sheikh Mujib, also known as Bangabandhu (Friend of Bengal), was released from a Pakistani prison and appointed Bangladesh's first prime minister. The country's constitution was based on Mujib's four principles—democracy, socialism, secularism, and nationalism. In the first years of Bangladesh's independent administration, the common bond of Islam was no longer emphasized, replaced by common linguistic heritage. In those years, Sheikh Mujib experienced difficulty in moving the nation forward economically, a problem further exacerbated by the famine of 1974. Overwhelmed by the challenges of position as head of state, in 1975 Mujib amended the constitution to make himself president for five years with full executive authority. He then created the Bangladesh Krishak Sramik Awami League and outlawed all other political parties. Mujib also organized a paramilitary force, the Rakhi Bahini, which became well known for its intimidation tactics. Though Sheikh Mujib was a charismatic figure in the independence strug-gle—among the most charismatic figures of twentieth-century South Asia—he faltered as president. After independence, in the face of great economic problems, Mujib resorted to repressive measures, abandon-ing his longtime fight for democratic governance. Many observers per-ceived Bangladesh's economic problems as Sheikh Mujib's failure, and on 15 August 1975, he and members of his family were assassinated in their Dhanmondi home.

After Mujib's death, several military coups and countercoups oc-curred. Not until the 1980s did the Awami League regain popular-ity under the leadership of Sheikh Mujib's daughter, Sheikh Hasina. Sheikh Hasina revived the Awami League's prodemocracy and pro-socialist platform. In June 1996, the Awami League regained power, and Sheikh Hasina became the prime minister. Significantly, another political party came into prominence in the late 1970s. Ziaur Rahman, one of Bangladesh's most decorated military officers during the inde-pendence war, became chief martial law administrator and president of Bangladesh and founded the Bangladesh National Party (BNP). In an attempt to distance himself from Mujib's government and failure, Ziaur Rahman amended the constitution to make Islam rather than secularism one of the country's guiding principles. In terms of law, this gesture did not translate into any change for Bangladesh, but in terms of collective identity it signaled a major shift away from the nation-alism for which the country had fought and on which it had been founded. Today, the Awami League, headed by Sheikh Mujib's daugh-ter, and the BNP, headed by Khaleda Zia, Ziaur Rahman's widow, con-tinue to dominate the political stage. The two parties exert differing brands of nationalism.

Crucial to the success of nationalism is the construction of a single sustainable national culture that bonds people together in a convinc-ingly imagined community. Traditions are created, intentionally sculpted to promote a particular nationalism.[5] As Eric Hobsbawm rightly points out, invented traditions "are highly relevant to that comparatively recent historical innovation, the 'nation,' with its associated phenomena: nationalism, the nation-state, national symbols, histories and the rest."[6] It is therefore directly pertinent to the discussion here. As long as the community commemorates these traditions, nationalism is reinforced and secured. Yet Bangladesh today is experiencing an emerging nationalism based on religious identity as expressed by the BNP as well as another nationalism based on secular Bengali identity, which was the foundation of the independence movement. Complicating matters further is a third movement, fundamentalist in nature, that promotes a global Islamic culture. Fundamentalists strive to move Bangladesh toward a state governed by Islamic values, a process discussed in detail in chapter 5.

Nationalism is necessarily based on a variety of common bonds, such as secularism, ethnic unity, religious unity, and sometimes a combination of these factors. In her work on Israeli nationalism, Yael Zerubavel demonstrates that Israeli culture and identity offer in significant ways a direct contrast to American or non-Israeli Jewish culture. The relative strength of Israeli nationalism in the country's formative years was its leaders' ability to create a collective identity constructed by connecting Palestinian Jewish events in the twentieth century with Jewish myths from antiquity. The Zionists created a "Hebrew national culture" that stood in direct contrast to a counterimage they also created of non-Israeli Jews. Zerubavel considers the role of holiday celebrations, festivals, monuments, memorials, songs, stories, plays, and education as the means of transmitting and reinforcing the collective memory that promotes a national Hebrew culture. The dominant themes of this master narrative are courage, victory, and return to the ancient homeland. Zerubavel argues that collective memory is crucial to creating and sustaining a national identity. She demonstrates that a nation-state relies on nationalism, national symbols, and collective memory to reinforce its unique form of imagined community, whether it is based on religion, ethnicity, language, or secularism.[7]

Bangladesh was founded on a secular nationalist unity based on Bengali language and ethnicity, necessarily in direct contrast to the nationalism on which Pakistan was founded. This situation bears some parallels to Zerubavel's suggestion that Israeli nationalism was con-

structed in direct contrast to some other notion of Jewishness that is a
negative image of the Jewish experience in exile.

Inventing Secular Traditions and Rituals:
Ekushey and the Erection of *Shaheed Minar*

From the beginning of Pakistani statehood, language was hotly debated. Muslim scholars and leaders logically believed that Urdu should
be the lingua franca because it had gained a reputation as the cultural
symbol of subcontinental Muslims. However, just as swiftly, Bengali
Muslims raised their objections, arguing that the new nation had more
Bengali speakers than Urdu speakers. Furthermore, Bengali Muslims
regarded Urdu as the language of the elite, not the language of the
majority of Muslims in what would become the eastern province.
To no avail, a Bengali linguist at Dhaka University, Dr. Muhammad
Shahidullah, advocated that both Urdu and Bengali should be declared
national languages.

In fact, Bengali leaders made many attempts between 1947 and 1948
to persuade the central government to make Bengali one of the state
languages. All proposals were summarily rejected, and on 26 February
1948, the All Party State Language Committee of Action was formed
in the eastern province. In March 1948, nearly seven months after independence, the committee organized a *hartal* (general strike) to protest
the government's policy on language. On 21 March, Muhammad Ali
Jinnah visited Dhaka, where he declared publicly,

> For official use in this province, the people of the province
> can choose any language they wish. The question will be de-
> cided solely in accordance with the wishes of the people of this
> province alone, as freely expressed through their accredited repre-
> sentatives at the appropriate time and after full and dispassionate
> consideration. There can, however, be only one lingua franca—
> that is, the language for intercommunication between the various
> provinces of the state—and that language should be Urdu and
> cannot be any other. The state language therefore must obviously
> be Urdu, a language that has been nurtured by a hundred million
> of this subcontinent, a language understood throughout the

length and breadth of Pakistan, and above all a language that more than any other provincial language embodies the best that is in Islamic culture and Muslim tradition and is nearest to the languages used in other Islamic countries. It is not without significance that Urdu has been driven out of the Indian Union and that even the official use of the Urdu script has been disallowed.[8]

This declaration was followed by debate and attempts to de-Sanskritize Bengali, even to the extent of introducing Arabic script for the Bengali language. The Pakistani government created twenty adult education centers in various locations in East Pakistan to introduce this new script. The central government's attempts to Arabicize Bengali demonstrate not only that officials viewed Urdu as a Muslim language but also that they viewed Bengali as a Hindu language and therefore in stark contrast to their vision of the nation. The West Pakistanis evidently viewed the common culture of Bengali Hindus and Bengali Muslims as a potential threat to national unity. No progress was made on resolving the language issue when on 26 January 1952, the ruling Muslim League announced that Urdu would be the official state language in all of Pakistan. Following this declaration, political leaders from East Pakistan declared 21 February the new State Language Day. In response, the central government banned all processions and demonstrations for that day. In defiance of this order, Dhaka University students led demonstrations, which resulted in violent clashes with police and military forces. Several students and other participants were killed, hundreds were injured, and some estimates suggest that hundreds or even thousands more were arrested. Two days later, people erected a column (*minar*) at the site near Dhaka Medical College where some of the students and other Bengalis had been killed. Construction began in the afternoon, and the structure was finished by midnight. Bengalis subsequently came to recognize 21 February as Shaheed Dibash (Martyrs' Day), more commonly known as Ekushey (Twenty-first). Bangladeshis continue to commemorate Ekushey, which has come to represent the beginning of a struggle to celebrate Bengali language and ethnicity as well as a symbol of resistance and the beginning of the struggle for independence. Within a few days after the 1952 incident, people from all over Dhaka were paying homage to those who had sacrificed their lives for the sake of their mother tongue. By 26 February the police had destroyed the monument. Nevertheless, processions occurred all over the province, with participants demanding that Bengali be recognized as a state language.

On 20 February 1953, students at Eden College and Dhaka Medical College planned to observe the first anniversary of Ekushey. They began to construct a *shaheed minar* (martyrs' column) at Siddique Bazaar but were eventually prohibited from completing it by several faculty members who supported the central government's position. Though the monument was destroyed, at midnight on 21 February, demonstrators chanted slogans proclaiming Bengali the state language. People also came to lay wreaths at the site of the demolished *shaheed minar*. The students also organized a musical celebration at Britannia Cinema Hall. Since the tragic clash with police in 1952, many poems had been written about the event. Abdul Gaffar Choudhury's poem was set to music composed and sung by Abdul Latif that evening, and the piece became the most celebrated Ekushey song, "Amar bhaiyer rakte rangano" (Colored with the blood of my brother). "Amar sonar bangla" (My golden Bengal), composed years earlier by Rabindranath Tagore (d. 1941) and later the Bangladeshi national anthem, was also sung that evening. A spontaneous general strike also occurred in East Pakistan in observance of Ekushey, and processions took place around the province. In Dhaka, the main procession ended at Armanitola, where a public meeting was held. The speakers included the charismatic Sheikh Mujib, acting secretary of the Awami League. The speakers made several demands, among them that Bengali be declared a state language and that political prisoners be released.

The site, near Dhaka University and the Medical College, extemporaneously became a sacred site. Since 1953, Bengalis have made pilgrimages to that site during February, especially on Ekushey. The site and date have been transformed into spatial and temporal loci of holiness on which justification for the eventual birth of Bangladesh would be based. This newly formed sacred space and event identified two imagined communities, one a common oppressor and the second the Bengali nation (encompassing many religious communities). Bengalis' economic and political marginalization fed a growing frustration in the eastern province. Bengali leaders expressed the sentiment that West

Pakistan was exploiting the eastern province, and the issue of national language further inflamed Bengali resentment. Those killed on 21 and 22 February 1952 included not just members of the aspiring intellectual elite but also victims who cut across all social classes—an employee of Dhaka High Court, the son of a mason, and the son of a farmer. All of the victims shared a Bengali identity, a point that is highlighted at each annual Ekushey observance. The tragic 1952 events rallied Bengalis around a common purpose: the protection and preservation of their culture as exemplified in the monument, the commemorative events, and the activities inspired by the clashes with police.

A collective memory of that tragic day, with the numerous forms of commemoration that commenced in 1953, has contributed to Bengali secular identity. The temporary *shaheed minar* that was erected and then demolished several times has been succeeded by a permanent monument near Dhaka University and Dhaka Medical College. Artist Hamidur Rahman designed the present *shaheed minar*, which comprises five columns. The central, largest column bends at an angle toward the other columns and is widely regarded as representing a mother bestowing love, affection, and protection on her children.[9] The region of Bengal is the mother, and the children are the martyrs and ultimately all Bengalis—that is, anyone born in the region and speaking the language. The monument serves, therefore, to reinforce a natural bond between land and people, a bond central in creating a secular nationalist sentiment. Many Bangladeshis see the *shaheed minar*'s numerous destructions as a powerful reminder of the oppression that the region's people have overcome. Bangladeshis continue to visit the monument site on Ekushey to lay wreaths. In fact, after Bangladesh gained independence, the annual observance of Ekushey developed into a monthlong commemoration.

Days before Ekushey, the *shaheed minar* area is cleaned, and women gather to create *ālpanās* (paintings, typically made of rice paste, on floor or wall surfaces) at the site. On Ekushey, men, women, and children dressed in traditional Bengali garb visit all night long beginning at midnight. Pilgrims proceed barefooted to the *shaheed minar* and to the Azimpur graveyard, burial site of the martyrs (as those who died on 21 and 22 February are always called). The participants wear black badges and walk silently or sing "Amar bhaiyer rakte rangano." When

Shaheed minar

they reach the *shaheed minar*, they lay wreaths. Also at the *shaheed minar*, a stage is decorated and artists sing. One of the first wreaths is laid by the prime minister, followed by other dignitaries and the general public. By morning, the *shaheed minar* typically is blanketed with colorful marigolds, dahlias, and roses deposited by the many pilgrims.

A rich collection of commemorative literature about Ekushey includes songs, poems, plays, novels, and short stories. For nearly a month before the festival, Bengali culture is celebrated in schools, on Bangladeshi television, and at cultural centers throughout the country, especially the *shaheed minar* and the Bangla Academy, which was established in 1955 to cultivate research and study of Bengali culture, inclusive of all religious practices. The Bangla Academy is a national research institute located at Burdwan House, the residence of the former chief minister of East Pakistan, whom Bengalis regard as ultimately responsible for the violent clash that occurred on Ekushey. The academy remains as a constant reminder of Bengali struggle, sacrifice, and eventual victory over oppression. Throughout the years of united Pakistan, when Bengali leaders battled to exert more power in the central government, the Bangla Academy provided an important source of Bengali cultural inspiration. The academy consists of several departments, including a press that publishes works in all areas of Bengali literature in both English and Bengali. The academy also houses a rich library and a Bengali folklore research wing, and its biggest annual cultural event is a monthlong Ekushey book fair.

Since Bangladesh gained independence, the commemorative events held on the occasion of Ekushey have grown tremendously to include plays, Bengali dance programs, the annual award of the Ekushey Padak for outstanding contributions to Bengali culture, children's painting competitions at the *shaheed minar*, national poetry festivals, and concerts. Newspapers and magazines print articles and stories celebrating Bengali culture and especially Ekushey, with contributors including adults, children, and Bengalis living abroad. People eat traditional Bengali fare and hold cultural gatherings in their homes and communities. Fashion shows celebrate traditional Bengali garb with styles incorporating the Bengali alphabet or Ekushey motifs.

These commemorative events reaffirm Bengali cultural importance and teach the younger generation why the nation struggled for independence. The struggle for independence has always been directly linked to Ekushey, which reinforces a secular national identity by affirming bonds with Bengalis regardless of religious identity. The religious minority status that inspired the creation of Pakistan is viewed as an insufficient bond when compared with ethnic identity and common language. Ekushey reminds Bengalis that regardless of their religious differences, Muslims, Hindus, Buddhists, and Christians suffered West Pakistani violence and oppression. Ekushey, with all its invented traditions, is the source of a political myth that fed Bengali secularism and independence, and the result is the common slogan "Our identity is in Ekushey."[10]

Linking Ekushey with the Liberation Struggle

War broke out on 25 March 1971, and India soon became involved in the conflict, enabling a victory for Bangladesh. On 16 December the

Pakistani army surrendered to the Mukhti Bahini (Liberation Forces). Every year on the occasion of Independence Day and Victory Day, the story of the liberation struggle is retold in Bangladesh's Bengali- and English-language newspapers. Wreaths are also laid at the National Monument, dedicated to the estimated one to three million Bengalis who lost their lives during the war. All retellings directly connect the liberation war and 21 February 1952. All those who died in 1952 and those who died during the war— including intellectuals, men, women, children, and the liberation forces—are remembered as martyrs to the cause. What began as a struggle to have Bengali language and culture recognized became a struggle to gain freedom from oppressors likened to their British predecessors. Indeed, both Independence Day and Victory Day are celebrated with Bengali cultural programs.

The dedication of the National Monument occurred on the eleventh anniversary of Victory Day. The monument was designed by Moinul Hossain and is located twelve miles from Dhaka, in Savar. It is triangular in shape and composed of seven separate triangles that represent the seven historic events that led to liberation, beginning with 1952. The other important dates—1954, 1958, 1962, 1966, 1969, and 1971—commemorate significant confrontations between Bengali leaders and the central government and massive strikes in the eastern province. The monument thus includes not only a symbolic reminder of the sacrifice for freedom but also a direct link between 1952 and independence. The years since 1952 are punctuated only by the remembrance and ritual commemoration of other events that further reinforce a myth about independence. The National Monument gives the myth of Bengali struggle and eventual victory a plot structure: there is a beginning suppression of Bengali culture and a successful conclusion to the story—independence.

But also tied to the sacrifice and liberation theme is the affirmation of a bond between land and people, which is achieved in many ways, including national flag, anthem, and the most celebrated Ekushey song. The national flag was created by a Dhaka University student, Shib Narayan Das, and was first flown on 2 March 1971 at a student league meeting at the university. The center features a yellow map of Bengal within a red circle that represents the sun, all on a green back-

Two views of the National Monument in Savar. (Photos by Sufia Uddin)

ground. The flag provides a visual reminder of the relationship between people and land, and the national anthem, "Amar sonar bangla," praises the beauty of the Bengal landscape.

My Bengal of gold, I love you
Forever your skies, your air
Set my heart in tune
As if it were a flute,
In spring, oh mother mine,
The fragrance from
Your mango groves make me
Wild with joy—Ah, what a thrill!
In autumn, oh mother mine,
In the full-blossomed paddy fields,
I have seen spread all over sweet smiles!
Ah, what a beauty, what
Shades, what an affection
And what a tenderness!
What a quilt have you spread at the feet of
Banyan trees and along the
Banks of rivers!
Oh mother mine, words from
Your lips are like
Nectar to my ears
Ah, what a thrill!
If sadness, oh mother mine
Casts a gloom on your face,
My eyes are filled with tears![11]

As with the *shaheed minar*, the anthem features the image of the land as mother, affectionate, nurturing, and loving, and here too, the narrator responds with love and affection.

This bond between land and people is juxtaposed with another image of the united Pakistan era and with Bengal's relationship with West Pakistan. The national myth of Bengali struggle, oppression, and eventual liberation is made successful also by the perpetuation of a collective memory of West Pakistan as violent, colonial, and communal. The

Bengal national myth of struggle parallels Zerubavel's description of the Israeli myth of struggle, in which Hebrew national culture is juxtaposed with a negative portrayal of Jewish life and culture in exile. In the Bangladeshi myth of struggle, those historic events that aid in shaping this picture of life during the Pakistan era are highlighted, and the horrors and battles associated with them are emphasized to construct a collective memory of struggle. This struggle is represented by the seven triangles of the National Monument and in the repetitive nature of the retelling of the story of Bangladesh's birth.

It is also important to consider what the story or myth omits, and why. The retellings and the rituals that remind Bengalis of their nation's birth contain almost no mention of Indira Gandhi's government and military involvement in the war for liberation. They also include little mention of the millions of Hindu Bengalis who fled across the border to India and the Awami League's only minimal efforts to protect the Bengali Hindus. This is not atypical of any national myth-making effort. In fact, it would not serve the purpose of creating a secular national myth to include historical events that do not suggest that the myth is founded purely in justice, sacrifice, and all that is deemed good and secular.

Moreover, Bangladesh has more than sixty ethnic minorities. These groups are neither Bengali nor Muslim, yet Bangladesh is their native home. The largest minority groups—the Chakmas, Santals, Marmars, Tripuras, Garos, and Biharis— and many other smaller ethnic groups have no representation and therefore no influence in national politics. They are obviously excluded by the religious nationalists and Islamists as well as by the ideology of Bengali nationalism. At a public meeting in Rangamati of the Chittagong Hill Tracts in 1975, Prime Minister Sheikh Mujib implored the minority communities to forget the past and embrace Bengali culture.[12] Despite having been dominated by other ethnic groups, Bengalis were not willing to create a more inclusive national ideology that embraced the many minorities. Many of these groups had received promises from the future Bangladeshi government during the independence struggle and consequently had taken up arms in the Mukti Bahini (Freedom Fighters) but became disillusioned after independence.

Linking a Secular, Tolerant Bengal with a Precolonial Past

Creating this bond between land and people constitutes an important nationalist strategy. After establishing this bond, nationalist strategies must necessarily suggest that the "national" community has legitimate claims to the land. Though the nation may have only recently realized its "true" self, to create the heir of legitimacy, it must suggest older roots or more specifically "natural" bonds to the land. As Hobsbawm points out, this attachment to land is a seeming paradox, given the newness of "nationhood" and the effort to justify it as having roots in antiquity, but it makes sense when we acknowledge the value attributed to history as evidence of the truth.[13] Through emphasis and omission, communities employ historical evidence to create a specific collective memory that legitimizes the existence of the new nation-state. Claims to early roots help citizens conceptualize a collective memory that supports nationalism.[14]

Pride in language and affirmation of its long history and tradition, which are central to Bengali nationalism, are easily conveyed and transmitted to younger generations through education in history of the language, Bengali culture, land settlement, and the civilization-building mission. An essential component of the Bengali-medium curriculum is the study of ancient, middle, and modern periods of Bengali history, Bengali language, and genres of literature and their creators. Since its establishment, the Bangla Academy has played a central role in meeting this goal, not only preserving information on Bengali language and culture but also promoting this knowledge throughout the wider community. The academy does so with its publications (including textbooks) and programs as well as with its sponsorship of research on the earliest Bengali literature, including folk literature and culture.

The Bangla Academy also has played a central role in the celebration of Pahela Baishakh (Bengali New Year's Day), sponsoring cultural programs to mark the occasion. Pahela Baishakh is a secular holiday that became increasingly popular during the united Pakistan period as a symbol of resistance to what Bengalis regarded as a form of cultural imperialism. During Ayub Khan's regime during the 1960s, he banned the singing of Tagore's songs (known as *Rabindra sangeet*) in an effort to promote Bengali Muslim cultural integration with West

Pakistani Muslim culture. The plan backfired because it left no space for Bengali-informed Muslim culture, which the government considered less than and distinct from "proper" Muslim culture. According to the government, early reformers during the British colonial period had failed to correct this problem. As the preceding chapter discussed, these reformers finally accepted Bengali as the language for reforming Muslim ritual practice yet hoped to reject the Bengali host culture. This attitude further solidified the Bengali bonds with Bengali culture. Many Bengali Muslims interpreted Ayub Khan's act not only as cultural imperialism but even as supporting religious fundamentalism. During this period, Sufia Kamal, a Bengali poet and activist, organized a women's movement calling for Ayub's resignation. The Bengali Music organization, Chhayanat, responded to Ayub's policy by organizing a *Rabindra sangeet* program at Ramna Park on the occasion of Pahela Baishakh. Rabindranath Tagore, from a landowning Brahman family, had always been one of Bengal's most celebrated poets, but in some ways he gained even more importance during the cultural resistance period. Tagore, his music, and his religious tolerance became symbols of Bengali national consciousness. Tagore's songs have become a part of Bengali New Year celebrations, with the biggest gatherings held at Ramna Park, the Bangla Academy, and Dhaka University. His works have become the most symbolic protest tradition in response to what secularists perceive as religious fundamentalism.

Prior to 1961 in East Pakistan's urban areas, Pahela Baishakh was not much celebrated. The Bengali calendar is an agricultural calendar, marking the cropping and harvest seasons, which are of little concern to urban dwellers. In less populated areas, village fairs selling products of the home cottage industry typically were held during this time, and the previous year's debts were paid off and new accounts were opened in books called *halkhata*. In 1961, a new tradition began, combining traditional practices of the *halkhata* and the fairs with the celebration of Bengali music and culture. At Ramna Park, musical concerts begin at sunrise. Bengalis dress in traditional garb, men in kurtas and women in red and white saris with fresh flowers in their hair. Crowds congregate for the festivities, the live traditional Bengali music, and the fair. Among the urban middle class, Pahela Baishakh is heralded by an early morning meal of *panta bhat* (day-old rice preserved in water overnight and eaten in the morning with green chilies and salt), hearkening back to the traditional rural life of the ancestors of many of the city dwellers. Picnics at Ramna Park consist exclusively of traditional Bengali cuisine. After these festivities, many members of the urban middle class visit shops, whose proprietors offer customers flowers and boxes of Bengali sweets.

Such invented traditions as the transformed Bengali New Year suggest that the past is kept alive and relevant to the present and that it aids the imagined community in preserving its group identity. The past referenced on Pahela Baishakh is precolonial and Bengali. Using and selecting historical information and reviving as well as transforming traditions create new traditions that legitimate a particular collective memory—in this case, a memory that supports a Bengali national consciousness and a bond with the land. Divergent interpretations of past events certainly can come into direct conflict with the collective memory of the larger community, but as Zerubavel points out, these interpretations can coexist with the dominant political myth. In the case of Israel, the countermemories reflect the growing diversity of the national community.[15] After the dominant collective memory comes into doubt as a result of changing social circumstances, the countermemory may again transform the collective memory and reshape the national myth, posing a serious challenge to the secular nationalist identity.

Contesting the Secular

In Bangladesh today, the secular national myth is threatened by several political factions. As one Bangladeshi scholar points out, "The legacy of 1952, consecrated by the deaths and sacrifices of 1971, provided the basis for the new state of Bangladesh where, through an ironical twist of history, the values of secular nationalism, with roots in language and soil, and democracy as an expression of the sovereignty of the people's will and economic justice, are under attack while 21 February is a Government supported orthodoxy along with the much greater event of the liberation war."[16]

The struggle over national identity can broadly be identified as between secular nationalists and religious nationalists, but other factions, such as the Jama'at-i-Islami Party, also have their own agendas.

Complicating matters even further, the secular nationalists and religious nationalists are the dominant powers whose interests are represented in the competing nationalisms, though other powers exist. Religious nationalism began to gain favor when Ziaur Rahman and his BNP amended two of the guiding principles of the constitution that Mujib had instituted. To the principle of socialism, Rahman added "economic and social justice." Profoundly more significant was his deletion of secularism and its replacement with "absolute trust and faith in Almighty Allah."[17] The ongoing battle over national ideology takes place in Parliament. Political mudslinging occurs, and government supporters make excuses for its inability to provide basic services to the public. The legislature is also the site of disputes about the way national holidays are celebrated or remembered in newspapers and popular journals.

Our investigation of nationalism, especially in the postcolonial regions of the world, leads to the question of why and under what conditions competing collective memories arise, since such competing memories can lead to the rise of competing nationalisms. With regard to Israel, Zerubavel argues that the competing collective memories represent the country's growing diversity., Israel has received Jewish immigrants from around the world and thus constitutes a rather unusual case. In the former British colonies of South Asia, no tremendous influx of immigrants accounts for the competing collective memories—most of the population was born in the region defined as Bangladesh. Bangladesh seemingly was founded on a solid base of collective struggle based on ethnic unity against what most Bengalis regarded as the oppressor. Yet some Bangladeshis apparently no longer find viable or legitimate the reasons that justified the country's independence. First we will examine some of the signs that indicate the move away from Mujib's secular nationalism, and then we will explore the conceivable motivations for this development.

After the war, Mujib maintained close ties with India. Some opponents of the Mujib government suggested that Mujib might be selling out Bangladesh to India and feared a future dominated by that country.[18] After Zia, a decorated hero of the independence war and the person who declared Bangladesh's independence on Chittagong radio, took over as president, his party came up with a most visible way of distinguishing his nationalism from that of Mujib's: the concept of "Bangladeshi" nationalism. In a way, this approach resolved the problem of what should distinguish Bangladesh from West Bengal, India. Under Zia, Bangladesh became recognized and celebrated as a predominantly Muslim nation; therefore, its culture was distinct from that of West Bengal. Not unlike Mujib's Bengali nationalism, Zia's Bangladeshi nationalism also emphasized the experience of the independence struggle as a significant difference between West Bengal and Bangladesh. International observers and historians such as Muhammad Ghulam Kabir have suggested that Zia was motivated by a desire to unify the country and to further assert Bangladesh's sovereignty. But Bangladesh already had a national ideology. Many people saw the problem as the fact that religion was part and parcel of Bengali culture, so religious identity also had to be emphasized. Zia tapped into and embraced this undercurrent of society, a welcome change from the latter part of Mujib's reign.

Another significant change that represented an articulation of Bangladeshi nationalism was Zia's effort to gain the support of religious and conservative parties. These religious parties, such as Jama'at-i-Islami, the Muslim League, and Islamic Democratic Party, interpreted Zia's Bangladeshi nationalism as a form of Islamic nationalism.[19] To this end, as symbolic gestures toward Islam, Zia labored to strengthen ties with Islamic countries in the Middle East, made it customary for a Qur'an recitation to commence BNP meetings, and increased aid to Bangladesh's madrassas.

On 30 May 1981, during a visit to Chittagong, Zia was assassinated, supposedly by a disgruntled military officer.[20] Major General Hussain Muhammad Ershad, Zia's chief of staff who was relatively unknown outside military circles, became president. Ershad chose to rely heavily on support from religious and conservative parties because he had no support base among Awami Leaguers and BNP politicians. Like Zia, Ershad continued to propagate Bangladeshi nationalism with an emphasis on Islam, an unsurprising tack considering the new president's reliance on the religious Right. Ershad made English and Arabic compulsory in primary schools, a move that many Dhaka University students protested and that religious conservatives and fundamentalists celebrated. On 7 June 1988, Ershad amended the constitution to proclaim Islam the state religion of Bangladesh. Although Ershad catered to the religious parties, he was also well known for sparing no expense to spend time with his *pir*. Ershad was the most famous disciple of Pir Atroshi.[21] Though Sufism constitutes an important part of Islamic life, nineteenth-century reformers had criticized the *pir*-disciple relationship, and the religious Right, represented by parties such as the Jama'at-i-Islami, opposed Sufi practices including the *pir*-disciple relationship.

By 1986, Ershad had retired from the military and continued to govern Bangladesh as a civilian president. The opposition parties nevertheless continued to view Ershad as a military dictator, and after eight years of his rule, pressure from the international community and the paralyzing effect of ongoing national *hartals* forced Ershad to step down and relinquish power to a caretaker government. Subsequent elections brought the BNP to power, with Khaleda Zia, widow of Ziaur Rahman, as prime minister. In 1996, the Awami League returned to power for a five-year term, which was followed by a government formed by a coalition between the BNP and several religious parties.[22]

What is most striking about these elections is the nature of the mudslinging by the various parties. Depending on who is in power, national holidays are celebrated differently—so differently that the festivities clearly indicate how the competing nationalisms are articulated. On the last day Sheikh Hasina was in office in June 2001, several newspapers published full-page special supplements. One paper, the *Independent*, called the special section, "Five Years of Development, Five Years of Success." The upper left-hand corner featured a picture of Sheikh Mujib, while the upper right-hand corner bore a picture of Sheikh Hasina with the famous Awami League phrases "Jai Bangla" (Victory to Bengal) and "Joi Bangabandhu" (Victory to the Friend of Bengal). The slogans and pictures directly link the Awami League with the victorious liberation struggle, while the BNP opts for the slogan "Bangladesh Zindabad" (Long Live Bangladesh). The *Independent*'s supplement was a full-page celebration of the successes of the Awami League, including biting criticisms of the BNP. For example, the paper stated, *despite* inheriting a weak economy from the BNP, the Awami League had made great strides in a number of areas, listing the many accomplishments attributed to Sheikh Hasina and her government. The statement suggests that Sheikh Hasina and her party played an important role in the United Nations Educational, Scientific, and Cultural Organization's decision to declare 21 February International Mother Language Day. The supplement ended with the declaration that the Awami League had upheld "the true history of the war of liberation to the new generation."[23] This statement and many others like it in newspaper editorials and letters to the editor and government statements provide explicit evidence of the struggle over how Bangladeshi history should be interpreted to serve the collective memory and therefore the nationalist ideology.

The final paragraph of the Awami League's outgoing statement blamed its predecessor governments and the opposition parties for inhibiting Bangladesh's further development:

> The present government had to spend 2 years to remove the anomalies created everywhere by the previous governments. When the government began to proceed in a planned way towards development and progress, the opposition parties started creating obstacles, initially by boycotting parliament sessions. They even appealed to the development partners to stop aid to Bangladesh. Development activities had been disrupted repeatedly in the last 5 years because of frequent hartals [strikes],[24] blockades and other destructive activities by the opposition. But they could not stop the overall development of the country due to the well-planned policies and coordinated efforts of the government. The period of Prime Minister Sheikh Hasina's government has been marked by success and development. In recognition of her successes the Prime Minister was conferred with honourable degrees from famous universities and with dignified awards from national and international organisations which has enhanced the image of the country in the world immensely.[25]

As elsewhere in the world, newspapers in Bangladesh have become a vital instrument of the political parties. On national holidays, the party in power in Bangladesh also customarily publishes statements in the English and Bengali newspapers to convey the party's interpretation of historical events pertaining to Bangladesh's independence. For example, on 18 April 2002, when the BNP was again in power, the *Daily*

Star printed an article in its "Focus" section under the title, "Teliapara: Springboard of the Liberation War." This historical piece highlights the military's important role in the struggle for independence. Teliapara, on the border with the Indian state of Tripura, served as the first headquarters of the Mukti Bahini, the place where the military organized and negotiated with the Indian government to gain its assistance. According to the article, the "pioneers of the liberation war" gathered at the Shalbagan Tea Estate in Teliapara to formulate a military strategy. The article prominently mentions Ziaur Rahman, highlighting the BNP founder's role in the liberation struggle. Awami League accounts, by contrast, emphasize Mujib's role.

On the day prior to this large spread on Teliapara, the paper ran a short article on Mujibnagar Day. Though the article began on the front page, it was allotted only a two-by-three-inch space and was continued on page 11. The article reminds the reader that on this day in 1971, the first Bangladeshi government in exile had been formed, with Sheikh Mujib as president and "supreme commander of the armed forces."[26] The piece reminds readers that Sheikh Mujib was unjustly arrested and imprisoned and points out that the Mujibnagar government led the war of independence. The staff correspondent reports that the Awami League will be commemorating the event with special programs, including Sheikh Hasina's laying of a wreath at the portrait of her father, Sheikh Mujib, at the Bangabandhu Bhaban, located in Dhanmondi residential area of Dhaka. It was the home of Sheikh Mujib and the place where he and most of his immediately family were assassinated. It now stands as a shrine and museum to Sheikh Mujib. The BNP leaders do not commemorate this event, just as the Awami League does not commemorate the events that highlight Zia's role. The article ends with accusatory comments from Sheikh Hasina: "The Mujibnagar Day has returned to us with a new perspective and requiring a fresh pledge. Distortion of the national history is going on in its worst form,' she said. Hasina added that the distortion that began after the Bangabandhu's killing in 1975 had continued barring the 1996–2001 period (when the A[wami] L[eague] was in power). 'In fact, the practice of distorting the history of liberation war has now got a new dimension with the BNP-Jama'at coalition government conspiring to destroy the national tradition and culture."[27] Many secularists voice concern regarding the BNP-

Jama'at coalition. In a letter to the editor of the *Daily Star*, a reader from Dallas, Texas, Golam Sarwar, lambasted the Jama'at-i-Islami for wanting to make the study of Arabic compulsory in elementary education:

> It does not take much to see why this absurd issue of making Arabic compulsory in Bangladeshi schools has surfaced at this time. The Jama'atis have become a part of the current BNP government. They are not here only to be a passive junior partner of the bigger party. They want to advance their cause as much as they can, as quickly as they can. A very effective way of doing so is making Arabic compulsory in schools. Once it is done, it becomes very difficult for a subsequent government to take Arabic out because the same Jama'atis will then stir up religious sentiments among people in the name of "holiness" of Arabic. In a way it is very much like Ershad's making Islam the state religion of Bangladesh. It was a cheap political move by a rather irreligious person, but who can do anything about it now? Introduction of Arabic at a base level in the society would serve as a bulwark for the Jama'atis for other future political agendas. The ultimate plan of the Jama'atis, given the opportunity, is to destroy Bangla language and culture and replace it with Arabic and it definitely helps to have population where a lot of people know Arabic and worship it for its purported holiness.[28]

These comments reflect the tensions in Bangladeshi society between the secularists on the one hand and the religious Right and fundamentalists on the other. In addition, the publication of this letter demonstrates that journalistic freedom and criticism of the government have a place in Bangladeshi society. Nevertheless, the government gets the lion's share of the press. The government has threatened to shut down newspapers and to imprison journalists they criticize the government too forcefully. The religious Right has also attempted to intimidate journalists, some of whom have even received death threats.[29] According to one scholar at a prominent university in Bangladesh, "Newspapers enjoy an overt freedom, but their freedom is controlled in clandestine ways. Government normally controls the distribution of advertisements, especially government ads. There are other ways to control freedom of the press and journalists. Sometimes they are bribed or threatened. It is not very difficult for the government to negotiate with the owners of the newspapers, whose primary concern is business, not journalism. But still, some of our press people are courageous enough to fight. They try to uphold their professional freedom."[30]

In July 1998, Matiur Rahman, editor of one of Bangladesh's leading Bengali-language dailies, *Bhorer Kagoj*, resigned. The Nepal-based *Himal* magazine reported that his resignation was attributed to the December 1997 appointment of the publisher, Saber Hossain Chowdhury, as deputy minister in Sheikh Hasina's cabinet.[31] This led to government pressure on the newspaper whenever articles were published that did not present the Awami League government in a positive light. The English-language *Daily Star* quoted Rahman as stating, "I believe in an independent media and in the independent role of the editor. This has been my cardinal principle in journalism. Partisan politics and independent journalism cannot function together."[32] Prior to the publisher's participation in politics, *Bhorer Kagoj* had earned a reputation for writing bold articles that criticized both government and opposition parties, exposing wrongdoing and defending the rights of religious minorities and the principle of secularism.

One freelance journalist described the problem of journalistic freedom in Bangladesh: "The Bangladeshi press enjoys more freedom than any other Muslim country—I guess even more than Turkey. The problem is not that of freedom but conflict of interest of the newspaper owner and the journalists. First of all, not even one newspaper has any guidelines for recruiting journalists. You see, every day the newspapers publish job advertisements for government and nongovernment sectors but never for the newspaper industry. Second, only one or two newspapers give good salaries to their workers—except *Ittefaq*. There is no job security at any of the newspapers. Then, the owners of 99 percent of the newspapers are rich businessmen. Naturally, they don't want to upset the government too much or else their business may get hurt."[33]

In 2003, the BNP government has placed some journalists under arrest; however, the Supreme Court has granted them bail. In addition, the three caretaker governments have also made great strides to protect journalistic freedom. In 1991 Justice Shahabuddin Ahmed made it extremely difficult for the government to shut down newspapers. In 1996, Justice Habibur Rahman Shelley legalized the Internet, which has provided a rich source of information and communication for both journalists and the educated general public, with cybercafes located throughout Bangladesh's metropolitan areas. Furthermore, in 2001, Justice Lotifur Rahman's caretaker government complicated the procedure for imprisoning journalists.

The political parties and religious communities clearly see news publication as an important means by which to communicate their perspectives to the wider Bangladeshi community. Although literacy in Bangladesh is quite low (40 percent of the general population, according to UNICEF),[34] discussion of politics and community issues constitutes an important element of Bengali culture. Every day, publishers post newspapers on cement walls at different locations throughout Dhaka. During their daily activities, people—particularly men—pause to read the posted newspapers, providing even those who do not purchase papers with access to the information they publish. This information then becomes an important source for Bengalis' *adda* (casual conversation).

Homogeneity and Nationalism

Based on an examination of newspaper journalism in Bangladesh, the observer would logically conclude that the battle over nationalist ideology is between secularists on one side and conservative Muslims and fundamentalists on the other. However, the situation is much more complex than that. In *Bangladesh from Mujib to Ershad: An Interpretive Study*, Lawrence Ziring holds political and economic stagnation accountable for Bangladesh's ills. These factors are certainly important, but competing imaginings of nationhood also constitute a central factor. How does Bangladesh define itself? Is it founded on ethnic unity, as the Awami League suggests, or is it founded on language as well as religion? In his celebrated works on nationalism, Partha Chatterjee suggests that the 1905, 1947, and 1971 partitions of Bengal have been a major factor in creating varying imaginings of community. Ziring too acknowledges the problem of partition: "What Bangladesh has witnessed in less than two decades of sovereign, independent existence, is not so much formative dislocation, the pangs of organization and transition, but rather the fitful rage of a severed body part, an append-age that still has movement, but not necessarily political life."[35] These partitions demonstrate what Chatterjee insightfully recognizes as the "fragility of nationalism," which lies in the fact that a community can be imagined in a number of ways by the very nature of being imag-ined.[36]

One of the major causes of nationalism's fragility is the assertion of a homogeneity, of a collective political voice, that does not truly ex-ist in the minds of the citizens. On the surface, Bangladesh appears to be a relatively homogenous society. The overwhelming majority of the population is both Bengali and Muslim. Religious nationalists have suggested that this fact distinguishes not only Bengalis from Pakistanis but also Bangladeshis from West Bengalis, who are mostly Hindu. Even if we do not count the Adivasi populations of the Chittagong Hill Tracts, Sylhet, Mymensingh, and elsewhere, with their distinctive languages, customs, and religious culture, diversity exists among the Bengali Muslims. However, all we see in an examination of invented traditions, commemorations, interpretations of particular events, and the intentionality behind the commemoration of a specific combina-tion of events is the struggle between religious nationalists and secu-larists. Yet more diversity exists than is represented by the BNP and Awami League. That diversity has no voice in the public sphere because it has no power. Talal Asad has suggested that the "public sphere is a space *necessarily* articulated by power."[37] Therefore, though the minor-ity groups in Bangladesh may protest and hold public demonstrations, no one really listens to their grievances. Having voice is not enough. Having a listening audience that engages and responds is also required. Bangladesh's minorities receive little if any space in the public sphere and instead are mostly ignored or viewed as a minor problem.

Leaders with financial resources, a willing cadre of followers, and know-how protect and uphold various imaginings of community. But these two nationalist movements do not protect some group interests. Who are the Muslims of Bangladesh? There are those of the religious Right, many of whom are represented by the Jama'at-i-Islami Party, which despite its small size seeks the establishment of Islamic law in Bangladesh.

Other Muslims in Bangladesh, such as those involved in Tablighi Jama'at, are very conservative and strict in their adherence to ritual life yet do not have a political agenda. Maulana Muhammad Ilyas (1885–1944) attended Deoband and started this movement during British rule in India; the group focuses on spiritual revival, encouraging what Maulana Muhammad Ilyas believed was a more authentic Islamic life filled with worship and praise of God.[38] The movement focuses on missionizing, which Ilyas believed was the duty of all Muslims, not just prophets and religious leaders. Those involved with the Tablighi Jama'at travel from mosque to mosque, emphasizing the need for faithful observance of ritual duties. The Tablighi Jama'at has no overt political agenda but simply seeks to spread observant practice of Islam. Every January, Tablighi Jama'at members gather in Tungi, Bangladesh, for what is purportedly one of the largest gatherings of Muslims in the world. From its small beginnings in India, this movement has become a worldwide phenomenon, with networks in North America, Europe, Africa, and other parts of Asia. Tablighi participants believe that their global Islamic movement propagates a culture that is closely identified with the Islam of the Prophet Muhammad. Tablighi Jama'at will be discussed in greater detail in chapter 5.

In contrast to those involved with Tablighi Jama'at are Muslims who venerate Sufi saints, a practice condemned by the Tablighi Jama'at and Jama'at-i-Islami. Like measuring membership in Tablighi Jama'at, determining how much of the population venerates Sufi saints or has membership in Sufi orders is nearly impossible, as the level of association with these institutions and the *pirs* varies with each devotee. Nevertheless, Sufi tradition has a long history in Bangladesh, and the *pirs* constituted the main avenue by which Bengalis were introduced to Islam, as discussed in chapter 1.[39] The shrines to revered saints and the *darbars* (a Persian term meaning "court," referring to the room where the *pir* receives visitors) of living *pirs* brim with activities and are part of the fabric of Bengali society in Bangladesh.

Like the national myths, Muslims who venerate Sufi saints commemorate personal myths about the saints' relationship to the people and land of Bengal. Chapter 1 provides an account of an oral tradition of Saint Shah Jalal's arrival in Bengal. All over Bangladesh there are shrines to Shah Jalal and other saints, some of them still quite popular.[40]

The most highly regarded saints of Bangladesh are Shah Jalal of Sylhet, Bistami of Chittagong, and Khan Jahan Ali of Khulna. The common theme among all of the stories of these saints' arrival in Bengal is the "civilizing mission." They arrive in Bengal, introduce Islam, and thus set the course for the construction of community there. All of these saints are said to be from points west of Bengal, especially the Middle East, and reportedly arrived in Bengal at the request either of the Prophet Muhammad or of their *shaikh*. They all have fantastic powers typically associated with control over wild animals such as tigers, snakes, and crocodiles that is crucial for the civilization-building mission in Bengal, which was dense untamed forest prior to human settlement.

Other common elements of these oral and written hagiographies include the performance of miracles that saved lives, the ability to breathe life either into oneself or another, and the power to travel great distances in a matter of seconds. The stories suggest that the miracles convinced people of the power of the saints and especially of the power of Allah, causing people to "convert" to Islam. These saints and their devoted followers constructed mosques and *mazars* throughout Bengal. These sites became local sacred sites and the locations for the offering of *ziyarat* (visitation).

In some ways, these *mazars* serve as an extension of the sacred center of the Islamic world, Mecca.[41] Muslims regard Mecca, the home of the Ka'ba, as the house of God built by Ibrahim and his son, Isma'il. All Muslims direct their daily *salat* (obligatory prayers) toward Mecca, and it is the focal point of the hajj. To turn toward Mecca in prayer and to make the pilgrimage to Mecca are physically symbolic gestures of the desire to be nearer to God. The *mazars* become miniature sacred centers in that the saints are believed to be saints because they have achieved some desired nearness to God. Their fantastic powers are proof of the blessings they have received. Muslims believe that these saints have powers to enable them to assist others on this difficult journey.

Many Muslims around the world view visiting a shrine as a means by which to connect with God and his friends (*waliullah*). This point is controversial for many conservative Muslims, especially those influenced by the Muwahhiduns (commonly referred to as Wahhabis), but also for fundamentalists. According to the Wahhabis, Islam has no sainthood and Muslims need no intercessor on their behalf. They can communicate directly with God, especially through the strict performance of the Five Pillars.

As chapters 2 and 3 discussed, Sufi practices have come under fire since the nineteenth-century. Many shrines in Bangladesh today post signs indicating correct decorum, which includes praying to God on the saint's behalf but never asking the saint for assistance. Signs also warn visitors that prostrating (*sajda*) at saints' tombs is forbidden and that vows must not be performed at shrines and that saints must not be venerated in any way. In reality, performing vows is common, and the signs merely appease more conservative Muslims.

Some Muslims acknowledge the saints but criticize some of the shrines' activities. A man at the shrine of Shah Jalal informed me that he had been appalled by the conduct of a previous visitor, who had kissed the shah's tomb and then walked backward down the steps, careful not to show his back to the tomb. My informant said that he had told the other man that his behavior was inappropriate and un-Islamic, but the man responded, "It is between me and Hazrat Shah Jalal." Thus even visitors to the shrines have diverse beliefs about appropriate behavior and how the saints should be regarded.

Despite this diversity, saints and Sufi traditions undoubtedly constitute important elements of Bengali Islam. Before commencing political campaigns, many of Bangladesh's politicians visit *mazars* around the country. In addition to Pir Atroshi of Faridpur, to whom President Ershad was devoted, other living *pirs*, including Anwar Chowdhury of Dhanmondi, Dhaka, who is known as Sher-e Khwaja, are well-known political power brokers on the subcontinent.[42] Dormitories, airplanes, and office buildings are often named after saints, a testament to their popularity. In fact, there was a move in Sylhet to rename the district Jalalabad, after Shah Jalal. Like the annual gathering of the Tablighi Jama'at in Tungi, those who revere saints meet each year, especially on the occasion of the saints' *urs* (death anniversary). One of the largest such gatherings is held at Maijbhander in Chittagong on the tenth of the Bengali month of Magh, and it is significant that a Bengali rather than Islamic calendar date is used. These saints and sacred sites affirm an Islamic history of Bangladesh and bring Bangladesh into a global Islamic history.

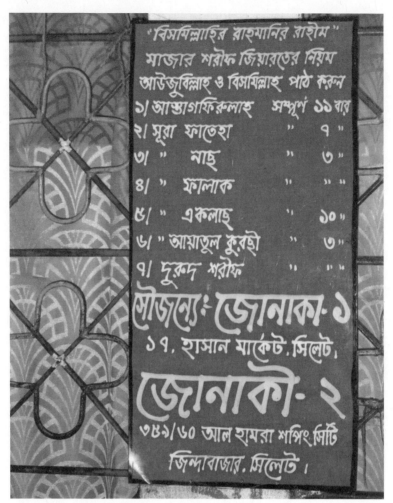

This signboard at a shrine requests that pilgrims perform *ziyarat* appropriately and describes a proper *ziyarat*. (Photo by Sufia Uddin)

Those who maintain some level of adherence to the Sufi saint tradition in Bangladesh cut across all classes and communal lines. Many Hindus visit Sufi shrines and are welcomed. The Maijbhandaris, who are well known for their *dhikr* (remembrance of God) and music, include many Hindu musicians who compose songs and sing the praises of these saints. Though the overwhelming majority of saints in Bangladesh are male, there are female saints such as Bonbibi of the Sundarbans, *faqirs* who claim Sufi lineage or some other Islamic religious affiliation.

However, many of the women *faqirs* play a different role in society, being regarded as healers or providers of unconventional remedies. Many advertise their services in Bengali-language newspapers, claiming their legitimacy and authority by linking themselves through kinship ties or master-disciple relationships to holy men.

Bangladeshi Islam has a rich tradition of diversity, from the conservative to the self-proclaimed strictly apolitical to the diverse Sufi practitioners. Despite the fact that most Bangladeshis regard themselves as Muslims, tensions at times arise between the different peoples as a result of the contrasting ways Islam is practiced. Therefore, it would be incorrect to assume that simply because many Bangladeshis consider themselves Muslims, they would be satisfied with religious nationalism or with the goals of the religious Jama'at-i-Islami and other Islamist political parties.

Secularism protects many Bangladeshis' diverse practices, especially those that have come under fire in the nineteenth and twentieth centuries. To conclude that all secularists are non-Muslims is to blur the complicated dynamics of the country's religious life. Many foreign journalists and other visitors to Bangladesh assume that the rise in madrassa education indicates a rise in "fundamentalism." The fact of the matter is that madrassa education is less costly than Bengali-medium schools, and many impoverished families have only enough resources to send their children to madrassas. In an April 2002 article in the *Far Eastern Economic Review*, Bertil Lintner assumed that madrassa education in Bangladesh was the source of all radicalism; therefore, if madrassas were becoming more common in the country, a serious threat of radicalism existed.[43] A little more than a month later, Ruth Baldwin published an article in *The Nation* that cited Lintner's article as evidence for the contention that a "more insidious threat is posed by the exponential growth of madrassahs [in Bangladesh], or religious schools, in the last decade. . . . These are described by a retired high-ranking civil servant as a 'potential political time bomb.'"[44] Journalists too often assume that as in Pakistan and Afghanistan, Bangladesh's madrassas provide their students only with radical political fodder. In fact, Bangladesh has some English-language madrassas as well as universities governed by Islamists and Muslim conservatives that offer degrees in computer science and English but no courses on Islam.

Lintner also incorrectly assumes that the Bangladeshi government has no control over madrassas. In fact, the government oversees the curriculum of a limited number of state-funded madrassas, which provide some students with their only opportunity to receive an education. Like the Bengali-medium schools, the government-funded madrassas are overseen by an education board. In government-funded madrassas, students take exams in either Bengali or English but also study Arabic. Since the 1990s, these madrassas have admitted girls. In addition to courses in religious studies, students study science, humanities, computer science, and business administration. Thus, even Bangladesh's madrassas provide evidence of diversity.

Conclusion

Whether nationalism is secular or religious, it is indeed fragile. The nation is imagined into existence in several ways, and its fragility lies within the potential of multiple imaginings, which are numerous but not infinite. They are constrained by the dominant cultures within which they are created and communicated; one is the universal (Islam), and the other is the local (Bengal). The creativity or imaginings happen where these two phenomena interact to create a regionally informed Islamic way of life. Islam and Bengal are interpreted and articulated through material culture, values, and norms. Each individual member of a community articulates a particular imagining shaped by the cultural context within which he or she lives. The productions of these individuals not only describe a vision but are themselves the visions.

Each imagining is supported and preserved by traditions—specifically, by what Hosbawm refers to as "invented traditions." This term refers to traditions with ideological rather than pragmatic purposes whereby old images and symbols are employed in novel ways.[45] The repetition of the tradition serves crucial functions, keeping alive a particular ideology. Commemoration educates youth about ideology and instills in them the emotional attachment to that particular imagining of the nation. For Bangladesh, the myth of secular nationhood begins with the events of 1952 and ends with independence in 1971. The justification for independence is the preservation of a distinct Bengali culture, with its rich literary and artistic heritage that predates the formation of Pakistan. The traditions and commemorations that support a secular nationalism are those that incorporate elements of an older Bengali culture such as the ritual consumption of *panta bhat* on Pahela Baishakh, whose present form took shape during the period of resistance to Pakistani cultural imperialism. In fact, all of the national holiday[46] celebrations incorporate some Bengali cultural activity, such as the singing of *Rabindra sangeet*. Nationalism is at once both powerful and fragile. Power and meaning are derived from the repetition and commemoration.[47] Nationalism's fragility arises when it is contested by alternative imaginings that are supported by their own constructions of a countercollective memory and are accompanied by the supporting ritual commemorations. The contestation begins with the introduction of a competing and compelling collective memory. Just as the secularists mentally constructed their version of Bangladesh, so too could other imaginings be constructed based on other interpretations of the Bengali past, as the BNP has done. Like the Hindu nationalists in India who understand Islam to be foreign to their country, Muslim nationalists in Bangladesh seek to exclude Hindu and Adivasi citizens.[48] The ultimate danger of nationalism lies in the fact that it is often based on some imagined conception of the homogeneity of race, religion, or ethnicity.

The BNP and the Awami League are the two political parties through which competing nationalisms are articulated in Bangladesh. Since independence, the BNP's incorporation of Islam as an important element in national ideology attests to the growing contestation of Bengali secularism. These two groups promote a religious (or, more accurately, religioethnic) nationalism by more narrowly defining Bengaliness to exclude West Bengalis and non-Muslims and other ethnic minorities.

To some extent, the BNP now relies and Ershad previously relied on the religious conservative parties to gain enough popular support to govern. Though the religious fundamentalist parties have formed a coalition with the BNP, they do pose a threat to the party's brand of religioethnic nationalism. For the fundamentalists, this religioethnic nationalism does not necessarily go far enough. Although it acknowledges a Muslim identity, it might seem only a token gesture. What distinguishes the BNP from the fundamentalists is that the party is very much committed to the idea of a nation-state that is founded also on the people's bond to the land of Bengal. As will be discussed in the next chapter, the religious fundamentalists do not agree with the idea of nationalist ideology. What makes nationalism, be it secular or religioethnic, even more unstable is the impact of globalization and transnational bonds.

five

The Contested Place of Nation in *Umma* and Globalizing Efforts

Freedom:
You are Tagore's ageless poetry,
His immortal songs.

Freedom:
You are Kazi Nazrul, wild-haired sage
Trembling with the thrill of creation.

Freedom:
You are
that meeting at the martyr's monument
On the eternal Twenty-First of February.

Freedom:
You are the stormy dialogues
In teashops and open fields.

Freedom:
You are the fierce storm
Flapping its wings across the sky.

Freedom:
You are the breast of the Meghna river
In the month of Shravan.

Freedom:
You are my father's soft *jainamaz*
On which he says his prayers.

Freedom:
You are the trembling of my mother's
white sari drying in the courtyard.
—Excerpt from "Freedom,"
    by Shamsur Rahman

Shamsur Rahman is one of Bangladesh's most celebrated contemporary poets. This excerpt from his poem "Freedom" provides a glimpse of his ability to capture the emotions many Bangladeshis feel when they think of their nation. Rahman fought in the war for Bangladeshi independence, and many of his poems reflect his experience during the freedom struggle and the ideals of the secular-minded Bangladeshis. The images he conjures and the emotions these poems evoke do not, however, reflect the views of Islamists. Though many Islamists would claim to be loyal citizens of Bangladesh, they would not share such secular ideals. Instead, they would distance themselves from many of the nonreligious customs to which the poem refers and would instead prefer to draw connections between themselves and other Muslims around the world, connections that have been facilitated by the advent of the global age.

Technological advancements have made the world a smaller place, more connected and interdependent. The instant accessibility of the world through the Internet, the European Economic Union with its porous borders, increased movements of peoples around the world, and global markets are all ways in which the world is more closely tied and instantly connected. "Globalization" is a term primarily used to discuss this new world economy, global governance, and media, but globalization also affects local cultures in a number of ways. As I argued in chapter 4, nationalism and regional group identity politics are not driven by fundamentalism. However, if Islamists become involved in regional conflict, they do so as part of their effort to move closer to creating an Islamic state, not as an affirmation of nationalist goals. Though the term "fundamentalism" was first coined to refer to a Protestant movement in the United States, it came to represent an identifiable comparative phenomenon that constitutes a rejection of many modern values yet is a product of modernity.[1]

The idea of a nation-state is one of the products of modernity. Fundamentalists do not necessarily advocate but must inescapably acknowledge the nation-state. When internal conflict occurs between groups that question nationhood, it is often the result of the production of competing visions of nation. Religious, ethnic, and linguistic divisions among groups within the nation-state are highlighted and intentionally interpreted as communal differences to such an extent that these groups envision the constitution of the nation-state in contesting ways. National borders do not necessarily have to change for some of these groups to realize their vision of the nation-state, but how the community within a specific geographical region is imagined is subject to change. The ways in which communities create nations are based on numerous and competing visions of a nation's history, where some historical events are highlighted and others ignored. We have seen how nation-states are undermined from within by competing nationalisms; however, migration patterns and global religious networks also have the potential to undermine nationalisms. Before examining patterns specific to Bangladesh, we will briefly discuss some of the ways that religious voices articulate themselves in the global context.

In the introduction to their book *Religions/Globalizations: Theories and Cases*, Dwight N. Hopkins and his coeditors suggest that globalization "points to a series of social processes whose outcomes remain speculative."[2] The cultural impact of globalization is still being examined. A primary interest lies in determining whether globalization has homogenizing or diversifying impacts.[3] Which conditions foster homogeneity, and which foster diversification? In Hopkins's volume, contributors from the field of religious studies explore the link between religion and global networks. Some contributors explore the positive; others consider the negative. My point is not to determine whether globalization and religion interact in ways that benefit the world but to interrogate how religion has gained prominence in the public sphere of the global context. Under what conditions does religion undermine that product of modernity called nationalism?[4] Global religious networks can and do inspire competing visions of community. This view greatly contrasts with contemporary beliefs about transnational influences such as Samuel P. Huntington's and Benjamin Barber's civilizational model of the conflict of globalization and parochialism.[5]

Political scientist Benjamin R. Barber uses the term "McWorld" to refer to globalization, defining it as homogenization, with its integrative modernization, aggressive economic activity, and cultural globalization. He juxtaposes that world to "jihad," which he suggests represents religious fundamentalists' attempts to counteract the homogenizing effects of McWorld by way of its own "parochial" tendencies. Barber contends that any religious fundamentalist who resists McWorld falls within the scope of jihad. Furthermore, he argues that a dialectical relationship exists between McWorld and jihad. In other words, globalism faces off against religious parochialism. In fact, he argues that jihad intensifies as McWorld culture expands its global reach. Barber's theory is interesting in the way it brings under the microscope capitalism, privatization of formerly public services in democracies, and the way this privatization has begun to undermine democracy and subvert national borders.

However, Barber's theory has limited applicability, in particular with regard to global networks.[6] He exploits the Islamic term "jihad" and stereotypically colors the process he refers to with images of violence, chaos, and instability: "Jihad pursues a bloody politics of identity."[7] Second, his approach is problematic in that it conflates two distinct phenomena, mistakenly referring to both regional and religious conflicts and the battle of nationalist ideology under the rubric of "jihad." Rather than making a sweeping assumption of a dialectic between McWorld and something called jihad, one could more accurately pinpoint a dialectical relationship that exists between nationalism and transnationalism. Nationalist ideology is being undermined in particular ways by global religious networks of people who seek to assert their notions of orthodoxies. Fundamentalists and extremists ultimately have no interest in safeguarding nationalisms that do not publicly acknowledge and adhere to religious doctrine.

This dialectic of nationalism and transnationalism certainly represents the postcolonial moment; indeed, in broader terms it constitutes a dialectic between the universal and the particular or the global and the local. Understanding this dialectic is further complicated by the fact that each of these categories (global/local, local/particular) contains multiple interacting values, norms, and traditions. Furthermore, the new media of the global age have several impacts, which Dale Eickelman and Jon Anderson term the "thickening of ties" to communities in the diaspora. The ties also occur horizontally between Muslim and non-Muslim communities. News media, Internet cafes, and personal ties across the globe enhance the rapid spread of ideas. Eickelman and Anderson also point out that the notion of the local also becomes more dynamic and complex as a result of by global interaction. Finally, the new technologies have given greater voice to extremists, those who wish to impose their own notions of orthodoxy on others.[8] Extremists' speeches and declarations appear repeatedly on CNN, Fox News, and Internet sites in the United States as well as on al-Jazeera in the Middle East.

Global religious networks use the new media of globalization in a variety of ways. Evangelical and fundamentalist movements in the United States have found cable and satellite television an important means of converting people around the world—that is, of realizing their global mission. For example, Pat Robertson's Christian Broadcasting Network (CBN) invests twenty million dollars annually in international outreach programs. CBN also broadcasts an international version of the *700 Club* in more than forty countries. Christian radio broadcasting internationally amounts to more than twenty thousand hours of programming per week in more than 125 languages.[9] Despite these impressive numbers, however, Berit Bretthauer finds that mass media alone do not have a significant impact on conversion. Instead, many conversions occur based on personal contact and exchange. Nevertheless, the mass media constitute a vital component of American Christian fundamentalists' missionary goal. Bretthauer demonstrates that the mass media, which are dominated by themes about conversion experience, are useful in combination with local and personal attempts to convert worldwide.[10] The media create local networks of people around the world, often through development programs: "Think globally. Act locally. This is what American telepreachers do."[11] Missionizing certainly is not new, but the new technology available to these groups makes achieving their goals much easier. This is just one example of the global reach of religious communities and how one community utilizes the technology of the global age to achieve its aim. Numerous other religious communities around the world use the new technologies of the globalized world to convert, raise funds, and attempt to create "normative" or homogenous religious cultures.

Religious groups also employ the media in an attempt to influence governmental domestic and foreign policy. Jerry Falwell, a visible and vocal Christian evangelical, has often employed the media to rally support among Americans on issues of foreign policy toward the Muslim world. In an October 2002 appearance on CBS's *60 Minutes*, Falwell declared the Prophet Muhammad a terrorist and implied that the

Christian Right influences U.S. foreign policy with regard to Israel and Palestine. Said Falwell, "There are 70 million of us, and there's nothing that would bring the wrath of the Christian public in this country down on this government like abandoning or opposing Israel on a critical matter." American Christian fundamentalists and evangelists see government policies as a means of protecting their Christian global interests.

The missionizing emphasis of many religious movements also provides a source of great conflict and tension between and within religious communities. In his study of Muharram rituals in Trinidad, Frank Korom highlights the globalizing forces that exist in tension with local Hosay practices and attempt to influence a more "orthodox" observance of Muharram.[12] Shi'i missionaries from Canada attempt to bring Trinidadian Muharram rituals in line with their ritual performance in Iran because the missionaries view the Iranian practices as orthodox. The missionaries' efforts meet with a complex mixture of both resistance and acceptance in Trinidad. The Canadian missionaries hope to build a Shi'i cultural center, a madrassa, and a mosque, but in exchange Trinidadians who participate in Hosay are being asked to make Hosay more "orthodox," even though they see their practice of Hosay as correct.[13] Trinidadian local culture and customs are being threatened by the same outsiders who also constitute a possible source of financial support.

Resentment of Christian missionaries has recently grown in India. For example, the Vishva Hindu Parishad (VHP) seeks to counter the influence of Christianity and Islam by welcoming into the Hindu fold those Indian Muslims and Christians willing to "convert." It can be argued that the notion of conversion to Hinduism is itself a modern practice. In addition to its efforts to Hinduize India, the VHP extends its reach to Hindus abroad, even those whose families have lived outside India for generations. The global ties the VHP wishes to foster with those who identify themselves as Hindu support and reinforce the group's modern concept of Hinduism as both civilization and nation. Thus, the VHP supports a Hindu-based nationalism that equates the Indian nation with Hindu civilization, subsuming under that umbrella Buddhist, Jain, and Sikh traditions. Huntington also refers to India as a Hindu civilization. Increasingly in the United States, West Indian

Hindus are reconnecting with their Hindu identity through study of Hindu cultural traditions and closer ties with India. The VHP encourages these ties, which well serve the organization's ideological goals.

All over the world, even in the West, religion has reemerged as a dominant means by which individuals and communities primarily identify and politically ally themselves, whether through nationalism or fundamentalism. Transnational religious loyalties sometimes undermine state structures in this new global context when the state ideology does not privilege the notion of orthodoxy touted by some religious groups.[14] Globalization's impact on culture (in the broad sense—that is, including religious culture) is not the same everywhere. The foregoing examples suggest some of the complex possibilities for religion's role in transnational networks. I turn now to the transnational Muslim networks and movements of people—specifically, to the Tabligh Jama'at and the Jama'at-i-Islami, the primary transnational networks operating in Bangladesh today. In addition, I will address the increasing patterns of outmigration of Bangladeshis for work and pilgrimages, which also has its influence on Bengali and Bangladeshi nationalisms and on the nation's sovereignty. Global religious networks undermine nationalism only when they seek to create an Islamic state governed by a particular interpretation of Islamic orthodoxy and shari'a through their participation in the political process of the nation-state. The Tabligh Jama'at does not do so, while the Jama'at-i-Islami does.

Tabligh Jama'at

The Tabligh Jama'at is an important transnational Islamic movement with widespread and growing appeal. The group seeks to call Muslims to more "orthodox" behavior. Though the movement was founded in British India, it now has influenced Muslim practice all over the world. In South Asia, a somewhat analogous organization to the Tabligh would be the VHP. Both groups aspire to reignite the religious life of the people. The VHP's network extends well beyond India's borders, with centers in more than twenty-five countries where Hindu traditions are practiced.

Tabligh Jama'at is avowedly apolitical and thus differs markedly from another transnational movement, the Jama'at-i-Islami. In fact, members of the Jama'at-i-Islami are frustrated that the Tabligh is no ally in politics, as it is and always has been unwilling to participate in political debates.[15] In fact, Tablighis typically support the Awami League. In this way, the Tabligh also diverges significantly from the VHP. Where the Tabligh is avowedly apolitical, the VHP overtly supports Hindu nationalism by working in close association with the Bharata Janata Party.

The Tabligh Jama'at focuses on individual piety. It was founded in the 1920s by Muhammad Ilyas Shah (d. 1944) with the objective of teaching nonpracticing Muslims of the subcontinent how to perform daily *salat* and how to live a Muslim life more in line with that of the Prophet Muhammad. Today, the Tabligh's goals have been transformed to meet what its members understand to be the current needs of the *umma*. Under the leadership of Muhammad Ilyas Shah's son, Maulana Muhammad Yusuf, from 1944 to 1965, the movement became transnational, spreading rapidly after 1945, when the first teams of missionaries were sent to Syria, Iraq, Egypt, and England.[16] Wherever there are Muslims in the world, Tablighi participants find their mission. The Tabligh Jama'at currently is active in the Arab world, Malaysia, Indonesia, Myanmar, Turkey, Japan, East Africa, West Africa, Europe, South Africa, and North America.[17] The group's goal is not only to encourage individual Muslims to respond more actively to the *da'wa* (the call) but also to reject the materialism its members associate with the West.[18] More recently, the Tabligh's mission has come to include conversion of non-Muslims to Islam.

Those involved in the Tabligh have influenced changes in praxis through their gatherings such as the one in Tungi, Bangladesh, where more than one million Muslims from all over the world congregate each year. The Tabligh's participants also make an impact by traveling to study and pray with other Muslims around the world. An expanding network of Tabligh missions around the world is not concerned with ethnic, national, or racial boundaries.[19] The Tabligh Jama'at focuses primarily on the religious practices of the Muslim *umma*, seeking to expand it and make it more observant of ritual life according to their very sober, supposedly nonregionalized, practices that hearken back to Muhammad's time. They do not preach against nationalism or any political ideology. For the Tabligh participants, *dar al-Islam* is a way of being that seeks to replicate the piety of the first community of Muslims. The Tabligh's spread has resulted in large part from its grassroots nature (a view that every Muslim is obligated to preach) and its focus on travel to teach, study, and pray with other Muslims. Those associated with Tabligh Jama'at are asked to commit three days in a month to spreading the movement's message and to go annually on *chillas* (forty-day missions). Many Tablighi members visit the movement's headquarters, the Nizamuddin center in Delhi, for further religious studies.

The Tabligh Jama'at does not concern itself with national sovereignty and ideology: does that make the group's fundamentalism a threat to the nation-state? Though the movement is transnational and fundamentalist in its rejections of "Western materialism," it is also apolitical and pietistic in nature, thus posing no direct threat to the articulations of the nation-state. For the Tabligh Jama'at, one can be both pious Muslim and loyal citizen of a nation that does not identify with Islam. Indeed, the Tabligh Jama'at presupposes a lack of proper ritual observance and so seeks to revive Muslim practices and to spread Islam. The movement's historically apolitical nature has made it so successful. Many governments in the Muslim world naturally view the movement as a stabilizing factor because it does not question the notion of state authority or legitimacy.

Jama'at-i-Islami

The Jama'at-i-Islami is the most influential Islamist political party in Bangladesh today. The group has formed a strategic coalition with the ruling Bangladesh National Party (BNP). The rise of religious nationalism gradually led to the reemergence of Islamist parties in public life, despite ideological differences between the two camps.[20] Religious nationalists needed the Islamists to gain a foothold in national politics. Talal Asad has observed that the differences between Arab nationalism and Islamism arise from the fact that "the Islamist project of regulating conduct in the world in accordance with 'the principles of religion' (*usul ud-din*), and from the fact that the community to be constructed stands counter to many of the values of modern Western life."[21] Religious nationalists see Islam as well as the idea of the nation as part of their identity marker. Unlike the political Islamists, religious nationalists do not seek to impose an Islamic form of governance, as chapter 4 demonstrated with regard to the BNP. Though political Islamists may participate in the nation-state's political process, they do not celebrate nationalism but merely acknowledge and work within the structure of the state to achieve their goals. In fact, Islamism poses serious challenges to the democratic forms of the nation-state. Political Islamists want to create an Islamic polity guided by *usul ud-din*.[22] The Jama'at-i-Islami is a political Islamist organization, very different from the Tabligh Jama'at. Because of the Tabligh's apolitical nature, it has gained much wider popularity in Bangladesh than have the political Islamists.

The Jama'at-i-Islami's reentrance into Bangladeshi public life began several years after the country gained independence, when the party was forced to readjust its original goals as set out by its founder, Maulana Sayyid Abul 'Ala Maududi (d. 1979). His career began with his work as editor for several Urdu magazines and journals, including *Madina*, *Taj*, and *Jamiyat*. In the early 1920s he supported nationalism, but when the Khilafat movement died, he changed his position. Maududi concluded that the Turks and Egyptians had become misguided, which led him to become suspicious of Indian nationalism. He then regarded Indian secular nationalism as simply a cover for Hindu nationalism. Maududi feared that under the guise of secularism, Muslims would suffer at the hands of Hindus. He rejected not just Hindu nationalism but even the secular goals of the Muslim League. Though the league was a political party that claimed to protect the interests of the subcontinent's Muslims, the Jama'at-i-Islami did not agree with the league's agenda. Maududi held specific ideas about how Islam should be practiced, an issue that was of less concern to the league. He criticized Sufism and other Islamic movements as practiced on the subcontinent, including the traditional *'ulama'*, whom Maududi viewed as unable to tackle contemporary problems.[23] He published these views whenever possible, especially noted in the monthly *Tarjuman al-Qur'an*, which he edited from 1933 until his death. He also wrote books on Islam, including *Al-jihad fil Islam*, which gave him wide recognition in the Islamic world. In 1941, Maududi and other young Muslim men founded the Jama'at-i-Islami.

During this era, Maududi created what he saw as the only ideology that fostered an Islamic way of life in an Islamic state. To have this Islamic state, the people had to become Islamized; the Islamization of the government and consequent enforcement of the shariʿa would follow. He regarded this process as a revolution, but it would begin with the people, not with a state structure. In many ways, this ideology was based on modern ideas. The Jamaʿat-i-Islami became a political party that participated in the democratic system. Maududi also believed that the government must follow the will of the people. Though in his ideal Islamic state, the laws of the state would be based on shariʿa, it could be implemented only if it were the will of the people. The implementation of shariʿa should happen only after the people had become fully Islamized. In this way, the government would be implementing but not forcing God's will.[24] Maududi relied heavily on the organizational structure of the party to bring about this revolution. The Jamaʿat-i-Islami in Bangladesh believes that since Bangladesh is overwhelmingly Muslim, the country should abide by the laws of God as Jamaʿat-i-Islami interprets them. According to the group's leaders, "The aims and objectives of the Jamaʿat-e-Islami Bangladesh are to achieve the pleasure of Allah and salvation in the life hereafter by making ceaseless efforts to establish the Islamic social order in Bangladesh."[25] The organization does not try to mislead citizens about its intentions. Instead, it puts a great deal of effort, through extensive publications, public meetings, and presence in the public sphere, into proselytizing to other Muslims and non-Muslims. It also challenges existing Bangladeshi governmental policies and cultural traditions deemed "un-Islamic."

The Jamaʿat-i-Islami has organizations and parties in India, Bangladesh, Pakistan, Sri Lanka, and North America. It is not simply a political party but an organization with an exclusive membership and a strong organizational structure from the local to the national level, with elections as an essential component. The head of the organization is the *amir*, who is elected by the direct vote of full-fledged members. The *amir* is the chief executive of the party who is advised by the central Majlis-i-Shura, a committee elected by the members every three years. Each country's organization relies heavily on a committed group of members. Membership in the Jamaʿat-i-Islami is open to all adult males and females who are committed to the goals of the party and whose lives reflect the party's view of an Islamic way of life. Members found to violate these values and doctrines are swiftly expelled. Members justify the party's exclusive nature through the view that the organization constitutes much more than a political party—it is an ideological movement seeking to build a perfect *umma*.[26]

Another important wing of the Bangladeshi organization is its students' chapter, Islami Chhatra Shibir (ICS), founded in 1977. The student wing maintains a presence in more than 60 percent of the high schools in twenty-one districts and is highly visible on college and university campuses.[27] Becoming a member of the student organization requires several steps: the first level of membership is worker, the second level is comrade, and the third level is member. To reach full member status, individuals must demonstrate a full commitment to and active practice of the Muslim way of life prescribed as orthodox by the organization. Like its parent organization, the student wing demands active commitment to the moral and ritual life as defined by the organization.

Between 1941 and 1947, the Jama'at-i-Islami focused on creating a strong organizational basis with a clear understanding of how Islam should be applied to all aspects of life.[28] Maududi opposed the move to create an independent Pakistan, just as he opposed any form of nationalism. In his view, a truly Islamic way of life could not be bounded by a nationalist ideology, with its territorial borders. Nevertheless, many former colonies sought national independence, so Maududi had to reconcile himself with this changing world. When independence arrived, more than half the Jama'at-i-Islami members became citizens of Pakistan, while the remainder became citizens of India. The Jama'at-i-Islami's main goal in Pakistan was to create a nation-state governed only by the principles of Islam. At times, Maududi's efforts to make Pakistan an Islamic state put him at odds with the central government; at other times, he found himself at odds with the traditional 'ulama'. Despite being imprisoned on occasion and even sentenced to death at one point, he continued his efforts to transform Pakistan. In 1963, the Jama'at-i-Islami founded the Islamic Research Academy, whose main goal was to counter the influence of the modernist Central Institute of Islamic Research headed by Fazlur Rahman. The Jama'at-i-Islami worked then and continues to work today to sway public opinion in a number of ways.

The Jama'at-i-Islami disseminates its views and teachings through its participation in government protests, *waz mahfil*, its student wing, and the literature and audio cassettes it publishes. The Jama'at-i-Islami has reading rooms throughout the country, enabling interested persons to read the works of Maududi and other supporters of the organization's agenda. Twenty-first-century religious movements all over the world eagerly adopt technology of the global age to facilitate their missions. The Jama'at-i-Islami, like the BJP in India, has maintained informative Web sites that are open to the world. According to Jama'at-i-Islami's Web site,

> As a conscious citizen:
> You must not remain indifferent to what is happening in your country.
> You must take notice of the people who have organised themselves to rule over your country upholding secularism, socialism, etc. instead of Islam.
> You must not fail to foresee the consequences if these forces succeed.
> As a Muslim:
> You must work for establishing Islamic social order in your country.
> You must join an organisation to accomplish this gigantic task.[29]

It is significant that Jama'at-i-Islami does not necessarily advocate the establishment of a local Jama'at-i-Islami in other countries; rather, it advocates any kind of Islamic social order.

The organization has worked very hard to disseminate its ideas in publications. It has produced traditional literature and was one of the first Islamist groups in Bangladesh to employ genres ordinarily the terrain of the secular litterateur. Though the Jama'at-i-Islami still publishes instructional texts, biographies, and translations of classical Islamic texts, it now also sponsors the publication of novels. Affiliated authors write fiction that contains themes related to Islam and promotes Jama'at-i-Islami views, selling these works primarily at Jama'at-i-Islami–linked publishing houses.

These novels form part of the Jama'at-i-Islami's effort to Islamize secular discourse, notes Mainmuna Huq. Huq suggests that these authors attempt "to socialize, politicize, and culturalize the religious imagi-nation" by employing Islamic themes or historical events or struggles such as the Palestinian-Israeli conflict to glorify particular conceptions of jihad, martyrdom, and Islamic life in the framework of genres that formerly constituted the domain of secular writers.[30] The authors in-sert into these struggles fictional heroic figures who embody the Islamists' ideals. These writers also pen romance novels, a very popu-lar genre in Bangladesh. These works differ little from secular romance novels except that the Islamist works contain hadith and Qur'anic verses and commentary. The Jama'at-i-Islami and other Islamists likely have turned to secular genres such as the novel because the more tra-ditional instructional texts, translations, and biographies have become less popular. Given the wide readership that novels enjoy, the Jama'at-i-Islami and similar organizations hope to reach a larger audience with their vision of Muslim life. This strategy of adopting the novel to create a particular image of Islam and of Muslim life is subtle, and the extent of its effectiveness in changing the way Muslims behave in Bangladesh cannot be answered here. This approach certainly carries a particular vision of Islam into the literary terrain, inserting Islam into the Bengali cultural realm. The novels by Islamists are sold exclusively in Islamic bookstores but sit side by side on the shelves with other novels, thus broadening the potential audience.

The Jama'at-i-Islami thus has remained open to new strategies for spreading its message both in Bangladesh and outside the country. As the organization grew after Maududi's death, it evolved somewhat to include the attitudes and beliefs of its newer generation of members, which sometimes conflict with its founder's ideas. In Bangladesh, the organization has allegedly backed violence and terror, which its founder did not advocate as a means of perfecting the *umma*. This vio-lence, some would argue, dates back to the group's collaboration with Pakistan during the liberation war.

Prior to Bangladesh's independence, the Jama'at-i-Islami was gaining members in West Pakistan but found little support in the eastern prov-ince. In 1955, Ghulam Azam, a teacher of political science at Carmichael College in Manipur, was the leader of the East Pakistan division of the Jama'at-i-Islami. Rafiuddin Ahmed notes that Ghulam Azam had previously been an active supporter of the language movement, for which he was imprisoned. Though Maulana Maududi worked to build an Islamic state in Pakistan, he soon realized that his only chance of gaining any support among Bengalis was to demonstrate some support for the recognition of Bengali as a national language. When, in February 1956, Maududi traveled to East Pakistan for the Islamic constitutional conference, he publicly announced his support for Bengali as a national language.[31] Nevertheless, the Awami League of East Pakistan received the overwhelming support of the Bengalis because of its emphasis on Bengali ethnic identity and secularism, which Ghulam Azam diligently opposed. During the war for independence, Ghulam Azam, as a representative of the Jama'at-i-Islami, lobbied against partition, and after the war he attempted to persuade Middle Eastern governments not to recognize the newly independent Bangladesh.[32] Though he had previously opposed the formation of Pakistan, when a Muslim homeland was created, he did not want to see it partitioned. Instead, he saw this as an opportunity to bring about the revolution.

When the Awami League began its agitation for independence from Pakistan, the Jama'at-i-Islami was the only political party in the eastern province to oppose the move. The group did so in hopes that a united Pakistan might be transformed into an Islamic state. Though the Jama'at-i-Islami supported Bengali language recognition, it would not support full autonomy for the Bengali people, which would go against the principle of oneness of a religious community. Bengali members of the Jama'at-i-Islami went so far as to collaborate with the central government during the war. Their student wing took up arms against the Mukti Bahini, a fact that today's hard-line secularists never forget.[33] After independence, Bangladesh's judiciary charged the Jama'at-i-Islami with war crimes. Sheikh Mujib also banned religious parties from participating in politics. Nevertheless, the party would soon regain political standing in Bangladesh.

The devastating failure of the secular government led many to question Mujib's four principles (secularism, socialism, nationalism, and democracy), although the major causes of the government's failure included the abandonment of democracy, Mujib's iron-fisted governance, the lack of international support, and natural disasters. In July 1978, Ghulam Azam returned to Bangladesh from his exile in Pakistan and England. The new government clearly did not view him as a traitor, and the strength and unity on which Bangladesh had been founded had been weakened during Mujib's rule. With the approval of the Jama'at-i-Islami organization in Lahore, a chapter was established in Bangladesh in 1979. The Jama'at-i-Islami organization in Bangladesh follows the same membership structure as the chapters in Pakistan and India.

Having recognized the reality of Bangladesh's sovereignty, Ghulam Azam was forced to rethink the possibilities for the Jama'at-i-Islami in the former East Pakistan province. President Ziaur Rahman not only permitted religious parties to participate in politics but sought their support of his regime. For the Jama'at-i-Islami and other religious parties, Zia's form of Bangladeshi nationalism represented a lesser evil than Mujib's secular nationalism. At least with Bangladeshi nationalism based on emphasizing Islam as the national religion, the religious parties believed they would have an opportunity to make Bangladesh an Islamic nation. The ability to form religious political parties quickly provided Islamists with entry into the political sphere, and the Jama'at-i-Islami has actively participated in national politics since 1979. Both Zia and Ershad sought the financial support of oil-rich Arab countries, thereby playing into the hands of the Jama'at-i-Islami.[34] As Enayetur Rahim has pointed out, "The ensuing competition among political parties to publicly display their loyalty to Islam by recourse to various pseudo-religious rituals, such as holding the *milad* in the offices of various political parties including the Awami League [and] official *iftar* parties during the month of Ramadan, demonstrated the importance of the Islamization of politics spearheaded by the Jama'at, and equally pursued by the successive military regimes of Zia and Ershad."[35] Sheikh Hasina undertook a highly publicized pilgrimage to Mecca in an attempt to demonstrate that she was an observant Muslim, though politically she believed in secularism. Though the Jama'at-i-Islami has never gained a majority of seats in Parliament, the party has gained enough influence to move Bangladesh in the direction of an Islamic polity, as evidenced by such high-profile gestures toward Islam. Both the BNP and the Awami League politicians have been eager to publicly demonstrate their observance of Islamic rituals. The Jama'at-i-Islami is not naive regarding the BNP's motivations. As one senior Jama'at-i-Islami member, Abdul Qader Mullah, put it, "We have an alliance with

BNP. We differ from them in 10–15 per cent of ideology. We are allied to them, because the Awami League manifesto is in favour of secularisation. They do not believe in total religion. Islam is a total code of life—education, welfare, social and economic life. The A[wami] L[eague] believes the relationship between man and God is private. BNP believes in Islamic values. They do not practise, but at least they pay lip-service."[36] The Jama'at-i-Islami currently sees its alliance with the BNP as mutually beneficial. The Jama'at-i-Islami has "a profound appreciation of the failure of man-made systems and ideologies prevailing in the world which have subjected man to exploitation, repression, corruption and suffering."[37] Yet the BNP believes it has the upper hand in this alliance.

The Jama'at-i-Islami focuses a great deal of energy on organizing and training its youth members, who participate extensively in politics and wield strong influence over Bangladesh's cultural life. Clashes often occur among various student groups, and the ICS is well known for its intimidation tactics, though the Jama'at-i-Islami publicly denounces the use of coercion and violence. On Ekushey 1990, I was in Jessore at a women's development organization, and several women who worked there set up a makeshift shrine of flowers in the garden in remembrance of those who died on Ekushey. When the women began singing songs to mark the occasion, several members of ICS stopped the activities, claiming that what the women were doing was un-Islamic. The women, fearful of the threat the ICS members posed, had no choice but to heed the warning. The students did not care that some of the women who had gathered were Christian but wanted everyone to observe and respect a narrow interpretation of Islam.

Though the ICS and the Jama'at-i-Islami have backed away from their political position on independence, members of these organizations are noticeably absent at major secular and national celebrations in Dhaka; at smaller gatherings, however, group members are present in an attempt to disrupt activities. The ICS has been implicated in a number of violent attacks, murders, and incidents of torture. Many of Bangladesh's universities and colleges are coeducational, and the ICS has been known to try to intimidate young female students deemed to be behaving in an "un-Islamic" manner. In 1999, UDICHI, a well-known cultural organization, planned a major cultural event with international guests in attendance at which a bomb was detonated, killing ten people and injuring many more. According to news reports in Bangladesh, the ICS was allegedly involved. In 2001, on Pahela Baishaikh (the Bengali New Year), a bombing occurred at the annual festivities at Ramna Park in Dhaka, with as many as twelve people killed and substantial numbers injured. Again, the ICS was implicated in the attack.

Many Bangladeshi Islamists condemn the celebration of secular holidays as well as the existence of monuments associated with those holidays. Other well-known Islamist political parties or coalitions of parties include Harkat and Islamic Oikko Jote, which have also been accused of committing violence for political aims. Though membership in these organizations comprises only a fraction of the overall population, their aggressive tactics make them formidable foes of secularists and nongovernmental organizations, many of whom have received death threats.[38] Among the most widely publicized controversies were death threats against outspoken secularist Taslima Nasreen, a medical doctor by training. Nasreen wrote newspaper columns about problems women face as a result of fundamentalist beliefs and practices and authored a novel, *Lajja* (Shame), on which Bangladesh's Islamists heaped criticism but which was lauded in India and the West. The fact that the author was a Muslim woman only added to the work's popularity abroad.

Political Islamists target any and all "un-Islamic" activities, including those that take women outside the home. Journalist Jeremy Seabrook has accurately portrayed the tensions between Islamists and secularist-oriented nongovernmental organizations, arguing that the secularists no longer effectively protect or represent the poor. Soon after Bangladesh's independence, nongovernmental organizations began to spring up to perform the functions that government was incapable of fulfilling, serving the poor through rural development, microcredit, and small business programs. According to Seabrook, "Micro-credit releases people from moneylenders, who enforce interest rates of 10 per cent per month. If people cannot pay, [the lenders] sequester the goods, houses, cattle or labour of the poor. Micro-credit disturbs traditional patterns of hierarchy and dependence. Rural elites, seeing their power diminished, are then ready to ally themselves with fundamentalists to restore their control over the poor. Indeed, this is a significant element in the rise in fundamentalism."[39] The elite and the Islamists create roadblocks that make it difficult for nongovernmental organizations to work with the poor, especially women. The effort to make women self-reliant and financially independent threatens traditional power dynamics.

Of serious concern to religious and ethnic minorities in Bangladesh is the escalating violence at the hands of Islamists and their supporters. Each year, an increasing number of Christians, Hindus, and Buddhists flee Bangladesh for India, seeking refuge from the violence.[40] According to the U.S. Committee for Refugees, the United Nations High Commissioner for Refugees, reported in 2002 that an estimated two hundred thousand Hindus and other religious minorities were displaced as a result of postelection violence, and between five thousand and twenty thousand Bangladeshi Hindus sought asylum in India.[41] All asylum seekers are not necessarily victims of religious violence, but many are, and many more fear it. In a publication released by Bangladesh's minister of state for planning, Dr. A. Moyeen Khan notes that according to census data, Bangladesh's Hindu population dropped from 18.5 percent of the country's total in 1951 to 13.5 percent in 1961 to 10.5 percent in 1991.[42]

The Jama'at-i-Islami carries out all of its programs with support from sources both within and outside Bangladesh, with significant funding coming from the Middle East. The Jama'at-i-Islami depends on the financial contributions of its members, who are expected to donate 5 percent of their monthly income to the organization. Members and supporters also give *zakat* and other contributions during Muslim holidays, and the organization accepts donations from around the world. Funds from the Middle East to the Jama'at-i-Islami are constant and support its many activities, though exact figures are difficult to determine.[43] The Jama'at-i-Islami has established close ties to government officials and wealthy private citizens in the Gulf states and Iran. Moreover, as Rafiuddin Ahmed has noted, a great deal of financial support comes from Bangladeshis in the Gulf states, who have emigrated in search of paying jobs, which are scarce at home but plentiful in the Gulf region.[44]

Bengalis have also migrated to other places across the globe. As Katy Gardner has pointed out, as far back as the eighteenth century,

Bengalis found work as servants and ship workers in Britain.[45] Since the twentieth century, many Bangladeshis have made their way elsewhere in the world, including the United States, following varying migration patterns tied to the global labor market and immigration laws. These migrants not only provide foreign currency for Bangladesh but also shape expressions of Bangladeshi culture.

Moving Outside the Borders:
Bangladeshi Migrants and Pilgrims

In her illuminating anthropological study of emigration, Gardner challenges the conventional theory that male outmigration has only negative impacts on the community, leading to its destabilization and ultimately to more "modern" forms of culture. She points to F. G. Bailey and T. Scarlett Epstein's studies of migration patterns in India that focus on a breakdown of the joint family. She also considers the work on African migration, "linking it with agricultural decay, and 'detribalization.'"[46] In contrast to these earlier studies, Gardner demonstrates the uneven cultural transformations that take place globally and locally—that is, how migration patterns not only transform but also maintain ties to home. Her study reveals the relativity of hegemony and its contestation in local discourse. Gardner's study of Sylheti Bangladeshis demonstrates that maintaining ties with home is central to these migrants. Even after resettling their entire families in the United States, Britain, the Middle East, or elsewhere, emigrants maintain bonds with their places of origin. The Sylhetis visit their homes in Bangladesh, help others find work abroad, and build new houses in natal villages that reflect the wealth accumulated by working abroad.

Bangladeshi migrants also bring some cultural elements of Bangladeshi life to their homes abroad. In her study of ethnic foodways among immigrants in the United States, Susan Kalcik suggests that "traditional foods and ways of eating form a link with the past and help ease the shock of entering a new culture."[47] Consequently, immigrants open restaurants and grocery stores selling traditional foods. Bangladeshis abroad, like other immigrants, also establish houses of worship and cultural organizations—typically, societies to promote the celebration of Bangladeshi holidays. They also found mosques, where their children may learn about Bangladeshi religious beliefs. Many of these immigrants also want their children to learn the Bengali language.

With the assistance of local government officials, the Bangladeshi community in Oldham, near Manchester, England, created a replica *shaheed minar*. This monument testifies to the community's commitment to maintaining ties not only with its homeland but also with its culture. Gardner refers to this local and global relationship as a relationship between *desh* (land/home) and *bidesh* (foreign land). As families move to Britain and mosques are built, *bidesh* is transformed into *desh*. Likewise, *bidesh* influences *desh* in the form of goods, remittances, and ideas. In Gardner's view, *bidesh* is "a metaphor for power and advancement" but also represents all that is wrong with *desh*.[48] She concludes, therefore, that the exchange is uneven.

Gardner's study highlights many migrants' mixed feelings about Bangladesh. Bangladesh is poor, and even educated persons lack opportunity there. Bangladesh suffers frequent natural disasters and lacks public infrastructure, yet it is home; it is where Bangladeshis wish to be buried, and it is a source of pride. The land of opportunity abroad also is not perfect in terms of its dominant culture and religion, despite the importation of Bengali customs, foods, and religion. Nevertheless, the home abroad is made more livable by bringing Bengali customs and foods to the land of opportunity, by building mosques where men may worship and where their children may study Islam with other Bengali children who are taught by a Bengali Muslim teacher. Similarly, Bangladesh is improved by the importation of things not available locally, and emigrants' funds make possible the construction of much-needed roads, electrification, and appliances for the new pukka home in their natal village.

But while the West is a land of opportunity, Mecca is also another important locus of influence. Islam's sacred center influences the ideological transformations that many Bangladeshis abroad desire. Their wealth allows them not only to articulate what is lacking but also to implement changes to shape individual selves and community in ways they have come to appreciate with the experience of living abroad.

Mecca and Saudi Arabia have had a great influence on religious life in Bangladesh, but this is nothing new. What is new is the extent of that influence. As Gardner and others have noted and as nineteenth- and twentieth-century reform movements demonstrate, the many interpretations of Islam in Bangladesh come under fire from those who advocate an Islam that is more narrowly textually based and is culturally more Arab informed and thus, they believe, more orthodox. According to Gardner, "This co-exists with 'scientific' knowledge, linked to migration and notions of modernity. Both are largely monopolized by men from the wealthier households. With their access to what they present as 'core' knowledge, some individuals attempt to redefine the sacred and eradicate domains of belief and practice oppositional to their new order. Whilst involving local hierarchy, at another level this is part of a wider process in which meanings are moulded by external, global processes; the power relations are not only between individuals, but also between the village and *bidesh*."[49] The constant and increasing flow of Bangladeshi pilgrims to Mecca for the hajj exposes them to Middle Eastern, Arab-informed Islamic culture. Many Bangladeshis appropriate customs that they understand as more authentically Islamic customs. This is not surprising, given the nineteenth century's reformist emphasis on more authentic and orthodox practice and given the efforts of Islamist movements in the postcolonial period. Some of the key features that Islamists stress are *tawhid* (oneness of God) and *umma* (community). Islamists such as Jama'at-i-Islami members emphasize the notion of a common "Muslim culture," considering anything else un-Islamic or inauthentic.

Religiously speaking, to the Sylheti who has become a religious purist while working abroad or traveling to the Haramayn for pilgrimage, Bengali Islam is backward, full of superstition, and improper. The West constitutes a potential source of material wealth but is culturally foreign: Mecca and Islam are the sources of knowledge. The hajj is an important factor and has always been an important locus for the transmission of religious ideas. Along with the obvious transports of Arab clothing, dates, and Zum Zum water, pilgrims also bring back notions of orthodoxy. The *hajji* gains an honored status in his or her community, and if the pilgrim also has economic means, he or she gains the ability to articulate change.

Conclusion

Most of Bangladesh's Muslims believe that one can be a member of the world community of Muslims while being culturally Bengali. This majority of Bengali Muslims sees no conflict of interest: it is not considered *kufr* to study classical Bengali music, to listen to Tagore songs, or to fight for the protection of one's cultural heritage. Shamsur Rahman's poem reflects this sentiment. Rahman proclaims that freedom is many things, including the songs of Tagore and his father's *jainamaz* (prayer rug). Religious and ethnic culture do not conflict.

Though Bangladesh was conceived as a secular nation, with religion playing no role in governance, the role of Islam has become a highly debated issue. This change in political climate has resulted in large part because of the influence of transnational Muslim networks. This chapter has demonstrated that the technology of globalization transforms religious life locally and globally. The implementation of new technologies (for example, the Internet), the revitalization of existing ones (for example, print media and literary genres), and the increased movement of people around the world have played a part in these transformations. The idea of a global religious community may not be novel; however, people around the world now have tighter bonds than ever. People are instantly connected via the Internet, telecommunications, and images on television. Ideas are communicated and exchanged swiftly; people are connected by their awareness of a common bond; and international funds provide support for common visions. In many ways, globalization supports manifestations of particular imaginings of world religious communities. The new and more dynamic interactions of the global and the local complicate the local. Particular imaginings of community arise in the local when people are exposed to different articulations of what it means to be a member of a global community. They are exposed to other interpretations of (in this case) Islam, judging one more authentic than another. This leads to the desire to transform either one's own practice or those of the other. Like-minded individuals around the world then work together to support each other's programs for global change, as we have seen with the Jama'at-i-Islami and Tabligh Jama'at, which narrowly define Muslim community. It is not enough to call oneself a Muslim: Islamists expect other Muslims to share the same values. With new technologies at their fingertips, Islamists can more easily work to achieve their visions of the Muslim *umma*. Though Islamists may be a minority in Bangladesh, the ability to participate in that country's democratic process in conjunction with financial support from overseas enables the Islamists to move Bangladesh, however slowly, toward their goal. In 2004, Islamists persuaded the government to ban the sale and publication of all Ahmadi books. Islamists would also like to see the Ahmadi minority group declared non-Muslim. Without the funding that comes from abroad, many Islamists would be less active. However, even without funds, extremists still carry out programs of intimidation. The Jama'at-i-Islami does not view itself as extremist, nor does it admit to using violence; however, many Bangladeshis view the group as violent and have accused it of using violent tactics. Bangladeshi migrants also transform the local and the global through the movement of people, ideas, and wealth. Their travels have exposed them to other interpretations of Islam and have influenced their individual transformation of self and society. Together these factors have led to the contestation of nation as it was conceived in 1971 in Bangladesh.

With individuals and organizations creating divergent visions of themselves as members of a particular global community and with these divergent images of the *umma* informing conceptions of the nation-state, contestation and new configurations are inevitable. How the numerous global notions of Muslim *umma* and the local notion of community (nation) will be combined in the long run remains unknown. We do know that the global conceptions work against local (national) visions of community that were conceived in a secular form.

Competing Visions of Community

In the postcolonial world, religion has become a source of great contestation about how we shape the present world, a world that has been transformed by globalizing technologies. The study of Bengali Muslim visions of community in Bangladesh indicates that the politics of religious group identity is complex and cannot be defined simply in terms of a static, monolithic Islamic culture. An Islamic civilization has been viewed as monolithic in two ways: as a singular, common culture throughout the Muslim world and as a culture that has not changed in fourteen centuries. In fact, Islamic civilization represents dynamic and diverse societies of Muslims.

This study demonstrates through examination of literary evidence from the precolonial and colonial periods that universal Islamic ideals always have interacted with the local. Islamic ideals are necessarily interpreted and are bound to have multiple meanings in different cultural and historical contexts. In the postcolonial world, impacted significantly by global-ization, we must consider the relation between the global and the local; between cultural frames of reference; and between individual, com-munity, and power as a way of understanding who gets to articulate a particular vision of community. In the postcolonial world, tensions exist between national and transnational visions of community. As lit-erary evidence shows, visions of community in precolonial Bengal were not necessarily based on a simple designation of Hindu and Muslim. The many diverse people of Bengal oriented themselves in a number of categories, such as *ashraf* and non-*ashraf* status. Muslim rulers were not simply Muslims but were Turk, Afghan, Habshi, and Arab. As dis-cussed in chapter 1, Mukundarām Cakravartī's *Caṇḍī-maṅgal* (1589) described Muslim residents of a Bengali town according to occupation. Group identity was asserted in a number of complex ways that dur-ing the colonial period were reduced to "Hindu" and "Muslim." The conflation of the numerous visions of community into two categories became the source of religious nationalism in the twentieth century.

To understand the impact of the colonial experience, we begin with the way the British perceived the various communities under their rule in India. Being secularist does not mean that the British ignored religion or the religious beliefs of those whom they ruled. They were well aware of their religious beliefs, and they used religious differentia-tion in relation to themselves to make sense of community in South Asia. Despite Muslim rule in India for more than five hundred years, the British saw Muslims as foreigners, while the indigenous groups were considered Hindu regardless of language and ethnic differences. British law, governance, and missionary strategy created and fostered such visions of community. Indigenous peoples' responses to these ex-periences and interactions are evidenced most clearly in the literature they produced. While religion became a primary source of envisioning community, language and print technology interacted to particular-ize rather than universalize religious visions of community. There was Bengali Islamic literature, Urdu literature, and literature about Islam in other regional languages such as Gujarati and Tamil. A Muslim nation for all the world's Muslims was not a practical goal, so Muslim leaders of the subcontinent opted to have a subcontinental union. While Urdu became the language of a majority of subcontinental Muslims, Bengali continued as the language of choice among Bengali Muslims and was the language spoken by a large portion of the Pakistani population.

The existence of regional differences despite universal idealism among Muslims led to the desire to adopt and reshape nationalist ideology. We simply cannot assume that ideas born in Western societies—such as nationalism—will be adopted without being changed by the actors and the different historical context provided by colonialism. The many different groups of Muslims who ruled India in the British period were conflated into one: Muslim. Indeed, a great deal of the colonial experience transformed the way communities are envisioned in South Asia today. The historical fact of British emphasis on the broad religious groupings of "Muslim" and "Hindu" and its subsequent role in communal formation represents one example. Individual actors used literature to shape visions of community but in turn were shaped by the tensions between the universal (Islam) and the local (Bengal) as well as the colonial. The tensions between the universal and the local are evident in the criticisms directed at local practices that differed from those of Muslims in the Middle East. The colonial experience and cultural activity undeniably led to the rise of religious nationalism and thus to the current shaping of the nations of South Asia.

While group identity has always existed, the question is which marker of identity becomes prominent at any given time. In Bangladesh today, the struggle is over this question of religious versus ethnolinguistic identity. Both the religious and the ethnic were important factors in the colonial period. To communicate religious reform to the Muslims who did not know Urdu, Bengali had to be used. Only a limited number of imaginings of community are possible. The number of imaginings is limited to those that lie within the bounds of the creative tensions between Islam and the local regional culture. Within these creative tensions, Bengali *tafsirs* were created, as was a distinctive Bengali dialect for a popular audience, with Arabic, Persian, and Urdu influences. Though the possible visions of community are many, those with power articulate their visions while others remain muted.

Power is a crucial factor, for without it individuals and groups of people cannot assert alternative visions such as ones that include Bangladesh's many ethnic minorities. This power may be realized as money, status, or the willingness to use violence on others. Ethnic Bengalis continue to overwhelm the ethnic minorities of the Chittagong Hill Tracts region, despite the armed resistance of those ethnic minorities. In fact, little is known about these dwindling minority communities in Bangladesh and their efforts to be heard. It is not enough to have free speech; it is also necessary to be heard, a power of which the ethnic minorities of Bangladesh have little. Few people are interested in the plight of these minorities, so little is heard or discussed about them. The politics of those with power and their relations with those who lack it demonstrate that only visions of community that come to prominence are asserted because the group wields enough power to articulate it through processions covered by the media or the ability to enact legislation.

In Bangladesh, the only visions that make it to the public sphere of debate are Bengali ethnolinguistic nationalism, religious nationalism, and the more universal Islamist vision. The Awami League's ethnolinguistic nationalism is so successful because it taps into an affinity for the native language with a rich literary heritage known to many Bengalis because of its oral nature. In addition, the league has prospered because of the recent historical experience of exploitation that supersedes class and religious difference. The tragic deaths of several Bengalis in 1952 in their protest against Pakistani language policy remains a powerful symbol of Bengali language, so much so that a community of Bangladeshis has erected a replica *shaheed minar* in their adopted home of England. Bangladesh's religious nationalism also draws its strength from recent historical experience, specifically the failure of Mujib's government, which the religious nationalists have attributed to his secularism. The existence of these competing nationalisms in Bangladesh today demonstrates the fragile state of competing visions of community and how they are caught between universal Islam's pull and native ties to the region.

Nationalism, be it ethnic or religious, likely will remain contested because homogeneity does not exist in any nation. Diversity is not nonexistent but is hidden because of the power asserted by some over others. This hidden diversity is not an anomaly that can be ignored in an attempt to understand the politics of religious group identity. The assumption of or desire for homogeneity often leads to violence and persecution against the "minority" community. The minority may even be members of the same religious community as the majority but engage in observances of religious tradition that differ from those of the group that asserts "orthodoxy" in the public sphere. In Bangladesh, the practice of Islam is diverse, but the Islamists want to impose their view of orthodoxy on the majority of the country's Muslims. With global and local support via an alliance with the political party in power, the political Islamists such as the Jama'at-i-Islami have more leverage to assert their vision. However, political Islamists had to rethink their goals after the subcontinent was remapped in 1947 and again in 1971. An Islamist vision of community rejects regional or culturally informed interpretations of Islam. Islamists around the world advocate some kind of transnational or global Islam. Yet this so-called global Islam that they preach is really a Middle East–informed Islam. This is no surprise, partly because the Islamist movements are driven in large part by funds from the Middle East. Despite the fact that the founder of this organization, Maulana Sayyid Abul 'Ala Maududi, was a South Asian, he believed that true Islam as practiced by the Prophet Muhammad could not be interpreted through a regional lens. His reforms, like those of many others, would make Islam as practiced by South Asian Muslims more like Islam as practiced by Middle Eastern Muslims. Like Islam everywhere else, Islam in the Middle East certainly is not uniformly practiced. However, Islamists seek out like-minded Muslims and participate in an international network that has a very public profile, financial backing, and organization.

Muslims all over the world have looked to the Middle East for Islamic authenticity. Many Muslims see geographical proximity to the Middle East as evidence of religious authenticity and authority. During the 1800s, Shah Wali Allah sought a reform of Islamic practice on the subcontinent that removed regional differences but simultaneously made it more culturally like Middle Eastern Islam. Though his vision was not as strict as that of Wahhab, Shah Wali Allah still advocated a practice of Islam that was universal and not in any way distinctively Indian. Many more recent examples exist of individuals who consider legitimate only Middle East forms of Islam. As the introduction discusses, Muhammad Ali Jinnah stated in 1948 that Urdu "embodies the best that is in Islamic culture and Muslim tradition and is nearest to the languages used in other Islamic countries."[1] Even modernist Muslims such as Jinnah are sensitive to the notion of cultural hierarchy, and he is not unique. Many South Asians tend to equate authentic practice with geographical proximity to the Middle East.

Parallel and intersecting cultural tensions leave Bengali Muslims in a cultural bind. Bangladeshis today struggle between the desires to be Bengali and to be true Muslims. To pronounce oneself a Bengali is not to acknowledge being part of the larger Islamic world. People of this region have had to choose between being Muslims who reside in Bengal or being Bengali Muslims. The Islamists, a vocal minority, do not accommodate the existence of this tension, refusing to recognize the profound attachment to region and language. The Bangladeshi government wants to exude a culture that connects the nation with the Middle East, not with the non-Muslim Bengalis of South Asia. Inscribed in large Arabic script at the entrance to the Dhaka Cantonment are the words "Allah" and "Muhammad." In fact, a visitor to Bangladesh will see these words inscribed on buses, baby taxis, and rickshaws all over the country. Yet there also is a Bengali linguistic/cultural nostalgia. Love of the Bengali language runs deep in the hearts of Bengalis, who honor their language with great pomp and circumstance every February. Some Bangladeshis would even suggest that they have more in common with Bengalis across the border in India than they do with Muslims in Afghanistan. There is a sentiment of regret among Bengalis on both sides of the border over the question of the partition of Bengal that haunts many Bengalis today, with Hindus of Calcutta, for example, proudly proclaiming roots in Bangladesh.

The publication of the Qur'an and its commentary in Bengali was crucial because it fully affirmed a Bengali-informed Islam. The introduction of this literature led Bengali Muslims to read the Qur'an in their native language. It did not lead to a reformation in the manner of Martin Luther's, with the common person interpreting the Qur'an for himself or herself. However, it did affirm that the meaning of the Qur'an was largely accessible to native Bengalis in their own language and that being Muslim does not necessitate a denial of Bengaliness. The publication of the Qur'an in Bengali constituted a recognition that one need not be culturally illiterate in Islam if one had the ability to read about it. Significantly, the reverse is also true. One need not be culturally illiterate in Bengali culture to be a good Muslim, and this realization represented a breakthrough issue for secular Bengali Muslims. The desire for a secular government arose from the need to express Muslimness without having to turn one's back on Bengaliness.

In the final analysis, there is no such thing as a truly neutral Islam uninformed by local culture, be it Persianate, Meccan, Indonesian, or South Asian. I am not suggesting a divide between great and little traditions. Rather, there is only one Islam, and the diversity of practice lies in regional interpretation that exists in constant tension with universal visions of Islam that have the power and funding to assert themselves even though their numbers are relatively small. The overwhelming majority of Bangladeshis likely will continue to resist the imposition of an Islamist vision. A rich Bengali Islamic heritage exists in Bangladesh and will not easily be surrendered. This heritage is supported from the grassroots and thrives despite Islamists' efforts to reform it. Future research may determine to what extent these tensions will abound in other Muslim countries. Will religious nationalism take root in Bosnia and the former Soviet republics where there are Muslim majorities? It is possible, even likely that in Muslim countries all over the world, political Islamists and especially extremists will make their presence known and consequently will make secular nationalism more unstable. Globalization is indeed the great asset of Islamists and especially extremists.

Nations with Muslim majorities will have to contend with these issues for the foreseeable future. For example, while many of the former Soviet Republics—Azerbaijan, Uzbekistan, Tajikistan, Turkmenistan—build their young nations, they must determine the place of Islam in society. Though they may identify with Islam, they must continually ask what role it should play in public life. Should Islam inform the way government functions? To what extent will laws reflect an Islamic understanding? What ultimately determines whether Islam plays a role in public life and the nature of that role is the extent to which external and internal Islamists or even extremists influence government.

Appendix

BENGALI TRANSLATIONS OF THE QURʾAN AND TAFSIRS

1. William Goldsack. *Korān.* Calcutta, 1908–20. A translation by a missionary of the Serampore Mission in Bengal.
2. Maulana Abbas Ali. *Korān bāṅgla anubād.* Calcutta, 1909.
3. Maulavi Taslimuddin Ahmed Khan Bahadur. *Āmpārā.* Calcutta, 1909.
4. Abul Faisul Abdul Karim. *Korān śariph.* Mymensingh, 1914.
5. Abul Hayat Abdul Karim. *Korān śariph.* Calcutta, 1914.
6. Karim Baksh. *Korān śariph.* Calcutta, 1916.
7. Maulana Muhammad Ruhul Amin. *Korān śariph-āmpārā.* Calcutta, 1918.
8. Maulana Muhammad Akram Khan. *Korān śariph-āmpārā.* Calcutta, 1922. A complete edition was done in 1929 and Dhaka, 1956.
9. Taslimuddin Ahmad. *Korān.* Calcutta, 1922.
10. Sheikh Idris Ahmad. *Korāner mahā śikkha.* Malda, 1923, 1927.
11. Maulavi Iyar Ahmad. *Āmpārār korāner bāṅgla taphchīr.* Calcutta, 1923.
12. Muhammad Fazel Mukimi. *Korāner bāṅgla tarjamā.* Calcutta, 1924.
13. Taslimuddin Ahmad. *Korān.* Calcutta, 1925.
14. Shah Muhammad Abdul Majid. *Śamsul korān.* Comilla, 1926.
15. Maulana Muhammad Rahul Amin. *Korān śariph.* Calcutta, 1926–27.
16. Abdur Rashid Siddiqi. *Mahā korān kābba.* Paddanubad, 1927.
17. Abul Faisul Abdul Karim. *Baṅganubād korān śariph.* 1928.
18. Abul Fadl Abdul Karim Bin Sahib Ali. *Korān śariph.* Calcutta, 1930.
19. Muhammad Abdul Hakim and Muhammad Ali Hasan. *Korān śariph.* Calcutta, 1931.
20. Muhammad Aziz Hindi. *Korān śariph.* Noakhali, 1931.
21. Muhammad Gulam Akbar. *Taphsīr āmpārā.* 1931.
22. Haji Ali. *Korān kanikā.* 1931. A poetic translation of some of the shorter suras.
23. Khondakar Abul Faisal Abdul Karim. *Korān śariph pārā ām.* Calcutta, 1931. A poetic translation.
24. Kājī Najrul Islām. *Kābbe āmpārā.* Calcutta, 1932.
25. A. Bethik. *Korān śariph-pārā ām.* Calcutta, 1933.
26. Muhammad Abu Bakr. *Baṅganubād āmpārā.* Calcutta, 1934.

27. Maulana Muhammad Anisur Rahman. *Surā āl āshar er ban.ganubād o bistārita taphsīr.* Calcutta, 1934.

28. Muhammad Ajhāruddīn. *Korāner ālo.* 1935.

29. Bashanto Kumār Mukhopāẏ. *Pabitra korān prabeś.* Calcutta, 1937.

30. Āl-Hāj Muhammad Nakībuddīn Khān. *Korān majid.* Calcutta, 1938.

31. Māulānā Phajlul Karim Ānoẏārī. *Ummul korān.* Dhaka, 1938.

32. Abul Faisal Muhammad Abdul Karim. *Āl korān.* Calcutta, 1938.

33. Muhammad Taimur. *Korān—pārā ām.* 1939.

34. Shaiẏed Muhammad Ishhāk. *Āmpārā-banganubād.* 1965.

35. Maulabhī Mohammad Śāmchul Hudā. *Neẏāmul korān.* Calcutta, 1940. A Bengali translation of various suras.

36. Begam Nūr Mahal. *Korān mukul.* Chittagong, 1941.

37. Māulānā Muhammad Śahīdullāh. *Mahābānī.* A Bengali translation of from suras *al-Fatiḥa to al-Fīl.* Dhaka, 1940–42.

38. Māulānā Mahīul Islām, A. B. M. Moslehuddīn, Ābdul Mujid, Mohammad Nurul Hak, Mohammad Śahīdullāh, Saiẏed Mīnul Hak, and Saiẏed Āśrāph Hosen. A Bengali translation with commentary in a monthly journal, *Taphsīrul korān.* Calcutta, 1941–88.

39. Maulabhī Nurul Islam. *Korān majider saral bāṅgla tarjamā o taphsīr.* Rajshahi, 1943.

40. Muphāt Mohāmmad Oẏāphī. *Āmpārār taphsīr.* Dhaka, 1945.

41. Muhāmmad Kudarat-I-Khudā. *Pabitra korāner pūt kathā.* Calcutta, 1945.

42. Molabhī Manīruddīn Āhmad. *Taphsīr hāphijil kāderī.* Rangpur, 1947.

43. Mohāmmad Osmān Gani. *Pabitra korān śarīph.* Calcutta, 1947.

44. Molānā Mohāmmad Raphikūl Hāsān. *Banganubād korān śarīph.* 24 Parganā, 1948.

45. Khān Bāhādur Ābdur Rahmān Khāṅ. *Pāṅch sūrā śarīph.* A Bengali translation of and commentary on five suras. Dhaka, 1948.

46. Muhāmmad Ābdul Kādir. *Kābbe korān.* Dhaka, 1948.

47. Māulānā Nūrūr Rahmān. *Taphsīre āśrāphī.* Dhaka, 1949.

48. Khān Bāhādur Āhsānullāh. *Banganubād pāṅch sūrā.* Dhaka, 1949.

49. Ābul Phajal. *Kurāner bānī.* Dhaka, 1949.

50. Monāoẏār Ālī. *Bamla āmpārā.* Sylhet, 1950.

51. Khān Bāhādur Ābdur Rahmān Khāṅ. *Āmpārā.* Dhaka, 1950.

52. Khān Bāhādur Ālhājj Ābdur Rahmān Khān. *Korān śariph.* Dhaka, 1952.

53. Molānā S. M. Ābdul Hāmid. *Sahaj āmpārā.* Rajshahi, 1953.

54. Golām Mostaphā. *Āl-korān.* Dhaka, 1957.

55. Muslim Ālī. *Kābbe āmpārā.* Rajshahi, 1957.

56. Muhāmmad Ābdur Rahim. *Surā phātehār taphsīr.* Dhaka, 1958.

57. Śāh Muhāmmad Siddik and Māolānā Ābduś Śukur Phārukī. *Taphsīre nesāriẏā.* East Pakistan, 1958.

58. Māolānā Ābdur Rahim. *Tāphhīmul korān.* Dhaka, 1958.

59. Muhāmmad Hāsān Ālī āl-Ālābhī. *Kābbe korān*. Dhaka, 1958.

60. Māolānā Mohāmmad Raphikul Hāsān. *Korān śarīph*. Calcutta, 1960.

61. Hāphej Āljijul Islām. *Pānje surār bangānubād*. Dhaka, 1960.

62. Māolānā Māhphujur Rahmān. *Bangānubād pānje surā majamuẏā ojiphā*. Chittagong, 1960.

63. Adha"pak Ākhtār Phāruk. *Ummul kurān*. Dhaka, 1961.

64. Māolānā Śāmsul Hak. *Hākkānī taphsīr*. 1961.

65. Molānā Ābdur Rahmān. *Korān o jīban darśan*. Chittagong, 1961.

66. Māolānā Mohāmmad Raphikul Hāsān. *Korān śarīph*. Calcutta, 1962.

67. Molbhī Ābdur Rahmān. *Korān śarīph—āmpārā*. Dhaka, 1962.

68. Ābul Hāśim. *Surā phātehār byākhyā*. Dhaka, 1962.

69. Khondkār Muhāmmadd Hosen. *Pāk sahaj tāphsīr*. 1962.

70. Māolānā Māhamudur Rahmān. *Tāphsīre surā iẏāsin*. Dhaka, 1963.

71. Muphtī Dīn Mohāmmad Khān. *Surā iusuph*. Dhaka, 1963.

72. Māolānā Mohāmmad Ālāuddīn Āl-Āyhārī. *Tāphsīre āl-āyhārī*. Dhaka, 1963.

73. Saiẏed Ābdur Rahmān. *Eḍbhans pepār in erābik*. Calcutta, 1964.

74. Śekh Māolā Bakhś. *Bāṃlāẏ āmpārā o kayekṭi surā*. Dhaka, 1964.

75. Muhāmmad Śāhidullāh. *Telāoẏāte kurān*. Dhaka, 1964.

76. Muhāmmad Ābdullāhil Kāphī āl-kurāẏśī. *Ummul kurān*. 1965.

77. Ācārya Binobābhābe. *Korān sār*. Calcutta, 1965.

78. Muhāmmad Ābdul Jabbār Siddikī. *Kurān kanikā*. Pabna, 1966.

79. Śāmsul Ulāmā Belāẏet Hosen. *Kurānul karīm-āmpārā*. Dhaka, 1966.

80. Māolānā Śāmsul Hak. *Pānje surār bangānubād*. Dhaka, 1966.

81. Kājī Ābdul Odud. *Pabitra korān*. Calcutta, 1966.

82. Śāmsul Ulāmā Belāẏet Hosen. *Āl-kurānul karīm*. Dhaka, 1967.

83. Ālī Hāẏdār Caudhurī. *Korān śariph*. Dhaka, 1967.

84. Hākim Ābdul Mānnān. *Pabitra korān-bāngla tarjamā*. Dhaka, 1967.

85. Māolānā Mīr Ābdus Sālām. *Mānab diśārī kurān majid*. Dhaka, 1968.

86. Māolānā Mohāmmad Sāīd Ibrāhimpurī. *Kurāner muktāhār*. Dhaka, 1968.

87. Māolānā Nūruddīn Āhmad. *Bāṃlā āmpārā*. Dhaka, 1968.

88. Mohāmmad Ābdul Bāri. *Kābye korān pāk*. Faridpur, 1969.

89. Māolānā Śāh Kāmrujjāmān. *Kholāshatul kurān*. Dhaka, 1969.

90. Muhammad Śahīdullāh. *Kurān prashanga*. Dhaka, 1970.

91. Molānā Mohāmmad Tāher. *Āl-kurān-tarjamā o taphshīr*. Calcutta, 1970.

92. Mailabhī Ābdur Rahmān. *Kāb'e korān pāk*. Chittagong, 1970.

93. Mohāmmad Chānāullāh. *Āmmā pārār taphshīr*. Calcutta, 1970.

94. Mohāmmad Śāhādāṭ Hochen. *Taphshīr hochāẏen*. Calcutta, 1970.

95. Māolānā Shaiẏed Āhmādullāh. *Āmpārār taphshīr*. Calcutta, 1970.

96. Śekh Ābdul Oẏāhed. *Korān śariph*. Calcutta, 1971.

97. Ānishur Rahmān. *Surā phātehār bishtārita taphshīr*. 1972.

98. Hāphey Śekh Āẏnul Bārī. *Ālkurānul hākim*. Calcutta, 1972.

99. Mohāmmad Śahīdullāh. *Āmmā pārār taphshīr*. Calcutta, 1974.

100. Mobārak Karīm Johar. *Korān śarīph.* Calcutta, 1974.
101. Māolānā Śāh Oÿālīullāh. *Pānj-surā o munājāte makbul.* Calcutta, 1975.
102. Oshmān Ganī. *Korān śarīph.* Calcutta, 1976.
103. Māolānā Muhiuddīn Khān. *Taphshīre māʿārephul-korān.* Dhaka, 1980.
104. Māolānā Muhāmmad Ābdur Rahim. *Āl-kurāner āloke unnat jībaner ādarś.* Dhaka, 1980.
105. Hāphey Śekh Āÿnul Bārī. *Taphshīre āinī.* Calcutta, 1981.
106. Ābdul Ājij Āl-Āmān. *B'bhārik jībane āl-kurān.* Calcutta, 1982.
107. Māolānā Mohāmmad Raphikul Hāshān, Māolānā Mohāmmad Śahīdullāh, Māolānā Śāÿkh Mājhārul Ishlām, Māolānā Shaiÿed Mīnul Hak, and Shaphi Lāÿek. *Pabitra korāner śāśta bānī.* Calcutta, 1983.
108. Molānā Kāyī Ābu Shāleh Śāmshul Ālam. *Surā phātehā.* Howrah, 1983.
109. Māolānā Ābdul Mānnān. *Āśrāphul kurān.* Chittagong, 1984.
110. Muhāmmad Mujībur Rahman. *Taphshīr ibne kāshīr.* Rajshahi, 1984.
111. Āhmad Śāmshul Ishlām. *Naitik charitra gaṭane kurāner śikkhā.* Dhaka, 1985.
112. Māolānā Kāji Khalilur Rahmān. *Pabitra korāner sharal bangānubād.* Calcutta.

Notes

INTRODUCTION

1. Jinnah as cited in Chakrabartī, *Bhāshā āndolaner dalilpatra*, 48.
2. Ibid.
3. See Partha Chatterjee, *Nation and Its Fragments*; Veer, *Religious Nationalism*; Veer, *Imperial Encounters*.
4. Sells, "Erasing Culture."
5. Asad, "Idea," 15.
6. Veer, *Imperial Encounters*, 9.
7. Asad, *Formations*, 1–17.
8. Veer, *Religious Nationalism*, 14–15.
9. Partha Chatterjee, "On Religious and Linguistic Nationalisms," 113.
10. Kakar, *Colors of Violence*, 186–87.
11. Asad, "Religion, Nation-State, Secularism," 191.
12. Huntington, *Clash*; Barber, *Jihad vs. McWorld*.

CHAPTER ONE

1. Stewart, "In Search of Equivalence," 286.
2. In 1599, eighty British merchants formed the East India Company. British parliamentary supervision of the company began with the Regulating Act of 1773.
3. Raja Ganesh's son's ascension was possible only after he converted to Islam and commenced religious studies under the tutelage of a famous and politically influential Chisti saint, Shaikh Nur Qutbi Alam.
4. Tarafdar, *Husain Shahi Bengal*, 34–35.
5. Ibid., 64.
6. Ibid., 72–77.
7. Ernst, *Eternal Garden*, 156.
8. Ibid., 156.
9. During the period of the early Arab conquests (632–945 C.E.) Muslim rulers also demonstrated no interest in converting Jews, Christians, and Zoroastrians to Islam, partly because the taxes collected from these groups were the main financial avenue for the support of military troops. See Lapidus, *History of Islamic Societies*, 43.

10. Eaton, *Rise of Islam*, 200.

11. Ibid., 19, 21.

12. Ibid., 195.

13. The title *ta'alluqdar* is given to one in possession of a *ta'alluq*, a portion of a revenue unit usually at the level between the *zamīndār* and the peasants.

14. Eaton, *Rise of Islam*, 223.

15. Akhtar, *Role*, 51, citing J. Shore's minute, April 1788, quoted in W. K. Firminger, ed., *The Fifth Report . . .* I, xlvii.

16. *Chaudhuri* and *ta'alluqdar* are titles common to both Muslims and Hindus of the landholding aristocracies. All the other titles are Muslim. *Shaikh* denotes a member of the *'ulama'*, while *khwāndkār* is a Persian title for Qur'an reciter. *Hājjis* are those who have performed pilgrimage. A *saiyid* claims descent from the Prophet, and the remaining titles simply indicate "holy man."

17. Stewart, "In Search of Equivalence," 261.

18. Eaton, *Rise of Islam*, 102–12.

19. Anisuzzaman, "Many Identities, Some Emphases," 156.

20. For a discussion of *ashraf*/non-*ashraf* class distinctions, see Rafiuddin Ahmed, *Bengal Muslims*, 5–21.

21. See Eaton, *Rise of Islam*, 100 n.21.

22. Ibid., 101.

23. Dimock, *Sound of Silent Guns*, 121–22.

24. Schimmel, *Islamic Literatures*, 2.

25. Ibid., 6.

26. Ibid., 1.

27. Ibid., 21.

28. Tarafdar, *Husain Shahi Bengal*, 264.

29. Eaton, *Rise of Islam*, 38, as quoted in Shamsuddin Ahmed, *Inscriptions*, 4:20.

30. Schimmel, *Islamic Literatures*, 21.

31. Subhan, "Arabic, Persian, and Urdu Literatures," 435.

32. Schimmel, *Islamic Literatures*, 4.

33. The *qadam rasul* in Gaur is believed to bear the Prophet's footprint.

34. Subhan, "Arabic, Persian, and Urdu Literatures," 434.

35. Hak, *Madh"yuger banglai muslim nitiśāstra katha*, 52.

36. Tarafdar, *Husain Shahi Bengal*, 267.

37. Eaton, *Rise of Islam*, 66. Increased usage of Bengali demonstrates that a clear boundary line no longer existed between *ashraf* and non-*ashraf*.

38. Ibid., 66.

39. There is no proof of a direct connection between rice cultivation and the growth of this literature. To establish such a connection definitively would be beyond the scope of this work and would require a detailed study of these early manuscripts.

40. Hak, *Madh"yuger banglai muslim nitiśāstra katha*, 53–85.

41. Many of these titles are quite common to multiple authors; therefore, I have not listed their names.

42. The most famous *Amir Hamza* was written in the eighteenth century jointly by Garibullah and Syed Hamza on the basis of an anonymous Urdu book.

43. Hak, *Madh"yuger banglai muslim nitiśāstra katha*, 169.

44. Rafiuddin Ahmed, *Bengal Muslims*, 86.

45. Ernst, *Shambhala Guide*, 178.

46. Hak, *Madh"yuger banglai muslim nitiśāstra katha*, 158–63.

47. Husain, *Descriptive Catalogue*, provides numerous descriptions of manuscripts from the fifteenth through the nineteenth century. Many of these manuscripts utilize these Sanskrit terms.

48. See Roy, *Islamic Syncretistic Tradition*.

49. Stewart, "In Search of Equivalence," 263.

50. Ibid., 276–77.

51. Ibid., 264.

52. Hak, *Madh"yuger banglai muslim nitiśāstra katha*, 28–91.

53. Ibid., 105–7. Unless noted otherwise, translations are my own.

54. *Mahājan*, *aparādh*, and *prabhu* are Sanskrit *tatsamas* (direct loan words), while *ekmane* is a Sanskrit *tadbhava* (a Bengali term derived from Sanskrit).

55. Hak, *Madh"yuger banglai muslim nitiśāstra katha*, 108.

56. Stewart, "Language of Equivalence," 384.

57. Ibid., 384–89.

58. Rafiuddin Ahmed, *Bengal Muslims*, 86.

59. See Eaton, *Rise of Islam*, 215–19, for a full description of the story.

60. Munshi Abdul Karim and Ahmad Sharif, *Descriptive Catalogue of Bengali Manuscripts in Munshi Abdul Karim's Collection* (Dhaka: Asiatic Society of Pakistan, 1960), 452.

61. Ibid.

62. Ibid., 91.

63. Hak, *Madh"yuger banglai muslim nitiśāstra katha*, 62–63.

64. Ibid., 65.

CHAPTER TWO

1. See Levtzion and Voll, *Eighteenth-Century Renewal and Reform*, 13.

2. In this early period, ʿAbd al-Wahhab did not wield the same influence as Shah Wali Allah; later in the nineteenth century, reformers were accused of being Wahhabis. This point will be explained in further detail later in this chapter.

3. Many eighteenth-century reform-minded scholars studied hadith and *tasawwuf* in religious centers such as the Haramayn, Damascus, Cairo, and Zabid in Yemen and then returned to their homelands to teach.

4. See Hermansen, *Conclusive Argument*, xxvi, for information on the importance of hadith studies. See Muhammad Akram Khan, "Back to the Qurʾan," 335.

5. The greatest expansion of the Mughal Empire occurred under the leadership of the Mughal emperor Aurangzeb (r. 1658–1707). He is also remembered for

contributing to its decline. He fought incessantly for its expansion but did so at the expense of a weakened empire. By 1724 the Deccan became effectively independent. The Mughals lost their hold on Kabul in 1739, Sind and Gujarat by 1750, Oudh and Punjab by 1754. In 1757 Delhi was sacked by Ahmad Shah Abdali, an Afghan.

6. Schimmel, *Islam*, 159.

7. In the seventh century, Husayn, a grandson of the Prophet Muhammad, was brutally murdered by the Umayyads at the Battle of Karbala for refusing to give the oath of allegiance to the Caliph Yazid ibn Mu'awiya. Annually, on the tenth of the Islamic month of Muharram, Shi'ite Muslims commemorate Husayn's martyrdom with prayer, elaborate processions of men performing self-flagellation, and reenactments of the battle of Karbala known as a *ta'ziya*.

8. In the sixteenth and seventeenth centuries, Shi'i influences became more prominent in Bengal. This trend was partly affected by the Persian traders who settled there, most of whom were Shi'i. Tarafdar states that particularly in the seventeenth century, a large influx of Persian Shi'i traders into Bengal occurred, some of them seeking refuge from Safavid rule in Persia. An example of epigraphic evidence for such Shi'i influence is an inscription of Sayf al-Din Abū'l-Muẓaffar Firuz Shah (1487–90), which names Muhammad, 'Ali, Fatima, Hasan, and Husayn. In Shi'i Islam, these five figures are known as the Panjetan Pak, or the five holy ones. Further reinforcing the notion that this is a Shi'i-influenced inscription is the fact that the first three caliphs are not mentioned. Shi'i influence is also evident in medieval Bengali literature: for example, Muslim characters who battle the snake goddess Manasā in Hindu epic poems known as Manasā Mangals are named Hasan and Husayn, the locality in which Muslims live is called Husainhāti, and a Muslim place of worship is a Hasanbāti. In addition, *marsiās*, or elegies, which began to be written in Bengal in the seventeenth century, are also a result of Shi'i influence. According to Ennamul Haq, Shaikh Faizullah's *Jaināler cautiśa* is the earliest example of this genre, possibly composed in the fifteenth century. Other *marsiās* titles include *Maqtul husain* by Muhammad Khan, *Karbala* by Abdul Hakim, *Maqtul husain* or *Janganama* by Garibullah and Yakub, and *Muharram parva* by Hayat Mahmud. During the month of Muharram, these stories were often recited in the homes of Muslims in the port city of Chittagong. See Schimmel, *Islam*, 47–50, on Shi'i influence; Tarafdar, *Husain Shahi Bengal*, 165–69, on literary and epigraphical sources. See also Haq, *Muslim Bengali Literature*, on literary sources of Shi'i influence.

9. The term *tariqa* denotes the Sufi way or path. After the thirteenth century, the term referred specifically to Sufi orders or brotherhoods. Sufi orders are distinguishable by their practices as well as their schools of thought. Each order has a common spiritual teacher to whom the members of the order trace their lineage. The Naqshbandiyya are named for Baha' al-Din Naqshband (d. 1389) of Bukhara, who emphasized silent *dhikr*, and the Qadiriyya are named for 'Abd al-

Qadir al-Jilani (d. 1165), a Hanbali jurist and preacher of Baghdad. See Baldick, *Mystical Islam*.

10. For a discussion of *taqlid*, see Hermansen, *Conclusive Argument*, xxix–xxxiii. *Taqlid* is an Arabic term that means "imitation." When used in legal terminology it refers to adherence to the legal rulings of one of the four Sunni schools of law. One who practices *taqlid* is one who abides by the rulings of one particular school of law on all matters.

11. *Ijtihad* is a legal technical term that refers to one method employed by a legal scholar to arrive at a legal ruling by way of reasoning through analogy. See Schacht, "Idjtihād."

12. Hermansen, *Conclusive Argument*, xxxii.

13. *Bāhās* and *munāẓara* are oral theological debates. The term *bāhās*, however, was used more widely in Bengal and is derived from the Arabic verb *baḥatha*, meaning "study," "examination," or "inquiry."

14. Both movements are treated later in the chapter.

15. Schimmel, *Islam*, 159.

16. The term "Hinduism" first arose in the early nineteenth century, derived from the Persian term "al-Hind" to refer to the region and "Hindu" to denote the people of that region. The term and what it represents in large part were constructed by the British in their efforts to identify a unified system of beliefs among the "heathens" of India. This conception of Hinduism was based primarily on the model of Brahmanical forms as the British scholars relied on Brahmans for advancing this Western conception of diverse indigenous practices. Richard King makes the point that the agency of Brahmans in the formulation of "Hinduism" should not be overshadowed by the endeavors initiated by Orientalist scholars. See King, *Orientalism and Religion*, 101.

17. See Ludden, "Orientalist Empiricism," 250–78.

18. Appadurai, *Modernity at Large*, 117.

19. Ibid., 126.

20. Jones, "Religious Identity," 80.

21. Hardy, *Muslims*, 67–68.

22. In 1616 Denmark had set up the Danish East India Company with settlements in Ceylon and Tranquebar on the Coromandel Coast. Missionaries came to these settlements at the request of the Danish king, Frederick IV, in 1705 to see to the religious well-being of Danish people. These Royal Danish Missionaries later extended their mission to include the conversion of local people. In 1755 the Serampore settlement on the Hoogly River north of Calcutta was established. At Carey's request, he was joined in Serampore by Ward, Fountain, Brunslow, and Marshman.

23. See De, *Bengali Literature*, 85–143.

24. Smalley, *Translation as Mission*, 45.

25. See Long, *Descriptive Catalogue*.

26. Some publications that James Long, in his descriptive catalog of books printed in the 1800s in Bengali, identified as "those Tracts, which are best adapted for general circulation among the Heathen and Musalman population of the country" include *The Great Atonement* (1837), *The Essence of the Bible* (1830), *The True, a Conversation between Rambari and Sadhu* (1830), *Hindu Objections Refuted* (1853), *The Voice of the Bible Concerning Idolatry* (1828), *Letters on Christianity and Hinduism* (1828), *Miracles of Christ* (1828), *Reasons for Not Being a Musalman* (1828), and *Muhammadan Ceremonies* (1828). He also included a listing of tracts directed to a "Native Christian" audience, such as *The Duty of Christians to Seek the Salvation of the Heathen* (1844) (Long, *Descriptive Catalogue*, 702–20). Books of this period include G. Mundy, *Christianity and Hinduism Contrasted* (1828) and Wilson, *The Hindu Religion* (1852), which Long notes "points out the bad character of the different Hindu gods, the Christian and Hindu incarnations contrasted, test of idolatry and need of revelation" (715). See also Karim and Sharif, *Descriptive Catalogue*, 458.
27. Sunil Kumar Chatterjee, "Serampore Missionaries," 125.
28. Potts, "Baptist Missionaries," 238.
29. The world, according to Muslims, is divided between *dar al-harb* and *dar al-islam*. *Dar al-harb* is the part of the world not under Islamic rule, while *dar al-islam* represents the part of the world inhabited by Muslims and governed by Islamic law.
30. Maitra, *Muslim Politics*, 32.
31. Rafiuddin Ahmed, *Bengal Muslims*, 42.
32. Hardy, *Muslims*, 58.
33. Rafiuddin Ahmed, *Bengal Muslims*, 42.
34. Hardy, *Muslims*, 53.
35. As is discussed later in the chapter, the designation "Wahhabi" used in India had negative connotations and had little to do with the reform efforts of Abdul Wahhab of Saudi Arabia.
36. "Karāmat 'Ali-," 217–18; Hardy, *Muslims*, 110–12.
37. Hardy, *Muslims*, 172.
38. Cole, "Sacred Space," 185.
39. Hardy, *Muslims*, 171.
40. Sanyal, "Are Wahhābis Kafirs?," 208.
41. During the nineteenth century in India, being called a Wahhabi, regardless of the validity of such a designation, was politically damaging to the accused. See Metcalf, *Islamic Revival*.
42. Sanyal, *Devotional Islam*, 236.
43. Sanyal, "Are Wahhābis Kafirs?," 210–11.
44. Sanyal, *Devotional Islam*, 237.
45. Metcalf, "Two Fatwas," 278.
46. Sanyal, *Devotional Islam*, 241. "Muwahhidun" is the self-chosen name of the followers of 'Abd al-Wahhab.

55. Wagner, "Munāẓara."

56. Sanyal, "Are Wahhābis Kafirs?," 205.

57. Many on the subcontinent affirmed that if a region is designated as *dar al-harb*, then *jumʿa* and *ʿid* prayers cannot be conducted in those areas. Until the close of the nineteenth century in much of Bengal, *jumʿa* and *ʿid* prayers were halted for this reason.

58. Sarkar, *Islam in Bengal*, 74.

59. Nevertheless, riots occasionally broke out at the close of these events, compelling the government to preclude particular *bāhās* from taking place, as reported in Bengali journals such as the *Mohāmmadi* (Rafiuddin Ahmed, *Bengal Muslims*, 81).

60. Ibid., 80.

61. Ibid., 100–104.

62. Anderson, *Imagined Communities*, 40.

63. Veer, *Religious Nationalism*, 78.

64. Ibid., 79.

65. Robinson, "Technology and Religious Change," 231.

66. Ibid., 234.

67. Ibid.

68. Ibid., 239.

69. Appadurai, *Modernity at Large*, 131.

70. Sweetman, "Unity and Plurality," 209–24.

71. As early as the 1730s, Muslims in Istanbul utilized the printing press (Robinson, "Technology and Religious Change," 233).

72. The term "reform" is how many of these thinkers saw what they did. However, it is used with reservations. Richard King, *Orientalism and Religion*, 86–95, persuasively argues that to call these movements reform movements implies the existence of a premodern form of "Hinduism" that they are modifying in some way, which then contradicts the idea of "Hinduism" being constructed in the nineteenth century. Perhaps more appropriately, they were actually reforming the idea of a precolonial Hinduism.

73. Metcalf, *Islamic Revival*, 203.

74. Schimmel, *Islamic Literatures*, 51.

75. Rafiuddin Ahmed, *Bengal Muslims*, 82.

76. The better-educated mullahs also contributed to this reform effort by writing *nasīhat nāmās*.

77. Rafiuddin Ahmed, *Bengal Muslims*, 85.

78. Ibid., 85–86.

79. Stewart, "Language of Equivalence."

80. Rafiuddin Ahmed uses the term "Musalmani Bengali," while Enamul Haq refers to "Dobhāṣī Bangla."

81. Rafiuddin Ahmed, *Bengal Muslims*, 93.

82. Goldsack, *Mussalmani Bengali–English Dictionary*, i.

83. *Kalema* is an Arabic term that literally means "word" and here refers to the recitation of the *shahada*, or the Muslim creed. *Namaz* is a Persian term for the Islamic five daily prayers, or *salat*. *Roza* is the Persian term for the obligatory fast, or *sawm*, of the month of Ramadan. *Zakat* is the Arabic term that refers to almsgiving. *Bait al-ka'ba* is the holy shrine in Mecca toward which Muslims pray. Finally, *kitab* is the Arabic term for "book" and here refers specifically to the Qur'an.

84. Anisuzzaman, *Muslim banglar samayikpatra*, 10.

85. Ibid., 15.

86. Ibid., 3.

87. See journals such as *Islam prachrak*, *Hedāyat islām*, *Ākhbār-e-eslāmiyā*, *Hāphej*, and *Sunnata al-jāmāta* for critiques of Bengali Islamic literature in the nineteenth century.

88. Metcalf, "Two Fatwas," 191; see also Anderson, *Imagined Communities*.

CHAPTER THREE

1. Some of the most widely available Urdu translations and commentary on the Qur'an were those by Shah 'Abd al-Qadir and Rafi' al-Din, both sons of Shah Wali Allah. Both also wrote works in Urdu on the Wahhabi controversy, the right of independent judgment, and religious duties.

2. Metcalf, *Islamic Revival*, 204.

3. Ibid., 203.

4. Naīmuddīn refers to an "audience who reads Bengali," not to Bengali Muslims, because in the nineteenth century Muslims identified themselves as Muslims rather than Bengalis. To identify oneself as Bengali was to admit indigenous ancestry or Hindu religious identity.

5. Whether his ancestors were from Baghdad cannot be determined. The result in any case is that having origins in Baghdad gives the author Arab heritage and therefore a great deal of authority in Bengal.

6. Literally, "those without a *madhhab*." This term had derogatory connotations. It was a phrase common in this period and was often used by Naīmuddīn in his attacks on specific Bengali reform movements such as the Tariqah-i-Muhammadiyahs.

7. Kādir, "Mohāmmad Naīmuddīn," 47.

8. Rafiuddin Ahmed, *Bengal Muslims*, 78.

9. One of his most well known fatwas was published in the journal *Ākhabāre islīmīyā*, which he edited.

10. Anisuzzaman, *Muslim banglar samayikpatra*, 5.

11. The Sudhakar group was an association of Muslim writers and intellectuals affiliated with the newspaper *Mihir o sudhakar*.

12. Kopf, *Brahmo Samaj*, 12–13.

13. Ibid., 133.

14. Cited in King, *Orientalism and Religion*, 104.

15. Ibid., 98–108.

16. Kopf, *Brahmo Samaj*, 133.

17. Ibid., 132–35.

18. Sastri, *Atmacarit*, 83. By this time, Girish Chandra Sen had moved to Calcutta and also lived at the ashram as a preacher.

19. Kopf, *Brahmo Samaj*, 268.

20. Keshab Chandra Sen substituted rice and water for the bread and wine of the Christian Eucharist. As Bengalis are not accustomed to drinking wine or eating the bread eaten by the British, Sen believed rice and water would be more meaningful to the Indians. See Kopf, *Brahmo Samaj*, 272–73.

21. Gaur Govinda Ray studied Hindu tradition, Protap Chandra Majumdar studied Christianity, Mohendra Nath Bose studied Sikh tradition, Aghore Nath Gupta studied Buddhist tradition, and Girish Chandra Sen studied Islam.

22. Sen, *Korān śariph*, 582.

23. Ibid., 9.

24. Ibid., 10.

25. Ibid.

26. Sen, *Korān śariph,* relies most heavily on *Tafsir husayni*, with approximately 1,277 references to this work. He makes 403 references to *Tafsir fa'ida*, only 7 to *Tafsir jalālayn*, and only 131 comments are made by Sen.

27. See Hermansen, *Conclusive Argument*, xxxviii.

28. The library of the India Office alone has ten copies of *Tafsir husayni*. See Ethé, *Catalogue*.

29. See Hardy, *Muslims*; Rafiuddin Ahmed, *Muslims of Bengal*; Metcalf, *Islamic Revival*.

30. Hardy, *Muslims*, 51.

31. Blumhardt, *Catalogue*, 4.

32. Gilmartin and Lawrence, *Beyond Turk and Hindu*, 1.

33. A *para* (Persian) or *juz'* (Arabic) is one of the external divisions given by early Islamic scholars to the Qur'an for monthly recitation. The Qur'an is divided into thirty parts or *paras*, one *para* to be read each day of the month, particularly during the holy month of Ramadan.

34. Other similar attempts occurred during the nineteenth century. Some authors even wrote Bengali with the Perso-Arabic script. None of these innovations were well received or lasted very long, and such attempts seem simply to have been ignored.

35. See Qur'an 74:30, "Over It Are Nineteen."

36. *Naīmuddīn, Korān śariph*, 3.

37. Ali, *Holy Qur'ān*, 21.

38. The Majusi (*Majūsī*, Ar.) caste or Magians were identified with the ruling elite of the Sāsānid Iran, where the Zoroastrian religion was the religion of the state. They are mentioned only once in the Qur'an, in sura 22:17. See Marony, "Madjūs."

39. The Sāyebīn (*Ṣābi'īn,* Ar.) are named three times in the Qur'an (2:62, 5:69, and 22:17). The Ṣābi'ūn are considered monotheists and among People of the Book. See "Ṣābi'ūn."

40. *Pir* (teacher) and *murid* (student) are Sufi terms commonly used in the Indian subcontinent. The *pir* (or *murshid*)–*murid* relationship is not limited to the Sufi teacher-student relationship but was highly criticized for the apparent worship of the *pir*. Communion with God was replaced by veneration and worship of the *pir*. The devotee views the *pir* as having special powers, or *baraka*. This *baraka* is passed to the *pir*'s descendants and is transmitted to the saint's tomb. Not only are the *pir* and his descendants worshipped, but so is the tomb of the saint. Around this saint/cult magic, astrology, and charms were introduced for the worshipper to achieve certain goals (Eaton, *Sufis,* xxx–xxxi).

41. Naīmuddīn provides the specific verses that one would need to recite.

42. *Phatuya ālamgiri* is Naīmuddīn's Bengali translation of the famous *Fatawa alamgiri* written at the request of the Mughal ruler Aurangzeb, also known as the Emperor Alamgir (d. 1707). *Fatwa alamgiri* is a compilation of Hanafi legal rulings on numerous subjects.

43. This term generally refers to the odd number of *rakas* said after the *'isha'* prayer.

44. The Rafi-yadayn is an offshoot of the Tariqah-i-Muhammadiyah religious reform movement. Because this group did not admit *taqlid* to any of the four schools of law, Naīmuddīn criticized it.

45. Rafiuddin Ahmed, *Bengal Muslims,* 94.

46. Anderson, *Imagined Communities,* 44.

47. Ibid., 40–42.

48. Metcalf, *Islamic Revival,* 209.

49. Muhammad Akram Khan, "Back to the Qur'an," 335.

50. In the introductions to many Bengali works by Muslims about Islam, the authors expressed their apologies for having no choice but to write about Islam in Bengali, as there were so many Muslims in Bengal who lacked a command of Arabic, Persian, or Urdu.

51. Makdisi, "Ethics."

52. Naīmuddīn, *Koran śariph,* 1–2.

53. Muhammad Shahidullah, principal of the Calcutta Madrassa, interview by author, April 1999.

54. A descriptive term applied to those *tafsir* that rely predominantly on the authority of the community.

CHAPTER FOUR

1. King, *Orientalism and Religion,* 2.

2. Stewart, "In Search of Equivalence"; Stewart, "Language of Equivalence."

3. For a fuller discussion of administration and martial law, see Uddin, "Awami League."

4. East Bengal was renamed East Pakistan in 1955.

5. Hobsbawm and Ranger, *Invention of Tradition*, 5–7.

6. Ibid., 13.

7. Zerubavel, *Recovered Roots*.

8. Jinnah as cited in Chakrabartī, *Bhāshā andolaner dalilpatra*, 48.

9. Sayeed Ahmed, "It Is My Mother's Face," 59.

10. Chowdhury, "Language Movement," 30.

11. Mahmood, *Meet Bangladesh*.

12. van Schendel, "Bengalis, Bangladeshis, and Others," 76.

13. Hobsbawm and Ranger, *Invention of Tradition*, 14.

14. Zerubavel, *Recovered Roots*, 214.

15. Ibid., 10.

16. Murshid, "Twentyfirst February," 24.

17. For a detailed discussion of the subtle changes imposed by the Zia regime, see Kabir, *Changing Face*, 196–202.

18. Ibid., 193.

19. Ibid., 200.

20. For details surrounding the death of Ziaur Rahman, see Baxter, *Bangladesh*, 103.

21. Mills, "Atroshi Urus," 83.

22. In October 2001, the Awami League won only 62 of the 300 seats in the Jatiya Sangsad (National Parliament), while the BNP, which had 191 seats. Prior to the elections, the BNP had set up a coalition with Islamist parties. The BNP's coalition partners—Jama'at-e-Islami, Jatiya Dal-Naziur, and Islami Oikya Jote— won a total of only 24 seats. Never before had any Islamist parties participated in a governing coalition in Bangladesh. Although the Awami League won only 62 seats, it won more of the popular vote than the BNP, whose platform was based on the coalition with the Islamist parties. Though support for the Awami League has waned, it remains the dominant opposition party. The remaining 33 seats are held by women appointed by the elected members.

23. Special supplement, *Independent*, 23 June 2001.

24. *Hartals* have become a symbol of democratic rights, but the strikes occur at the expense of the economy. Sheikh Hasina criticized the BNP for organizing *hartals* during the Awami League's rule, yet Sheikh Hasina and the Awami League have employed the same tactics to disrupt the BNP government.

25. Special supplement, *Independent*, 23 June 2001.

26. "Mujibnagar Day Today," *Daily Star*, 17 April 2002.

27. Ibid.

28. *Daily Star*, 15 February 2002.

29. "Bhorer Kagoj Editor Resigns over Interference in Newspaper Reporting," *Himal*, September 1998.

30. Interview, 14 June 2003.

31. *Himal*, now known as *Himal South Asia*, was founded by Kanak Dixit in 1989.

32. Cited in *Himal*, September 1998.

33. Interview, Dhaka, April 2002.

34. See <www.unicef.org/infobycountry/bangladesh_statistics.html> (accessed 20 November 2005).

35. Ziring, *Bangladesh*, 217.

36. Partha Chatterjee, *Nation and Its Fragments*.

37. Asad, "Religion, Nation-State, Secularism," 180.

38. Metcalf, "New Medinas," 111.

39. See Stewart, "In Search of Equivalence."

40. Uddin, "In the Company of *Pirs*."

41. Ibid.

42. I met with Anwar Chowdhury in July 2001 at his *darbar* in Dhanmondi.

43. Bertil Lintner, "A Cocoon of Terror," *Far Eastern Economic Review*, 4 April 2002.

44. Ruth Baldwin, "The 'Talibanization' of Bangladesh," *The Nation*, 18 May 2002.

45. I find it quite difficult to draw clear distinctions between traditions and invented traditions. Nevertheless, in terms of understanding the traditions associated with nationalism, I would agree with Hobsbawm's claim that the choice of traditions and their employment in novel ways seeks to affirm specific national ideologies. The use of the old (traditions that date prior to the formation of the nation-state) to justify the new (the national ideology) is crucial to naturalize the nation.

46. "National holiday" here specifically refers to those holidays that celebrate nationhood.

47. Clark, "Testing." In the context of medieval monastic life, Clark suggests that repeated rituals evoke emotional and cognitive states beyond the ordinary, quotidian experience.

48. Ludden, *Contesting the Nation*, 5.

CHAPTER FIVE

1. Lawrence, *Defenders of God*.

2. Hopkins et al., *Religions/Globalizations*, 3.

3. Ibid., 4.

4. Veer has shown that in the case of India, the Vishva Hindu Parishad's transnationalism has helped the cause of the Hindu nationalist movement, but other movements adamantly oppose nationalist ideologies (*Religious Nationalism*, 128).

5. Huntington, *Clash*; Barber, *Jihad vs. McWorld*.

6. Barber employs the term "jihad" to refer to all types of fundamentalism; however, his examples are overwhelmingly drawn from Islam, leaving the reader with the dangerous impression that "jihad" refers to religious violence and that nearly all religious violence is conducted by Muslims.

7. Barber, *Jihad vs. McWorld*, 8.

8. Eickelman and Anderson, *New Media*, xi–xiii.

9. Bretthauer, "Televangelism," 205.

10. Ibid., 206.

11. Ibid., 223.

12. Korom, *Hosay Trinidad*, 222.

13. Ibid., 226.

14. Ludden, *Contesting the Nation*, 2.

15. Mumtaz Ahmad, "Islamic Fundamentalism," 518.

16. Gaborieau, "Transformation," 125–26.

17. Ibid., 127–30.

18. Metcalf, "New Medinas," 123.

19. Ibid., 118–19.

20. Prior to the partition of Pakistan, Islamist parties existed, though often in a tenuous relationship with the central government.

21. Asad, "Religion, Nation-State, Secularism," 190.

22. Ibid.

23. Nasr, *Mawdudi*, 110–22. Nasr contends that at times Mawdudi and the Jama'at-i-Islami allied with the *'ulama.* To modernize, the Jama'at-i-Islami needed to become more traditional (124–25).

24. Ibid., 107.

25. <www.jamaat-e-islami.org/about/anintroduction.html> (accessed 29 September 2002). The Jama'at-i-Islami in both Bangladesh and Pakistan maintain informative Web sites.

26. Mumtaz Ahmad, "Islamic Fundamentalism," 491.

27. Ibid., 502.

28. Ibid., 467.

29. <http://www.jamaat-e-islami.org/about/anintroduction.html> (accessed 29 September 2002).

30. Huq, "From Piety to Romance," 132.

31. Rahim, "Bengali Muslims," 240.

32. Rafiuddin Ahmed, "Redefining Muslim Identity," 246.

33. Mumtaz Ahmad, "Islamic Fundamentalism," 503.

34. Rahim, "Bengali Muslims," 248.

35. Ibid., 254.

36. As quoted in Seabrook, *Freedom Unfinished*, 119.

37. <www.jamaat-e-islami.org/about/visioncommitment.html> (accessed 30 June 2003).

38. Mumtaz Ahmad, "Islamic Fundamentalism," 502.

39. Seabrook, *Freedom Unfinished*, 30.

40. "Unending Tragedy: Delhi Must Take up Minority Issue with Dhaka," *Statesman*, 16 November 2001.

41. See <www.refugees.org/data/wrs/03/country_reports/SouthNCentralAsia.pdf> (accessed 20 November 2005).

42. See <www.bbsgov.org/ana_vol1/religiou.htm> (accessed 22 November 2005).

43. B. M. Monoar Kabir, "Islamic Fundamentalism in Bangladesh: Internal Variables

and External Inputs," in *Religion, Nationalism, and Politics,* ed. Rafiuddin
Ahmed, 140–46.

44. Rafiuddin Ahmed, "Redefining Muslim Identity," 693
45. Gardner, *Global Migrants,* 39.
46. Ibid., 4.
47. Kalcik, "Ethnic Foodways," 37.
48. Gardner, *Global Migrants,* 281, 16.
49. Ibid., 229.

EPILOGUE

1. Jinnah as cited in Chakrabartī, *Bhāshā āndolaner dalilpatra,* 48.

Bibliography

Ahmad, Aziz. "Political and Religious Ideas of Shāh Walī-Ullāh of Delhi."
   Muslim World 52 (1962): 22–30.
———. *Islamic Modernism in India and Pakistan, 1857–1964*. London: Oxford
   University Press, 1967.
———. "Islamic Reform Movements." In *A Cultural History of India*, edited by
   A. L. Basham, 383–90. Oxford: Clarendon Press, 1975.
Ahmad, Mumtaz. "Islamic Fundamentalism in South Asia: The Jamaat-i-Islami
   and the Tablighi Jamaat." In *Fundamentalisms Observed*, vol. 1 of *The
   Fundamentalism Project*, edited by Martin E. Marty and R. Scott Appleby,
   457–530. Chicago: University of Chicago Press, 1991.
Ahmed, Rafiuddin. *The Bengal Muslims, 1871–1906: A Quest for Identity*. Delhi:
   Oxford University Press, 1981.
———. "Redefining Muslim Identity in South Asia." In *Accounting for
   Fundamentalisms: The Dynamic Character of Movements*, vol. 4 of *The
   Fundamentalism Project*, edited by Martin E. Marty and R. Scott Appleby,
   669–705. Chicago: University of Chicago Press, 1991.
———, ed. *Religion, Nationalism, and Politics in Bangladesh*. New Delhi: South
   Asian Publishers, 1990.
———, ed. *Understanding the Bengal Muslims: Interpretive Essays*. New Delhi:
   Oxford University Press, 2001.
Ahmed, A. F. Salahuddin. *Bengali Nationalism and the Emergence of Bangladesh:
   An Introductory Outline*. Dhaka, Bangladesh: International Centre for
   Bengal Studies, 2000.
Ahmed, Sayeed. "It Is My Mother's Face." In *Essays on Ekushey, the Language
   Movement, 1952*, edited by Syed Manzoorul Islam, 57–63. Dhaka,
   Bangladesh: Bangla Academy, 1994.
Ahmed, Shamsuddin, ed. and trans. *Inscriptions of Bengal*. Rajshahi, East Pakistan:
   Vavendra Research Museum, 1929.
Ahmed, Sufia. *Muslim Community in Bengal, 1884–1912*. Dhaka, Bangladesh:
   University Press, 1996.
Ahmed Khan, Muin ud-din. *History of the Fara'idi Movement in Bengal (1818–1906)*.
   Karachi: Pakistan Historical Society, 1965.
Ahsan, Syed Ali. *Essays on Bengali Literature*. Karachi: University of Karachi, 1960.

Akhtar, Shirin. *The Role of the Zamīndārs in Bengal, 1707–1772.* Dhaka: Asiatic
　　Society of Bangladesh, 1982.
Ali, A. Yusuf. *The Holy Qur'ān: Text, Translation, and Commentary,* Washington,
　　D.C.: Islamic Center, 1978.
Āmin, Mohammad Ruhul. *Korān śariph.* West Bengal, India: Majediya, 1939.
Anderson, Benedict. *Imagined Communities: Reflections on the Origin and Spread of
　　Nationalism.* New York: Verso, 1991.
Anisuzzaman. *Muslim banglar samiyikapatra (1831–1930).* Dhaka, Bangladesh:
　　Phajale Rabbi, 1969.
―――. *Creativity, Reality, and Identity.* Wiesbaden, Germany: Harrassowitz, 1973.
―――. *Muslim manas o banglā sahitya (1757–1918).* Dhaka, Bangladesh:
　　Cittaranjana Saha, 1983.
―――. "Many Identities, Some Emphases: The Case of Muslims of Bengal down
　　to the Eighteenth Century." In *Essays in Memory of Momtazur Rahman
　　Tarafdar,* edited by Perween Hasan and Mufakharul Islam, 149–69. Dhaka,
　　Bangladesh: Centre for Advanced Research in the Humanities, Dhaka
　　University, 1999.
Appadurai, Arjun. *Modernity at Large: Cultural Dimensions of Globalization.*
　　Minneapolis: University of Minnesota Press, 1996.
Asad, Talal. *The Idea of an Anthropology of Islam.* Washington, D.C.: Georgetown
　　University, 1986.
―――. *Genealogies of Religion: Discipline and Reasons of Power in Christianity and
　　Islam.* Baltimore: Johns Hopkins University Press, 1993.
―――. "Religion, Nation-State, Secularism." In *Religion and Nation,* edited by Peter
　　van der Veer and Hartmut Lehman, 178–96. Princeton: Princeton University
　　Press, 1999.
―――. *Formations of the Secular: Christianity, Islam, Modernity.* Stanford, Calif.:
　　Stanford University Press, 2003.
Azm, Sadik al-. "Islamic Fundamentalism Reconsidered, Part II." *South Asia Bulletin*
　　14 (1994): 73–98.
Baldick, Julian. *Mystical Islam: An Introduction to Sufism.* New York: New York
　　University Press, 1989.
Baljon, J. M. S. *Modern Muslim Koran Interpretation (1880–1960).* Leiden, the
　　Netherlands: Brill, 1961.
―――. *Religion and Thought of Shāh Walī Allāh Dihlawī, 1703–1762.* Leiden, the
　　Netherlands: Brill, 1986.
Barber, Benjamin. *Jihad vs. McWorld: Terrorism's Challenge to Democracy.* New York:
　　Ballantine, 2001.
Barrier, N. Gerald, ed. *The Census in British India: New Perspectives.* New Delhi:
　　Manohar, 1981.
Baxter, Craig. *Bangladesh: From a Nation to a State.* Boulder, Colo.: Westview, 1997.
Blumhardt, James Fuller. *Catalogue of the Hindustani Manuscripts in the Library of
　　the India Office.* Oxford: Oxford University Press, 1926.

Bretthauer, Berit. "Televangelism: Local and Global Dimensions." In *Religions/ Globalizations: Theories and Cases*, edited by Dwight N. Hopkins, Lois Ann Lorentzen, Eduardo Mendieta, and David Batstone, 203–25. Durham: Duke University Press, 2001.

Carey, William. *An Enquiry into the Obligations of Christians to Use Means for the Conversion of the Heathens*. London: Carey Kingsgate, 1792.

Chakrabartī, Ratan Lāl. *Bhāshā āndolaner dalilpatra*. Dhaka: Bangla Academy, 2000.

Chatterjee, Partha. *Nationalist Thought and the Colonial World: A Derivative Discourse?* London: Zed, 1986.

———. *The Nation and Its Fragments: Colonial and Postcolonial Histories*. Princeton: Princeton University Press, 1993.

———. "On Religious and Linguistic Nationalisms: The Second Partition of Bengal." In *Nation and Religion,* edited by Peter van der Veer and Hartmut Lehman, 112–28. Princeton: Princeton University Press, 1999.

Chatterjee, Sunil Kumar. "Serampore Missionaries and Christian Muslim Interaction in Bengal (1793–1834)." *Bulletin of Christian Institutes of Islamic Studies* 3 (1980): 115–32.

Choudhury, Abdul Gaffar. "Ekushey." In *Poems on the Twenty-first*, edited by Bashir al-Helal, translated by Kabir Chowdhury, 57. Dhaka: Bangla Academy, 1983.

Choudhury, Sujit. "Badshah: A Hindu Godling with a Muslim Background." In *Folkloric Bangladesh,* edited by Mustafa Zaman Abbasi, 61–69. Dhaka: Bangladesh Folklore Parishad, 1979.

Chowdhury, Kabir. "The Language Movement and the Bangla Academy." In *Essays on Ekushey, the Language Movement, 1952*, edited by Syed Manzoorul Islam, 26–30. Dhaka: Bangla Academy, 1994.

Clark, Anne L. "Testing the Two Modes Theory: Christian Practice in the Later Middle Ages." In *Theorizing Religions Past: Archaeology, History, and Cognition*, edited by Harvey Whitehouse and Luther H. Martin, 125–42. Walnut Creek, Calif.: AltaMira, 2004.

Cole, Juan R. I. "Sacred Space and Holy War in India." In *Islamic Legal Interpretation: Muftis and Their Fatwas*, edited by Muhammad Khalid Masud, Brinkley Messick and David S. Powers, 173–83. Cambridge: Harvard University Press, 1996.

David, S. Immanuel. "'Save the Heathens from Themselves': The Evolution of the Educational Policy of the East India Company till 1854." *Indian Church History Review* 18 (1984): 19–29.

De, Sushil Kumar. *Bengali Literature in the Nineteenth Century (1757–1857)*. Calcutta: Calcutta Oriental Press, 1962.

Denny, F. M. "Exegesis and Recitation: Their Development as Classical Forms of Qur'ānic Piety." In *Transitions and Transformations in the History of Religions*, edited by F. E. Reynolds and T. M. Ludwig, 91–123. Leiden, the Netherlands: Brill, 1981.

Dharmaraj, Jacob S. "A Brief Review of Alexander Duff, English Education, and

Colonial Connections in 19th Century India." *Indian Church History Review* 25 (1991): 73–87.

———. "Serampore Missions and Colonial Connections. *Indian Church History Review* 26 (1992): 21–35.

Dimock, Edward C. *The Sound of Silent Guns and Other Essays.* Delhi: Oxford University Press, 1989.

Eaton, Richard M. "Approaches to the Study of Conversion to Islam in India." In *Approaches to Islam in Religious Studies,* edited by Richard C. Martin, 106–23. Tucson: University of Arizona Press, 1985.

———. *The Rise of Islam and the Bengal Frontier, 1204–1760.* Berkeley: University of California Press, 1993.

———. *Sufis of Bijapur: Social Roles of Sufis in Medieval India.* Princeton: Princeton University Press, 1996.

Eickelman, Dale F., and Jon W. Anderson, eds. *New Media in the Muslim World: The Emerging Public Sphere.* 2nd ed. Bloomington: Indiana University Press, 2003.

Ernst, Carl W. *Words of Ecstasy in Sufism.* Albany: SUNY Press, 1985.

———. *The Shambhala Guide to Sufism.* Boston: Shambhala, 1997.

———. *Eternal Garden: Mysticism, History, and Politics at a South Asian Sufi Center.* Albany: SUNY Press, 1992.

———, trans. *Teachings of Sufism.* Boston: Shambhala, 1999.

Esposito, John. *The Islamic Threat: Myth or Reality?* 3rd ed. New York: Oxford University Press, 1999.

Ethé, Hermann. *Catalogue of Persian Manuscripts in the Library of the India Office.* Oxford: Oxford University Press, 1903.

Gaborieau, Marc. "The Cult of Saints among the Muslims of Nepal and Northern India." In *Saints and Their Cults,* edited by Stephen Wilson, 291–308. Cambridge: Cambridge University Press, 1983.

———. "The Transformation of the Tablīghī Jamā'at into a Transnational Movement." In *Travellers in Faith*, edited by Muhammad Khalid Masud, 121–38. Leiden, the Netherlands: Brill, 2000.

Gardner, Katy. *Global Migrants, Local Lives: Travel and Transformation in Rural Bangladesh.* Oxford: Clarendon, 1995.

Gellner, Ernest. *Nations and Nationalism.* Ithaca: Cornell University Press, 1983.

———. *Nationalism.* New York: New York University Press, 1997.

Gilmartin, David, and Bruce B. Lawrence, eds. *Beyond Turk and Hindu: Rethinking Religious Identities in Islamicate South Asia.* Gainesville: University Press of Florida, 2000.

Gottschalk, Peter. *Beyond Hindu and Muslim: Multiple Identity in Narratives from Village India.* New York: Oxford University Press, 2000.

Goldsack, William. *A Mussalmani Bengali–English Dictionary.* Calcutta: Banerjee, 1923.

Hak, Muj"āmmil Khandakār. *Madh"yuger musalim nītiśāstra kathā*. Dhaka: Bangla
    Academy, 1987.

Haq, Muhammad Enamul. *Muslim Bengali Literature*. Karachi: Pakistan
    Publications, 1957.

———. *A History of Sufi-ism in Bengal*. Dhaka: Asiatic Society of Bangladesh, 1975.

Hardy, Peter. *The Muslims of British India*. Cambridge: Cambridge University Press,
    1972.

Hasan, Perween, and Mufakharul Islam, eds. *Essays in Memory of Momtazur Rahman
    Tarafdar*. Dhaka, Bangladesh: Centre for Advanced Research in the
    Humanities, Dhaka University, 1999.

Hermansen, Marcia. *The Conclusive Argument from God: Shah Walī Allāh of Delhi's
    H.ujjat*. Leiden, the Netherlands: Brill, 1996.

Hobsbawm, Eric, and Terence Ranger, eds. *The Invention of Tradition*. Cambridge:
    Cambridge University Press, 1983.

Hopkins, Dwight N., Lois Ann Lorentzen, Eduardo Mendieta, and David Badstone,
    eds. *Religions/Globalizations: Theories and Cases*. Durham, N.C.: Duke
    University Press, 2001.

Huntington, Samuel P. *The Clash of Civilizations and the Remaking of World Order*.
    New York: Simon and Schuster, 1996.

Huq, Mainmuna. "From Piety to Romance: Islam-Oriented Texts in Bangladesh." In
    New Media in the Muslim World, edited by Dale F. Eickelman and Jon W.
    Anderson, 129–57. Bloomington: Indiana University Press, 1999.

Husain, S. S. *Descriptive Catalogue of Bengali Manuscripts*. Dhaka: Asiatic Society of
    Pakistan, 1962.

Ikram, S. M. "An Unnoticed Account of Shaikh Jalāl of Sylhet." *Journal of the Asiatic
    Society of Pakistan* 2 (1957): 63–68.

Islam, Syed Manzoorul, ed. *Essays on Ekushey, the Language Movement, 1952*. Dhaka:
    Bangla Academy, 1994.

Ivanow, Wladimir. *Concise Descriptive Catalogue of the Persian Manuscripts in the
    Collection of the Asiatic Society of Bengal*. Calcutta: Baptist Mission Press,
    1924.

———. *Concise Descriptive Catalogue of the Persian Manuscripts in the Curzon
    Collection, Asiatic Society of Bengal*. Calcutta: Baptist Mission Press, 1926.

Jones, Kenneth W. "Religious Identity and the Indian Census." In *The Census in
    British India: New Perspectives*, edited by N. Gerald Barrier, 73–102. New
    Delhi: Manohar, 1981.

Kabir, Muhammad Ghulam. *Changing Face of Nationalism: The Case of Bangladesh*.
    Dhaka, Bangladesh: University Press, 1995.

Kādir, Ābdul. "Mohammad Naīmuddīn." In *Baṅl ā Ekāḍemī Patrikā*, 1:43–66.
    Dhaka: Bangla Academy, 1959.

Kakat, Sudhir. *The Colors of Violence: Cultural Identities, Religion, and Conflict*.
    Chicago: University of Chicago Press, 1996.

Kalcik, Susan. "Ethnic Foodways in America: Symbol and Performance of Identity."
    In *Ethnic and Regional Foodways in the United States: The Performance of
    Group Identity*, edited by Linda Keller and Kay Mussell, 37–65. Knoxville:
    University of Tennessee Press, 1984.

"Karāmat 'Alī." In *Shorter Encyclopedia of Islam,* edited by H. A. R. Gibb and J. H.
    Kramers, 217–18. Leiden, the Netherlands: Brill, 1961.

Khan, Ahmad. *History of the Fara'idi Movement in Bengal (1818–1906).* Karachi:
    Pakistan Historical Society, 1965.

Khan, Mufakkhar Hussain. "A History of Bengali Translations of the Holy Qur'ān."
    Muslim World 72 (1982): 129–36.

———. *Pabitra kurān pracārer itihās o banganubāder śatabarsha.* Dhaka: Bangla
    Academy, 1997.

Khan, Muhammad Akram. "Back to the Qur'an." Translated by Sufia Uddin. In
    Modernist Islam (1840–1940): A Sourcebook, edited by Charles Kurzman,
    334–36. Oxford: Oxford University Press.

Khan, Shaukat Ali. *Catalogue of the Arabic Manuscripts.* Rajasthan, India: Arabic and
    Persian Research Institute, 1980.

King, Richard. *Orientalism and Religion: Postcolonial Theory, India, and 'the Mystic
    East.'* New York: Routledge, 1999.

Kokan, Muhammad Yousaf. "The Holy Quran in Tamil Translation." In *Islam in
    India: Studies and Commentaries,* edited by Christian Troll, 135–42. New
    Delhi: Vikas, 1982.

Kopf, David. *The Brahmo Samaj and the Shaping of the Modern Indian Mind.*
    Princeton: Princeton University Press, 1979.

Korom, Frank. *Hosay Trinidad: Muharram Performances in an Indo-Caribbean
    Diaspora.* Philadelphia: University of Pennsylvania Press, 2003.

Lacunza-Balda, Justo. "Translations of the Quran into Swahili, and Contemporary
    Islamic Revival in East Africa." In *African Islam and Islam in Africa:
    Encounters between Sufis and Islamists,* edited by David Westerlund and Eva
    Evers Rosander, 95–126. Athens: Ohio University Press, 1997.

Lapidus, Ira M. *A History of Islamic Societies.* Cambridge: Cambridge University
    Press, 1988.

Lawrence, Bruce B. *Defenders of God: The Fundamentalist Revolt against the Modern
    Age.* San Francisco: Harper and Row, 1989.

———. "Tracking Fundamentalists and Those Who Study Them: A Sequel to Sadik
    Al-Azm, 'Islamic Fundamentalism Reconsidered . . .'" *South Asia Bulletin* 14
    (1994): 41–50.

Levtzion, Nehemiah, and John O. Voll, eds. *Eighteenth-Century Renewal and Reform
    in Islam.* New York: Syracuse University Press, 1987.

Long, J. *A Descriptive Catalogue of Bengali Works.* Calcutta: Sanders, Cones, 1855;
    as reprinted in Dineshacandra Sen. *Bangabhāshāya o sāhitya.* Calcutta:
    Chattāpādhāy, 1943.

Ludden, David. "Orientalist Empiricism and Transformations of Colonial Knowledge." In *Orientalism and the Postcolonial Predicament: Perspectives on South Asia*, edited by Carol A. Breckenridge and Peter van der Veer, 250–78. Philadelphia: University of Pennsylvania Press, 1993.

———, ed. *Contesting the Nation: Religion, Community, and the Politics of Democracy in India*. Philadelphia: University of Pennsylvania Press, 1996.

Mahmood, Kalam, ed. *Meet Bangladesh*. Dhaka: Department of Film and Publications, Ministry of Information, Government of the People's Republic of Bangladesh, 1987.

Maitra, Jayanti. *Muslim Politics in Bengal: 1855–1906*. Calcutta: Bagchi, 1984.

Majumdar, R. C., H. C. Raychaudhuri, and Kalikinar Datta. *An Advanced History of India*. 4th ed. Madras: Macmillan India, 1978.

Makdisi, George. "Hanbali School and Sufism." *Boletin de la Asociacion Española de Orientalistas* 15 (1979): 115–26.

———. "Ethics in Islamic Traditionalist Doctrine." In *Ethics in Islam*, edited by Richard G. Hovannisian, 115–26. Lancaster, Calif.: Undena, 1985.

Mamoon, Muntassir. *The Festivals of Bangladesh*. Translated by Rajoshi Ghosh. Dhaka, Bangladesh: International Centre for Bengal Studies, 1996.

Marony, M. "Madju-s." In *Encyclopaedia of Islam*, edited by C. E. Bosworth, E. Van Donzel, W. P. Heinrichs, and C. Pellat, 5:1110–18. Leiden, the Netherlands: Brill, 1993.

Martin, Richard C., ed. *Islam in Local Contexts*. Leiden, the Netherlands: Brill, 1982.

Marty, Martin E., and R. Scott Appleby, eds. *Accounting for Fundamentalisms: The Dynamic Character of Movements*. Vol. 4 of *The Fundamentalism Project*. Chicago: University of Chicago Press, 1991.

———, eds. *Fundamentalisms Observed*. Vol. 1 of *The Fundamentalism Project*. Chicago: University of Chicago Press, 1991.

Massey, Ashish Kumar, and June Hedlund. "William Carey and the Making of Modern India." *Indian Church History Review* 27 (1993): 7–18.

Masud, Muhammad Khalid. "Apostasy and Judicial Separation in British India." In *Islamic Legal Interpretation: Muftis and Their Fatwas*, edited by Muhammad Khalid Masud, Brinkley Messick, and David S. Powers, 193–203. Cambridge: Harvard University Press, 1996.

———, ed. *Travellers in Faith: Studies of the Tablīghī Jamāʿat as a Transnational Islamic Movement for Faith Renewal*. Leiden, the Netherlands: Brill, 2000.

Masud, Muhammad Khalid, Brinkley Messick, and David S. Powers, eds. *Islamic Legal Interpretation: Muftis and Their Fatwas*. Cambridge: Harvard University Press, 1996.

Metcalf, Barbara D. *Islamic Revival in British India: Deoband, 1860–1900*. Princeton: Princeton University Press, 1982.

———. "Nationalist Muslims in British India: The Case of Hakim Ajmal Khan." *Modern Asian Studies* 19 (1985): 1–28.

———. "New Medinas: The Tablighi Jama'at in North America and Europe." In *Making Muslim Space in North America and Europe,* edited by Barbara Daly Metcalf, 110–30. Berkeley: University of California Press, 1996.

———. "Two Fatwas on Hajj in British India." In *Islamic Legal Interpretation: Muftis and Their Fatwas,* edited by Muhammad Khalid Masud, Brinkley Messick, and David S. Powers, 184–92 . Cambridge: Harvard University Press, 1996.

Mills, Samuel Landell. "The Atroshi Urus." *Journal of Social Studies* 63 (1994): 83–106.

Mottahedeh, Roy P. "The Clash of Civilizations: An Islamicist's Critique." *Harvard Middle Eastern and Islamic Review* 2 (1995): 1–26.

Muqtadir, Maulavi Abdul. *Catalogue of the Arabic and Persian Manuscripts in the Oriental Public Library at Bankipore.* 2 vols. Calcutta: Baptist Mission Press, 1908– .

Murshid, Khan Sarwar. "Twentyfirst February." In *Essays on Ekushey, the Language Movement, 1952,* edited by Syed Manzoorul Islam, 17–25. Dhaka: Bangla Academy, 1994.

Nadwi, Maulavi Muinuddin. *Catalogue of the Arabic and Persian Manuscripts in the Oriental Public Library at Bankipore.* Calcutta: Baptist Mission Press, 1962.

Naīmuddīn, Mohammad. *Jobdātal Masāyel.* Bangladesh, 1873.

———. *Koran śariph.* Mymensingh, Bangladesh: Akhbari Isalamiyay Sampadaka, 1887.

Nasr, Seyyed Vali Reza. "Mawdudi and the Jama'at-i Islami: The Origins, Theory, and Practice of Islamic Revivalism." In *Pioneers of Islamic Revival,* edited by Ali Rahnema, 98–124. Atlantic Highlands, N.J.: Zed, 1994.

———. *Mawdudi and the Making of Islamic Revivalism.* New York: Oxford University Press, 1996.

Potts, E. Daniel. "The Baptist Missionaries of Serampore and the Government of India, 1792–1813." *Journal of Ecclesiastical History* 15 (1964): 229–49.

Rahim, Enayetur. "Bengali Muslims and Islamic Fundamentalism: The Jama't-i-Islami in Bangladesh." In *Understanding the Bengal Muslims: Interpretive Essays,* edited by Rafiuddin Ahmed, 236–61. New Delhi: Oxford University Press, 2001.

Rahman, Muhammad Mujib. *Bangla bhāshāya kurān carca.* Dhaka, Bangladesh: Islamic Foundation, 1986.

Rahman, Shamsur. "Freedom." Translated by Prithvis Nandis. *Journal of South Asian Literature.* 9 (1974): 74–75.

Robinson, Francis. "Technology and Religious Change: Islam and the Impact of Print," *Modern Asian Studies* 27:1 (1993): 229–51.

———. *Islam and Muslim History in South Asia.* New Delhi: Oxford University Press, 2000.

Roy, Asim. *The Islamic Syncretistic Tradition in Bengal.* Princeton, Princeton University Press, 1983.

Ruhul Amin, Mohāmmad. *Korān śariph: saīka baṅganubad pārā āma.* Calcutta: Mājediya, 1918.

"Ṣābi'ūn." In *Encyclopaedia of Islam* (CD-ROM), 8:672a. Leiden, the Netherlands: Brill, 2003.

Śahīdullāh, Mohāmmada. *Kalikāta mādrasa kaleja o korana śaripher baṅgla anubād.* Calcutta: Bani Manzil, 1988.

Sanyal, Usha. "Are Wahhābis Kafirs? Ahmad Riza Khan Barelwi and His *Sword of the Haramayn.*" In *Islamic Legal Interpretation: Muftis And their Fatwas,* edited by Muhammad Khalid Masud, Brinkley Messick, and David S. Powers, 204–13. Cambridge: Harvard University Press, 1996.

———. *Devotional Islam and Politics in British India: Ahmad Riza Khan Barelwi and His Movement, 1870–1920.* Delhi: Oxford University Press, 1996.

Sarkar, Jagadish Narayan. *Islam in Bengal (Thirteenth to Nineteenth Century).* Calcutta: Ratna Prakashan, 1972.

Sastri, Sivnath. *Atmacarit: Ramtanu lahiri o hatkalin bangasamaj.* Calcutta: Saksarata Prakasan, 1979.

Schacht, Joseph. "Idjtihād." In *Encyclopaedia of Islam,* edited by C. E. Bosworth, E. Van Donzel, W. P. Heinrichs, and C. Pellat, 3:1026–27. Leiden, the Netherlands: Brill, 1993.

Schimmel, Annemarie. "Translations and Commentaries of the Qur'ān in Sindhi Language." *Oriens* 16 (1963): 224–43.

———. *Islamic Literatures of India.* Vol. 7 of *A History of Indian Literature.* Wiesbaden, Germany: Harrassowitz, 1973.

———. *Islam in the Indian Subcontinent.* Leiden, the Netherlands: Brill, 1980.

Seabrook, Jeremy. *Freedom Unfinished: Fundamentalism and Popular Resistance in Bangladesh Today.* New York: Zed, 2001.

Sells, Michael. "Erasing Culture: Wahhabism, Buddhism, Balkan Mosques." Updated version, 2 April 2003. <http://www.haverford.edu/relg/sells/reports/WahhabismBuddhasBegova.htm> (accessed 22 November 2005).

Sen, Bhai Girish Chandra. *Koran śariph.* Dhaka, Bangladesh: Shamla Book Depot, 1881–85.

Smalley, William A. *Translation as Mission: Bible Translation in the Modern Missionary Movement.* Macon, Ga.: Mercer, 1991.

Shaikh, Farzana. "Muslims and Political Representation in Colonial India: The Making of Pakistan." *Modern Asian Studies* 20 (1986): 539–57.

Stewart, Tony K. "The Language of Equivalence: Interpreting Bengali Muslim Literature from the Middle Period." In *Essays in Memory of Momtazur Rahman Tarafdar,* edited by Perween Hasan and Mufakharul Islam, 380–409. Dhaka, Bangladesh: Centre for Advanced Research in the Humanities, Dhaka University, 1999.

———. "Surprising Bedfellows: Vaiṣṇava and Shi-'a alliance in Kavi Āriph's 'Tale of Lālmon.'" *International Journal of Hindu Studies* 3 (1999): 265–98.

————. "In Search of Equivalence: Conceiving Muslim-Hindu Encounter through Translation Theory." *History of Religions* 40 (2001): 261–88.

Subhan, Abdus. "Arabic, Persian, and Urdu Literatures." In *History of Bangladesh, 1704–1971*, vol. 3, *Social and Cultural History*, edited by Sirajul Islam, 393–417. Rev. 2nd ed. Dhaka: Asiatic Society of Bangladesh, 1997.

Sweetman, William. "Unity and Plurality: Hinduism and the Religions of India in Early European Scholarship." *Religion* 31 (2001): 209–24.

Taher Saheb, Mahāmmad. *Al Kura-n tarjama- o taphasi-r.* Calcutta: Rabi ār Presa, 1970.

Tarafdar, Momtazur Rahman. *Husain Shahi Bengal, 1494–1538 A.D.: A Socio-Political Study.* Dhaka: Asiatic Society of Pakistan, 1965.

Thorp, John P. "The Muslim Farmers of Bangladesh and Allah's Creation of the World." *Asian Folklore Studies* 41 (1982): 201–15.

Troll, Christian W. *Sayyid Ahmad Khan: A Reinterpretation of Muslim Theology.* New Delhi: Vikas, 1978.

Uddin, Sufia. "Awami League." In *Encyclopedia of Islam and the Muslim World*, edited by Richard C. Martin, 1:90–92. New York: Macmillan, 2003.

————. "In the Company of Pirs." *In Dealing with Deities: The Ritual Vow in South Asia*, edited by Selva Raj and William P. Harman. Albany: SUNY Press, forthcoming.

Van Schendel, Willem. "Bengalis, Bangladeshis, and Others: Chakma Visions of a Pluralist Bangladesh." In *Bangladesh: Promise and Performance*, edited by Rounaq Jahan, 65–106. New York: Zed, 2000.

Veer, Peter van der. *Religious Nationalism: Hindus and Muslims in India.* Berkeley: University of California Press, 1994.

————. *Imperial Encounters: Religion and Modernity in India and Britain.* Princeton: Princeton University Press, 2001.

Veer, Peter van der, and Hartmut Lehmann, eds. *Nation and Religion: Perspectives on Europe and Asia.* Princeton: Princeton University Press, 1999.

Wagner, E. "Arabic Rhetoric and Qur'ānic Exegesis." *Bulletin of the School of Oriental and African Studies* 31 (1968): 469–85.

————. "Munāẓara." In *Encyclopaedia of Islam,* edited by C. E. Bosworth, E. Van Donzel, W. P. Heinrichs, and C. Pellat, 7:565–68. Leiden, the Netherlands: Brill, 1993.

Zerubavel, Yael. *Recovered Roots: Collective Memory and the Making of Israeli National Tradition.* Chicago: University of Chicago Press, 1995.

Ziring, Lawrence. *Bangladesh from Mujib to Ershad: An Interpretive Study.* New York: Oxford University Press, 1992.

Index

Sen, Girish Chandra; Sen, Keshab
Chandra
Bible society, 70
Bidesh, 175, 176
Biharis, 133
Bistami, Bayazid, 37, 147. *See also* Sufis
Bonbibi, 149. *See also* Sufis
Bosnia, 5, 16, 185
Brahma, 32, 36
Brahma Samaj, 71, 82, 84–88, 91, 95, 96,
111. *See also* Sen, Girish Chandra; Sen,
Keshab Chandra
Brunslow, D., 50, 195 (n. 22). *See also*
Christianity; Missionaries
Buddhists, 85–86
Burdwan House, 128. *See also* Bangla
Academy

Calcutta, 50–51, 61, 83–84
Calcutta Madrassa, 88. See also *Tafsir*
Caliph, 61. *See also* Ali, Karamat; Faraizi
Canada, 160
Carey, William, 41, 43, 49–50, 195 (n. 22).
See also Christianity; Missionaries
Central Asia, 18, 20, 23
Central Institute of Islamic Research, 166.
See also Jama'at-i-Islami
Chaitanya, 25. *See also* Brahma Samaj
Chakmas, 133. *See also* Adivasi
Chaudhuri, 24
Chillas, 163. *See also* Tablighi Jama'at
Chingiz Khan, 20
Chisti, 30. *See also* Chistiyya; Sufis
Chistiyya, 43, 45, 55. *See also* Sufis;
Al-Wahhab, Muhammad ibn 'Abd
Chittagong, 30, 37–38, 137–38
Chittagong Hill Tracts, 145, 147–48, 182
Choudhury, Abdul Gaffar, 126. *See also*
Shaheed Minar
Christianity, 70, 85. *See also* Christians;
Missionaries; Serampore
Christians, 6, 9, 43, 48, 51, 57, 65, 67, 71, 75,
86–87, 110–11, 129, 159, 171; critiques of,
75, 83; evangelism, 53; fundamentalism,

159–60; Christian missionaries, 43,
47–52 passim, 62, 83, 114, 195 (n. 22).
See also Brunslow, D.; Carey, William;
Christianity; Civilizing mission;
Fountain, John; Goldsack, William;
Marshman, J.
Civilizational clash, 11
Civilizing mission, 50, 147. *See also*
Christianity; Christians
Converts, 21, 27, 47, 191 (n. 9)

Danish colony, 50–51, 195 (n. 22). *See also*
Christianity; Missionaries; Serampore
Dar al-harb, 54, 81, 92, 198 (n. 57). *See also*
Jama'at-i-Islami
Dar al-Islam, 162
Darasbari, 30
Darvish, 24. *See* Sufis
Das, Shib Narayan, 130. *See also* Ekushey;
Shaheed Minar
Da'wa, 162. *See also* Tablighi Jama'at
Delhi Sultanate, 19
Deoband, 57–58, 78, 108, 146
Desh, 175, 176
Dhaka, 30, 61, 84, 124–25, 130, 141, 144,
148, 171–72
Dhaka Medical College, 125–27
Dhaka University, 120, 124, 125–27, 130,
135, 138
Dhanmondi, 141, 148
Dhikr, 149. *See also* Sufis
Dobhashi, 69. *See also* Mussalmani
Dutch, 41. *See also* Missionaries

East Bengal, 1, 54, 120. *See also* East
Pakistan
East India Company, 50–51, 191 (n. 2)
East Pakistan, 118, 121, 125–26, 128, 135,
168–69. *See also* East Bengal
Eden College, 126. *See also* Dhaka
University
Ekushey, 125, 127–30, 171
Ershad, Hussain Muhammad, 138–39, 148,
152, 170

Ethnolinguistic nationalism, 182
Evangelical movements, 159. *See also*
    Christianity; Missionaries
Eve, 36
Exegesis, 18, 91, 109; exegetical texts, 11. *See*
    also Naīmuddīn, Muhammad; Sen,
    Girish Chandra; *Tafsir*

Fakir, 71. See also *Faqir*; Saints; Sufis
Falwell, Jerry, 159–60. *See also* Christianity;
    Fundamentalism; Globalization;
    Missionaries
Faqir, 24, 149, 150
Faraizi, 54, 56, 62, 81. *See also* Faridpur;
    Shariatullah, Haji
Faridpur, 54, 148. *See also* Faraizi;
    Shariatullah, Haji
Fatwas, 56–58, 64, 82, 107, 199 (n. 9), 201
    (n. 42)
Fiqh, 26, 29, 80. *See also* Hanafi school;
    La-majhābis; *Madhhab*; Sunni schools
    of law
Five Pillars, 148
Fort Williams, 51, 77. *See also* Calcutta;
    Carey, William
Fountain, John, 50, 195 (n. 22). *See*
    also Carey, William; Christianity;
    Missionaries; Serampore
Frederick VI, 50, 195 (n. 22). *See also* Carey,
    William; Danish colony; Missionaries;
    Serampore
Fundamentalism, 15, 119, 123, 135, 147,
    150, 156–59, 161, 163, 173. *See also*
    Christianity; Falwell, Jerry; Hindu
    nationalism; Islamists

Gandak, 20
Gandhi, Indira, 133
Ganges River, 22, 24, 25, 106
Gangohi, Rashid Ahmad, 58. *See also*
    Deoband
Garos, 133. *See also* Adivasi
Gaur, 30
Al-Ghazali, 87

Global Islam, 11, 16; global Islamic culture,
    123
Globalization, 9, 156, 177, 185
Go-jiban, 60, 72, 81
Goldsack, William, 52, 70
Gosai, 33. *See also* Syncretism
Gospel, 43, 50, 83. *See also* Christianity;
    Missionaries
Gujarati, 59, 180

Habshi, 19
Hadith, 6, 28, 29, 35, 44, 52, 80, 106, 109.
    See also Sunna
Hājjī, 24, 192 (n. 16)
Hanafi school, 45, 81–80. See also *Fiqh*;
    La-majhābis; *Madhhab*; Sunni schools
    of law
Haramayn, 44, 58, 176. *See also* Mecca;
    Medina
Harkat, 172
Hartal, 124, 139, 202 (n. 24)
Heathen, 49–50, 115
Hijaz, 58. *See also* Haramayn; Mecca;
    Medina; Saudi Arabia
Hindi, 4, 7, 32, 64, 72, 108. *See also* Urdu
Hindu landlords, 55. *See also* Land grants;
    Ta'alluqdar; *Ta'lluq*; *Zamīndār*;
    Zamīndāri
Hindu nationalism, 152, 160, 162, 164. *See*
    also Bharata Janata Party
Hindustani, 72. *See also* Hindi; Urdu
Hosay, 160
Hossain, Moinul, 130. *See also* National
    Monument
Huq, Shamsul, 121. *See also* Awami League
Husayn, 32, 160. *See also* Karbala, Battle of
Husayn Shah, 19, 20, 30, 39
Hussain, Mir Mosharraf, 60, 72, 81

'*Ibadat*, 57, 103
ICS (Islami Chhatra Shibir), 166, 171–72
'*Id*, 54, 62, 78, 81, 198 (n. 57)
Identity politics, 8
Idolatry, 83

Ijtihad, 45
Ilyas Shah, Muhammad, 162. *See also*
    Tablighi Jama'at
Ilyas Shah, Shams al-Din, 19
Ilyas Shahi, 19, 30
Indian nationalism, 151, 164
Indic tradition, 21
Indigo planters, 55. *See also* Carey, William
Internet, 177
Invented tradition, 151
Iqbal, 46
Islamic civilization, 6, 7, 16, 179
Islamic cosmology, 33
Islamic language, 70
Islamic law, 10, 45, 80, 145. See also *Fiqh*;
    Hanafi school; *La-majhābis*; *Madhhab*
Islamic nationalism, 119, 138
Islamic nationhood, 9
Islamic Oikko Jote, 172, 202 (n. 22)
Islamic Research Academy, 166
Islamists, 4, 6, 15, 150, 156, 167, 172, 177,
    178, 182–85. *See also* Fundamentalism;
    Jama'at-i-Islami; Tablighi Jama'at

Jahiliyya, 34
Jalalabad, 148. *See also* Sylhet
Jama'at-i-Islami, 136, 141–50 passim, 161,
    163–74, 176–78, 183, 202 (n. 22), 203
    (n. 25)
Jesus, 32, 36, 83–84. *See also* Christianity;
    Sen, Keshab Chandra
Jihad, 54, 55, 58, 93, 157, 158, 167, 203 (n. 6).
    See also *Dar al-harb*
Jinnah, Muhammad Ali, 1–4, 8, 120, 124,
    183–84. *See also* East Bengal; East
    Pakistan; West Pakistan
Jobdātal masāÿel, 78, 79, 97, 107. *See also*
    Naīmuddīn, Muhammad
Jum'a, 54, 62, 78, 81, 198 (n. 57)

Kafir, 5, 7, 60, 81, 82, 102–4. See also
    Fatwas; *Kufr*; Wahhabis
Kamal, Sufia, 135
Kankurgachi, 85

Karbala, Battle of, 32, 194 (n. 7)
Khalifas, 55. *See also* Faraizi; Miyan, Dudu
Khan, Muhammad Akram, 116. *See also*
    Qur'an
Khan, Sir Sayyid Ahmad, 46, 59, 78
Khān, 24
Khan Barelwi, Maulana Ahmad Riza,
    55, 57, 58, 78. See also *Fatwas*; *Kafir*;
    Wahhabis
Khulna, 37, 147
Khwāndkār, 24, 192 (n. 16)
Kistbundy, 23
Korān śarīph, 89, 96. *See also* Naīmuddīn,
    Muhammad; Sen, Girish Chandra;
    Tafsir
Kosovo, 5, 16
Al-Kufi, Ali, 28
Kufr, 58, 177. See also *Fatwas*; *Kafir*;
    Wahhabis

Laili-majnun, 31, 38. *See also* Yusuf-
    Zulaikha
Lajja, 172
La-majhābis, 80, 199 (n. 6). See also *Fiqh*;
    Sunni schools of law
Land grants, 22–24
Liberation war, 141
Local languages, 63
Lodi Dynasty, 20
Luther, Martin, 184

Madhhab, 80, 199 (n. 6). See also *Fiqh*;
    Hanafi school; Sunni schools of law
Madrassa, 43, 150–51
Maghazi literature, 28, 31
Mahabharata, 7
Maheswar, 32, 36
Maijbhander, 148–49
Majlis-i-Shura, 165. *See also* Jama'at-i-Islami
Maktabs, 63
Marmars, 133. *See also* Adivasi
Marshman, J., 50, 195 (n. 22). *See also*
    Carey, William; Christianity; Danish
    colony; Missionaries; Serampore

Haramayn; *Mazars*; Mecca; Medina;
Ziyarat

Pirs, 18, 33, 105–6, 111, 139, 146, 201 (n. 40)

Pir Atroshi, 148. *See also* Sufis

Prabhu, 33–34, 193 (n. 54). *See also*
Syncretism

Print capitalism, 64, 108

Printing press, 49, 51, 59–60, 65

Print technology, 11, 64–66, 108, 180

Protestantism, 64, 108

Protestants, 83, 110

Public debates, 61, 63–64

Public sphere, 15, 165, 182–83

Punjabi, 32

Puranas, 84

Puthi, 7, 111

Qadis, 29

Qadiriyya, 43, 45, 55. *See also* Sufis; Al-
Wahhab, Muhammad ibn 'Abd; Wali
Allah, Shah

Queen Victoria, 85

Qur'an, 4, 6, 9, 18, 29, 31, 38, 44, 46, 52,
56, 77, 89, 94–116, 118, 184, 199 (n. 83),
200 (n. 33)

Qur'anic translation, 11. *See also*
Naīmuddīn, Muhammad; Sen, Girish
Chandra; *Tafsir*

Rabi'a, 87

Rabindra sangeet, 134–35, 152. *See also*
Tagore, Rabindranath

Rafi-yadayns, 80, 201 (n. 44). *See also*
Tariqah-i-Muhammadiyah

Rahman, Ataur, 121. *See also* Awami League

Rahman, Fazlur, 166

Rahman, Shamsur, 156

Rahman, Ziaur, 122, 137, 139, 141, 170. *See
also* Bangladesh National Party

Raja Ganesh, 19, 191 (n. 3)

Rajshahi, 61

Rakhi Bahini, 122. *See also* Sheikh Mujib

Ramadan, 103, 170, 200 (n. 33)

Ramayana, 7

Ramna Park, 135–36, 171

Ranade, M. G., 67

Rangpur, 30

"Religion of the sword" theory, 20

Religious nationalism, 4, 115, 136, 145, 163,
180, 182, 185

Revivalists, 43

Rice cultivation, 23–24. *See also* Sufis

Risālas, 31

Robertson, Pat, 159. *See also* Christianity;
Globalization

Roy, Ram Mohan, 67, 82–84, 88. *See also*
Brahma Samaj

Rumi, 29, 87

Ryots, 55. *See also* Miyan, Dudu

Al-Saghani, 28

Saints, 106, 118, 147–48; veneration of, 112

Saiyid, 24, 192 (n. 16)

Sajda, 118, 148. *See also* Mazar; Pilgrimage;
Tomb

Salafiyya, 4. *See also* Fundamentalism;
Global Islam; Transnational Muslim
networks

Salat, 147, 162, 199 (n. 83)

Samkhya philosophy, 33

Sanad documents, 23. *See also* Land grants

Sanskrit, 25, 101, 108, 111, 125

Santals, 133. *See also* Adivasi

Saudi Arabia, 4, 175

Sayyid Abu 'ala Maududi, 164–69, 183

Sayyid Ahmad, 46, 54–56

Secularism, 12, 118, 129, 150–51, 170, 177–
78; secular nationalism, 119, 136, 152,
185; secular nationalists, 137; secularists,
141

Semitification of Hinduism, 83

Sen, Girish Chandra, 82, 87–90, 93–98,
101, 110, 116, 200 (n. 26). *See also* Bharat
Ashram; Sen, Keshab Chandra

Sen, Keshab Chandra, 67, 82, 84–89, 200
(n. 20) *See also* Bharat Ashram; Korān
śarīph; Sen, Girish Chandra

Senas, 22, 25

Serampore, 50–52, 83, 195 (n. 22). *See also*
Carey, William; Missionaries

'Upavita, 84

Urdu, 2, 4, 7, 15, 32, 46, 56, 59–64 passim,
     67, 69, 72, 75–80, 87, 91–94, 108–11,
     113–16, 118, 119, 124, 125, 180, 181, 183,
     197 (n. 49)

Urs, 148

Usul ud-din, 163–64. See also Muhammad;
     Sunna; Sunni schools of law

Uzbekistan, 185

Vaishnava movement, 25, 68, 119. See also
     Shiva; Vedas; Vishnu

Vedantic philosophy, 84

Vedas, 83; Vedic religion, 24

Vishnu, 32, 36. See also Chaitanya; Shiva;
     Vaishnava movement; Vedas

Vishva Hindu Parishad, 160–62, 203
     (n. 4). See also Bharata Janata Party;
     Fundamentalism; Nationalism;
     Transnationalism

Vision of community, 10, 14, 57, 114, 116,
     180, 182

Al-Wahhab, Muhammad ibn 'Abd, 33,
     43–44, 65, 193 (n. 2), 196 (n. 46)

Wahhabis, 55, 57–58, 147, 196 (n. 41). See
     also Al-Wahhab, Muhammad ibn 'Abd

Wali Allah, Shah, 33, 43–45, 55, 65, 91–92,
     183

Waqf grants, 23, 78. See also Land grants

Ward, William, 50. See also Brunslow, D.;
     Carey, William; Civilizing mission;
     Fountain, John; Goldsack, William;
     Marshman, J.

Wazirs, 61

Waz mahfil, 57, 63, 167. See also Bāhās;
     Munāzara

West Bengal, 83, 120, 138, 152

West Pakistan, 3, 118–21, 125, 129, 132, 168

Yemen, 37. See also Shah Jalal

Yoga-kalandar, 31–32, 38. See also Ashraf
     Muslims; Non-ashraf Muslims

Yusuf-zulaikha, 30–32, 38

Zakat, 173, 199 (n. 83)

Zamīndār, 22–24, 37–38, 61, 63, 192 (n. 13).
     See also Ta'alluq; Ta'alluqdar

Zamīndāri, 22. See also Zamīndār;
     Ta'alluq; Ta'alluqdar

Zia, Khaleda, 122. See also Bangladesh
     National Party

Ziyarat, 147. See also Pilgrimages; Sufis;
     Tombs

Zulfiqar Ali Khan Bhutto, 121. See also
     East Pakistan; West Pakistan

Zum Zum water, 176

ISLAMIC CIVILIZATION *&* MUSLIM NETWORKS

Sufia M. Uddin, *Constructing Bangladesh: Religion, Ethnicity, and Language in an Islamic Nation* (2006).

Omid Safi, *The Politics of Knowledge in Premodern Islam: Negotiating Ideology and Religious Inquiry* (2006).

Ebrahim Moosa, *Ghazālī and the Poetics of Imagination* (2005).

miriam cooke and Bruce B. Lawrence, eds., *Muslim Networks from Hajj to Hip Hop* (2005).

Carl W. Ernst, *Following Muhammad: Rethinking Islam in the Contemporary World* (2003).